buying **affordable**
antiques

MILLER'S

KU-368-112

Created and designed by
Miller's Publications
The Cellars, High Street
Tenterden, Kent TN30 6BN
Telephone: +44 (0) 1580 766411
Fax: +44 (0) 1580 766100

Managing Editor: Valerie Lewis
Production Co-ordinator: Kari Moody
Project Co-ordinator: Léonie Sidgwick
Editorial Co-ordinator: Deborah Wanstall
Editorial Assistants: Melissa Hall, Joanna Hill, Maureen Horner
Designer: Philip Hannath
Advertisement Designer: Simon Cook
Jacket Design: Alexa Brommer
Advertising Executive: Emma Gillingham
Advertising Co-ordinator & Administrator: Melinda Williams
Production Assistants: June Barling, Ethne Tragett
Production Controller: Sarah Rogers
Additional Photography: Robin Saker
Indexer: Hilary Bird

First published in Great Britain in 2004
by Miller's, a division of Mitchell Beazley,
imprints of Octopus Publishing Group Ltd,
2–4 Heron Quays, London E14 4JP

© 2004 Octopus Publishing Group Ltd

A CIP catalogue record for this book is
available from the British Library

ISBN 1 84000 960 8

Illustrations: One Thirteen Ltd, Whitstable, Kent
Printed and bound by Lego SpA, Italy

Front Cover Illustrations:
Oak Wainscot chair, 18thC. **£600–720 / €890–1,050 / $1,050–1,250**
Silver melon-shaped teapot, c1761. **£400–480 / €600–710 / $710–850**
Two Chinese blue and white lidded vases, late 19th/early 20thC,
larger 25¼in (64cm) high. **£160–190 / €240–280 / $280–340**

Contents

6   Contributors
8   Periods & Styles
10 How to use this book
11 Introduction
12 Types of Wood

14   Furniture
64   Ceramics
132 Silver & Plate
166 Glass
192 Clocks, Watches & Barometers
218 Other Antiques
     Antiquities 219
     Architectural 224
     Arms & Armour 234
     Boxes 238
     Dolls, Teddy Bears & Toys 244
     Kitchenware 248
     Lighting 254
     Metalware 258
     Rugs & Carpets 262
     Scientific Instruments 266
     Sculpture 270
     Textiles 274
     Wooden Antiques 278

282 Glossary
283 Directory of Specialists
285 Directory of Auctioneers
286 Key to Illustrations
290 Index to Advertisers
291 Index

MILLER'S

Contributors

FURNITURE:

Mervyn Carey started his career in 1964 at the Harrods Auction Gallery before moving on to run the Fine Art Department of Geering & Collier until 1991, when he started his own auctions. Mervyn Carey holds five auctions a year and is a member of the Furniture History Society.

CERAMICS:

Hamish Wilson was given a small quantity of old coins by his grandmother when he was eight years old, and so not only started collecting coins but began hoarding anything that was old. He studied Fine Arts Valuation at University, where he specialized in Arts and Crafts glass. He is now a specialist valuer of British and European Ceramics and Oriental Works of Art at Dreweatt Neate auctioneers in Tunbridge Wells, Kent. He has a personal collection of Japanese woodblock prints.

SILVER & PLATE:

Daniel Bexfield has specialized in Silver for 22 years. He regularly contributes to BBC television and radio programmes and a variety of publications on the subject, including *Miller's Silver & Plate Buyer's Guide*. Daniel is also on the council of BADA. He carries an extensive range of stock at his premises in Burlington Arcade, London, W1.

GLASS:

Andy McConnell is a writer/historian specializing in antique glass. He is currently working on a book about affordable 20th-century glass, which is due to be published by Miller's in Autumn 2005. Readers wishing to contact him may do so through his website www.decanterman.com

CLOCKS, WATCHES & BAROMETERS:

Jeremy Sparks worked at a major international auction house between 1987 and 1999, eventually becoming Executive Director. He left to form Calcutt Maclean Standen Fine Art, of which he is now Managing Director. Calcutt Maclean Standen Fine Art holds three to four large fine art sales a year. Jeremy also has a personal interest in fine antique furniture.

ANTIQUITIES & SCULPTURE:

Mark Ellin is a fellow of the National Association of Valuers and Auctioneers (NAVA). He joined the family firm Burstow and Hewett when he left school and has 20 years' experience in auctioneering and valuation. His spare time is occupied with two young children and a passion for collecting antiquities.

ARCHITECTURAL:

Jon Griffith took over the running of his father's antiques business in 1981 and branched out into antique fireplaces in 1985. He currently runs a small business in Canterbury, Kent, 'The Victorian Fireplace' which specializes in fireplaces and fenders from Georgian through to contemporary pieces, and advises writers on the subject.

ARMS & ARMOUR:

Roy Butler has been interested in arms, armour and militaria ever since he came across a set of military headdress cigarette cards as a boy. His particular subjects are Waterloo, Napoleon and Nelson. He has 53 years' experience at Wallis and Wallis as Senior Partner, and holds nine militaria sales, eight toy sales and two connoisseur sales each year. He appears on British television in the *Antiques Roadshow* and lectures on various cruise lines.

BOXES:

Leslie Gillham is consultant and manager of Gorringes in Tunbridge Wells, Kent and has more than 35 years' experience in the world of auctioneering. Gorringes Auction Galleries have four salerooms in the South East of England, holding over 70 scheduled auction sales per year of Antiques, Fine Art and Collectables, together with occasional specialist and house sales.

DOLLS, TEDDY BEARS & TOYS:

Barbara Ann Newman developed her childhood interest in dolls, toys and teddy bears into a business in 1991. She exhibits at the major fairs in London and Birmingham as well as from her shop. She is particularly interested in late 19th-century German and French bisque-headed dolls and character dolls.

KITCHENWARE:

Jane Wicks' business in kitchenware grew from her own personal collection. She has been selling kitchenware from the 1920s to 1950s from her shop in Rye for the last 10 years and also has a regular stall in the Abergevenny building at the Ardingly Antiques Fair.

LIGHTING:

Glynis Braizer has been the auction manager at Lambert and Foster for 17 years and the valuer for the last 10, where they hold general antiques sales once a month. Her personal collections encompass furniture and porcelain figures.

METALWARE:

Derek Hodge is the auctioneer and valuer at Ibbett Mosely in Sevenoaks, Kent where he has worked for the last 45 years. The auction house was established in the 1940s and holds approximately nine general antiques sales a year.

RUGS & CARPETS:

Jonathan Wadsworth is a specialist dealer in antique and modern rugs and carpets. He is a former director of Sotheby's Fine Art Auctioneers, London, and now operates as an expert consultant to auctioneers and loss adjusters. He also lectures at home and abroad and has featured on, and devised challenges for, British television's *Great Antiques Hunt*. He also regularly contributes to Miller's publications.

SCIENTIFIC INSTRUMENTS:

Jim Hollands started out as a general dealer in antiques and collectables before becoming an auctioneer 25 years ago. He has been the auctioneer at the Rye Auction Gallery for the last six years, and has always found scientific instruments fascinating. He also currently collects local history ephemera.

TEXTILES:

Erna Hiscock started with a shop in New Romney, Kent. She opened her gallery on Portobello Road, London, W11 in 1990, which is open only on Saturdays and specializes in 17th- to 19th-century samplers and needlework. Erna also gives talks on samplers and needlework from this period.

WOODEN ANTIQUES:

Dianne Brick has been in the antiques trade for 20 years and has always been interested in wooden boxes, and this grew into an interest in Tunbridge ware. She has specialized in Tunbridge ware for the last 15 years, has a shop on Old Gloucester Street, London, WC1N and exhibits at fairs such as Olympia, London.

Dates	British Monarch	British Period	French Period
1558–1603	Elizabeth I	Elizabethan	Renaissance
1603–1625	James I	Jacobean	
1625–1649	Charles I	Carolean	Louis XIII (1610–1643)
1649–1660	Commonwealth	Cromwellian	Louis XIV (1643–1715)
1660–1685	Charles II	Restoration	
1685–1689	James II	Restoration	
1689–1694	William & Mary	William & Mary	
1694–1702	William III	William III	
1702–1714	Anne	Queen Anne	
1714–1727	George I	Early Georgian	Régence (1715–1723)
1727–1760	George II	Early Georgian	Louis XV (1723–1774)
1760–1811	George III	Late Georgian	Louis XVI (1774–1793) Directoire (1793–1799) Empire (1799–1815)
1812–1820	George III	Regency	Restauration Charles X (1815–1830)
1820–1830	George IV	Regency	
1830–1837	William IV	William IV	Louis Philippe (1830–1848)
1837–1901	Victoria	Victorian	2nd Empire Napoleon III (1848–1870) 3rd Republic (1871–1940)
1901–1910	Edward VII	Edwardian	

German Period	US Period	Style	Woods
Renaissance	Early Colonial	Gothic	Oak Period (to c1670)
		Baroque (c1620–1700)	Walnut period (c1670–1735)
Renaissance/ Baroque (c1650–1700)			
	William & Mary		
	Dutch Colonial	Rococo (c1695–1760)	
Baroque (c1700–1730)	Queen Anne		
Rococo (c1730–1760)	Chippendale (from 1750)		Early mahogany period (c1735–1770)
Neo–classicism (c1760–1800)		Neo–classical (c1755–1805)	Late mahogany period (c1770–1810)
	Early Federal (1790–1810)		
Empire (c1800–1815)	American Directoire (1798–1804)	Empire (c1799–1815)	
	American Empire (1804–1815)		
Biedermeier (c1815–1848)	Late Federal (1810–1830)	Regency (c1812–1830)	
Revivale (c1830–1880)		Eclectic (c1830–1880)	
	Victorian		
Jugendstil (c1880–1920)		Arts & Crafts (c1880–1900)	
	Art Nouveau (c1900–1920)	Art Nouveau (c1900–1920)	

How to use this book

It is our aim to make this book easy to use. In order to find a particular item, consult the contents list on page 5 to find the main heading – for example, Arms & Armour. Having located your area of interest, you will find that sections have been sub-divided alphabetically. If you are looking for a particular factory, designer or craftsman, consult the index which starts on page 291.

---

234 ARMS & ARMOUR

Arms & Armour

Bowie knife, with a cutlery handle, c1860, 13in (33cm) long.
£580–650 / €860–970
$1,050–1,150 MDL ⊞

Bowie knives

Bowie knives are usually classified as any large knife with a chipped point. They were particularly popular in America between 1840 and 1865 and are believed to have been designed by Rezin Bowie, brother of James Bowie who played a leading role in the Texas revolution of 1835. Bowie knives were designed to be used when fishing and hunting but there are stories of more sinister uses as well. Some of the most desirable knives were made in Sheffield and exported to America and the Hudson Bay Company, Canada. Bowie knives are very popular with American collectors.

Miller's compares...

A. Artillery hanger, with a brass hilt and ribbed grip, slight wear, the blade marked 'Art Fab De Toledo', Spanish, 1902, blade 27½in (70cm) long.
£175–195 / €260–290
$310–350 FAC ⊞

B. Infantry hanger, with a brass hilt and ribbed grip, marked with a crowned 'GR' cipher, slight wear, 1812, blade 23in (58.5cm) long, with original leather scabbard.
£400–450 / €600–670
$710–800 FAC ⊞

Item A is Spanish and was made in the early part of the 20th century. Item B is an English sword dating from the Napoleonic period, which adds significant value to this piece. English and French swords are more desirable to collectors than Spanish examples, thus increasing the price of Item B.

The look without the price

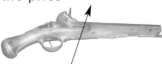

East India Company-style brass-mounted flintlock holster pistol, the barrel engraved with armoury inventory number 'S.L.3.79', Indian, 19thC, 17½in (44.5cm) long.
£180–210 / €270–310
$320–370 PFK ✦

If this pistol had actually been made by the East India Company it might have been worth £400–600 / €600–890 / $710–1,050. However, this piece still makes a good decorative item for a fraction of the cost.

Flintlock pistol, engraved 'Mabson and Labron', early 19thC, 6in (15cm) long. This pistol has the unusual and interesting feature of a hidden trigger. It also carries Birmingham proof marks which are less sought after than the well-known London marks.
£200–240 / €300–360
$350–420 HOLL ✦

Find out more in

Miller's Antiques Price Guide, Miller's Publications, 2004

Price guide
these are based on actual prices realized shown in £sterling with a € Euro and US$ conversion. Remember that Miller's is a price guide not a price list and prices are affected by many variables such as location, condition, desirability, whether it is a dealer ⊞ or auction ✦ price (see the source code below) and so on. Don't forget that if you are selling it is quite likely you will be offered less than the price range. Price ranges for items sold at auction tend to include the buyer's premium and VAT if applicable. The exchange rate used in this edition is 1.77 for $ and 1.49 for €.

Miller's compares
explains why two items which look similar have realized very different prices.

Information box
covers relevant collecting information on factories, makers, fakes and alterations, period styles and designers.

Caption
provides a brief description of the item. It explains, where possible, why an item is valued at a particular price.

Source code
refers to the Key to Illustrations on page 286 that lists the details of where the item was photographed. The ✦ icon indicates the item was sold at auction. The ⊞ icon indicates the item originated from a dealer.

The look without the price
highlights later items produced 'in the style of' earlier counterparts. It illustrates how you don't have to spend a fortune to have the original look.

Find out more in
directs the reader towards additional sources of information.

Introduction

Welcome to the 2005 edition of *Miller's Buying Affordable Antiques*, now in its third year of publication. The success of these *Guides* is primarily due to the careful process of selecting a balanced representation of the present-day market place. Each section has been overseen by an expert who is highly respected in their particular discipline. All have not only provided an interesting overview of their market but also reviewed the 1500 or more colour illustrations and their relevant prices.

We live in an age that appears preoccupied with the big story, the big event and in the case of the antiques world, the big price. The past three years have borne witness to some huge auction prices, all of which go some way to keeping the profile of the art and antiques world in the international public eye. Alas, it also helps perpetuate the ongoing myth that fine art and antiques is a playground where those who play invariably pay. I am delighted to be able to tell you that this book provides a welcome return to what I personally consider to be the real world of all things antique. So leave behind the stratosphere where £2,400,000 / €3,576,000 / $4,248,000 buys you a Roman glass cage cup c300 AD, put your feet on terra firma, open the pages of this guide and prepare to be pleasantly surprised.

Over the past few decades the asking prices for most antiques have risen, often at a steady rate and sometimes at a quantum leap. Consequently the past three years might be considered to have been a period of relative calm and stability as well as being an opportune time to have been out and about searching for pieces to collect in your particular field of interest.

Glancing through the pages of the furniture section I have found myself considering the feasibility of finding a large barn and then stacking it from the floor to the rafters with all that good-quality Georgian and Victorian brown furniture which continues to be unloved and unwanted at the time of writing. Maybe I should also consider filling the drawers with no end of Victorian brass candlesticks, table glass and dinner services.

All businesses rely upon a plentiful supply and a strong demand so I was intrigued to read a couple of recent articles in the British press suggesting that a falling demand in some areas was a result of changes in contemporary taste. There could well be an element of truth in this argument, after all the antiques business has always proved itself to be not only fickle but also cyclical. It's nothing new for successive generations to seek alternative collecting areas – just think in terms of 'goodbye Art Nouveau, hello Art Deco'. What I do think unlikely is that we are about to descend into a dark age of flat-pack furniture. Hopefully future trends will strike a happy balance between old and new, after all not many people want to find themselves living in a museum.

Despite the uncertainty of the market the omens are good for the 'antiqueholic' buyer. This guide is one such positive omen. Crammed full of the right advice from the right people, *Miller's Buying Affordable Antiques* offers an insight into a market eager to attract new buyers. So if you're new to the antiques scene, welcome to the party! **Eric Knowles, FRSA**

Types of Wood

Bird's-eye maple ▶

Bird's-eye maple, or American sugar maple, describes the very attractive figuring in maple. It was popular for veneers during the Regency period, and was also used in Victorian and Edwardian bedroom suites. The wood of the maple is whitish, and responds well to polishing. Bird's-eye maple is also popular today for picture frames.

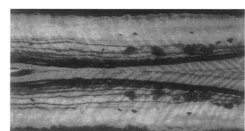

◀ Burr walnut

Burr walnut is the term used for walnut with knotty whorls in the grain where injuries occurred on the trunk or roots of the tree. It was often used in decorative veneers. Walnut is a close-grained hardwood, the colour varying between light golden brown to dark grey-brown in colour with dark streaks, often with a rich grain pattern.

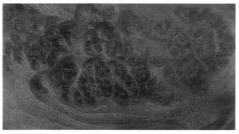

Calamander ▶

Calamander is a member of the **ebony** family and derives from Ceylon. Popular in the Regency period, it is light brown in colour, striped and mottled with black, and was used for veneers and banding. Calamander was also used in the manufacture of small decorative boxes. Ebony is close-grained, black in colour, and is resistant to decay.

◀ Elm

The English variety of elm is hard and durable, but liable to warp, and prone to woodworm. Chairs were made from elm from the Georgian period, and the seats of Windsor chairs were elm from the 18th century. The wych elm has a particularly attractive grain and polishes well. **Burr elm** was used for veneers and cabinet-work in the early 18th century.

Kingwood ▶

Kingwood is related to rosewood, which was first imported to Britain from Brazil in the late 17th century. It is a rich brown with purplish tones, giving it an alternative name of violet wood. Also known as princewood, it was used as a veneer or for parquetry decoration, particularly in France. From c1770 it was used for crossbanding and borders.

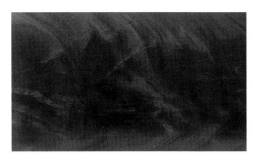

◄ Mahogany

Mahogany is a close grained hardwood, native to northern and central South America and the West Indies. It varies in colour from dark brown to red, and sometimes has a spotted effect. Furniture made from mahogany became very popular with cabinet-makers in Britain from the mid-18th century, followed by France and the rest of Europe. African mahogany, which is lighter in weight, was used from the 1800s onwards.

Oak ►

Oak is a slow-growing tree, taking between 150 and 200 years to reach maturity. The wood is hard and pale in colour, but darkens to a rich brown with age and polishing. Furniture made from oak is usually heavy and solid, and simple in design. From the middle of the 17th century oak was used mainly for the carcases of furniture and drawer linings, but became popular again in the late 19th century with the Arts and Crafts movement.

◄ Rosewood

Rosewood is a very dark brown hardwood, with an almost black wavy grain. The name comes from the scent released when the wood is cut. Rosewood was used for inlaid decoration in the 17th century, and for veneer, but was not used for making solid furniture until the early 19th century. It was also used for decorative banding and small panels from the late 18th century.

Satinwood ►

Satinwood was used widely for veneers and inlaid decoration, the pale colour making it particularly suitable for painting. The grain varies from plain to rich figuring, the latter having a more transparent grain under polish or varnish. Cabinet-makers of the 19th century preferred the West Indian variety, which is darker than the East Indian variety, and was used as a veneer in fine furniture from c1765. It was rarely used in the solid, and not for chairs until c1800. The Eastern type, imported in the late 18th century, was pale yellow and used mainly for crossbanding.

◄ Sycamore

Sycamore is a European wood related to the North American maple, and is as strong as oak. It is hard, milky-white, with a fine even grain with natural lustre. In medieval times furniture was made in solid sycamore, and from the late 17th century it was used in floral marquetry on walnut furniture. When quarter-sawn the figuring is known as **fiddleback**, as it was often used in the manufacture of violins. Sycamore treated with iron oxide or stained green or grey was known as **harewood.**

Furniture

'You have never had it so good!' Prime Minister Harold Macmillan's catchphrase from the late 1950s is equally appropriate when applied to today's furniture market. In particular, traditional British furniture of the range covered by this book has seen prices in retreat or remaining fairly static during the past decade, and noticeably so during the last three or four years. Therefore, now is a good time to consider what is on offer at affordable prices at auctions, antiques fairs and in dealers' shops.

As with many spheres of life, fashions change in the world of antiques, but the wide range available ensures that all tastes can be catered for. Those influenced by the current trend for minimalism can look for selected pieces among the more restrained furniture from the late Georgian period and the Sheraton revival, or even Arts and Crafts and Art Deco items to blend with their schemes. Items that particularly spring to mind are the various types of occasional table, from Sheraton and Edwardian examples with elegant square tapering legs, to late 19th-century pieces based on designs by E. W. Godwin and C. R. Mackintosh.

There does, perhaps, need to be a re-awakening of interest in more traditional furniture. While there are those that have not lost sight of the merits of oak, mahogany seems to be less popular nowadays and pine has recently fallen from fashion, resulting in lower prices, so now is a good time to pick up a bargain. Generally speaking, people need to realize that it is not necessary to own a Georgian property in order to house Georgian furniture satisfactorily. The elegance of pieces such as chairs, chests of drawers, corner cupboards and tables (including Louis XV- and XVI-style examples) from the 18th century and Regency periods can be shown to advantage in many types of property. Even the currently unfashionable bureau or davenport makes a suitable furnishing item for a sitting room. The comfort of Victorian upholstered chairs, together with the practicalities of dining and side tables and chests of drawers from that era need to be rediscovered and to be explained to the novice.

It is important to build up as wide a body of knowledge as you can, not only from television, books and magazines, but from visiting stately homes and the various establishments selling antiques. While the principal rooms of great houses will contain the finest items, look at the contents of the lesser rooms and servants' quarters. Such visits will add interest to the process of acquiring knowledge, and will help place furniture in the context of rooms and people.

So, armed with your newly-acquired knowledge and improved judgement, go confidently into the marketplace and buy what appeals to you. This book will give you a good idea of what is available and the price ranges – the value of any piece will be governed largely by its quality and condition. If you are buying at auction and the item requires restoration, do take into account the likely cost of this when bidding. Be aware that damage to inlays, marquetry and veneers such as cracking, splitting, scratches and stains can be expensive to repair and may not always be worth the investment. In this instance it is worth seeking specialist advice before making a purchase. Replacement handles can be relatively inexpensive as there are many modern reproductions to choose from, but a period example will always be preferable to serious collectors.

Mervyn Carey

Beds & Cradles

Bentwood cot, with turned spindle rails and supports, c1900, 37¼in (94.5cm) long.
£80–95 / €120–140
$140–165 SWO ⚒

◀ **Carved and painted four-poster bed,** with C-scroll and foliate decoration, 18thC, 53½in (136cm) wide. A certain amount of wear and tear is to be expected on an item of this age and this should not affect the value.
£320–380
€480–570
$570–670 JAA ⚒

Victorian bed, with carved head- and footboards, American, East Lake, 56in (142cm) wide. American-made items of furniture appeal to both US and Continental buyers as they complement the larger items of furniture which are fashionable there. Therefore, now could be a good time to invest in such pieces in the UK while prices are still low.
£165–195 / €240–290
$290–350 JAA ⚒

Oak and walnut cradle, French, mid-19thC, 47in (119.5cm) wide. Sleigh-shaped cradles are very collectable in the US and command a much higher premium than they would in the UK, where they do not have the same appeal.
£450–540 / €670–800
$800–960 JAA ⚒

Victorian child's mahogany bergère cradle, with arabesque hood, on a turned stand, 41in (104cm) long. This style of cradle is currently very popular in the UK market.
£460–550 / €690–820
$810–970 SWO ⚒

Benches

Miller's compares...

A. Ash and elm milking stool, Irish, c1880,
12in (30.5cm) high.
£30–35 / €45–50
$50–60 ByI ▦

B. Walnut bench, Italian, 17thC,
49¼in (125cm) long.
£600–720 / €890–1,050
$1,050–1,250 S(O) ⚒

Item A is a 19th century rustic, Irish bench made of various woods. Item B, however, is an older, more elegant Italian example, made entirely of walnut, which makes it more desirable and able to command a higher price.

► **Oak bench,** with adze marks, 19thC,
97in (246.5cm) long.
£160–190 / €240–290
$290–340 SWO ⚒

The look without the price

Louis XV-style banquette, by Haentges Frères, upholstered in silk, French, Paris, 19thC, 41¾in (106cm) long.
£360–430 / €530–640
$640–760 S(Am) ⚒

Louis XV-style furniture was extremely fashionable in the 19th century. A genuine Louis XV example could be worth 10 times as much as this banquette.

Walnut and fruitwood hall bench, with hinged seat, Italian, 19thC, 60¼in (153cm) wide. This is an ornate, good quality piece at a very reasonable price.
£960–1,150 / €1,450–1,700
$1,700–2,000 S(O) ⚒

Bookcases & Shelves

◄ **Pine bookcase,** 1900, 28in (71cm) wide. The popularity of the British pine market has decreased recently, hence the low price.
£70–80
€ 105–120
$125–140 DFA ⊞

Walnut bookcase, damaged, Italian, early 19thC, 58in (147.5cm) high.
£230–270 / € 340–400
$410–480 DN(BR) ✗

Miller's compares...

A. Set of mahogany waterfall hanging shelves, c1810, 30½in (77.5cm) high.
£310–350 / € 460–520
$550–620 F&F ⊞

B. Rosewood waterfall bookcase, 19thC, 36¼in (92cm) wide.
£530–630 / € 790–940
$940–1,100 B(Kn) ✗

Set of fruitwood open shelves, with five tiers and turned supports, 19thC, 31in (78.5cm) wide. Fruitwood can be more popular than oak. These shelves are particularly elegant and are good value for money.
£330–390 / € 490–580
$580–690 WW ✗

Item A is of a very plain design whereas Item B is a more decorative and substantial set of floorstanding shelves made of rosewood which is more desirable than mahogany.

Find out more in

Miller's Antiques Encyclopedia, Miller's Publications, 2003

► **Victorian walnut-veneered bookcase,** with adjustable shelves, 34in (86.5cm) wide.
£380–450 / € 570–670
$670–800 WW ✗

Late Victorian walnut breakfront open bookcase, with adjustable shelves, 67in (170cm) wide. Larger pieces of furniture have become less fashionable due to the small room sizes in contemporary homes, so good buys can be found.
£480–570 / €720–850
$850–1,000 SWO 🔨

▶ **Edwardian mahogany open bookcase,** 52in (132cm) wide.
£600–720 / €890–1,050
$1,050–1,250 B(Kn) 🔨

Mahogany bookcase, with adjustable shelves, c1860, 54in (137cm) wide. Adjustable shelving is always more desirable to purchasers because of its adaptability.
£780–940 / €1,150–1,400
$1,400–1,650 S(O) 🔨

Edwardian mahogany and kingwood crossbanded revolving bookcase, c1910, 19¾in (50cm) wide. The workmanship and the use of mahogany and kingwood adds to the quality of this bookcase, making it a desirable piece of furniture at a good price.
£840–1,000 / €1,250–1,500
$1,500–1,800 S(O) 🔨

The look without the price

Ebonized and parcel-gilt bookcase, fall-front missing glass, Italian, c1850, 86½in (219.5cm) wide.
£840–1,000 / €1,250–1,500
$1,500–1,800 S(O) 🔨

This item could have fetched £200 / €300 / $350 more if the bookcase had been complete, although it is still a functional piece. It is always worth checking restoration costs in advance of an auction, as the thought of repair bills might deter other bidders, and result in an opportune purchase.

Chairs

Miller's compares...

A. Pair of Victorian balloon-back bedroom chairs, with mother-of-pearl inlay and cane seats.
£40–50 / €60–70
$75–90 MCA ⚲

B. Pair of Victorian papier-mâché chairs.
£360–430 / €540–640
$640–760 L ⚲

Child's beech chair, c1900. Children's chairs are always popular with collectors.
£45–50 / €70–80
$80–90 Byl ⊞

Although the chairs in Item A have mother-of-pearl inlay, the chairs in Item B have cabriole legs, which is currently a feature more in demand, making it a more desirable purchase. The quality of the decoration in Item B also contributes to the difference in the realized prices.

Lady's mahogany Adam-style elbow chair, the pierced lyle splat carved with rosette and laurel swags, trade label for Jas Shoolbred & Co, early 20thC. This chair represents an excellent opportunity to buy a quality piece by a well-known maker at a relatively low price.
£110–130 / €165–195
$195–230 NSal ⚲

Edwardian mahogany open armchair, with boxwood stringing.
£80–95 / €120–140
$140–165 PFK ⚲

Mahogany open armchair, with later drop-in seat, all legs repaired, 18thC.
£100–120 / €150–180
$175–210 WW ⚲

Miller's compares...

A. Child's ash and elm training chair, c1900, 20in (51cm) high.
£140–155 / €210–230 $250–280 SDA ⊞

B. Child's beech and elm training chair, 1860–80, 20in (51cm) high.
£270–300 / €400–450 $480–530 SDA ⊞

Item A is a more modern piece and is a more commonly-found stick-back design. Item B is in better condition, which adds to the higher price.

Victorian walnut prie dieu, with barley-twist uprights and upholstered back, 38¼in (97cm) high. The Victorian prie dieu style was based on church chairs. The 'seat' was knelt on and a prayer book could be rested on the top of the back. They were later adapted for drawing room use.
£155–180 / €230–270 $270–320 DN(Bri) 🔨

Victorian walnut open hall chair, with barley-twist arms, supports and stretchers, the arms with carved lions.
£160–190 / €240–280 $280–330 WilP 🔨

▶ **Ash and elm hoop-back Windsor chair,** 19thC.
£160–190 / €240–280 $280–330 G(L) 🔨

Edwardian mahogany tub chair.
£160–190 / €240–280 $280–330 FHF 🔨

▶ **Oak side chair,** with later needlework, late 17thC.
£175–210 / €260–310 $310–370 WW 🔨

Find out more in

Miller's Late Georgian to Edwardian Furniture Buyer's Guide, Miller's Publications, 2003

Miller's compares...

A. George III child's elm high chair, with later adjustable footplate, 38¼in (97cm) high.
£180–210 / €270–310
$320–370 B(Kn) 🔨

B. Child's mahogany high chair, with a pierced splat and drop-in seat, early 19thC.
£500–600 / €750–890
$890–1,050 SWO 🔨

Item A is made of elm, which is less desirable than the mahogany of Item B. Item A is not entirely original as it has been repaired and is incomplete, whereas Item B retains its original restraining bar, thus making it the more valuable item of the two.

Victorian oak tub library chair, with leather upholstery, on barley-twist front legs. Original leather upholstery in good condition adds to the desirability of this piece. Reupholstery in leather would add greatly to the overall cost of a chair.
£180–210 / €270–310
$320–370 PFK 🔨

Children's furniture

Furniture made for children tends to follow contemporary fashion, mirroring the features found in full-size, adult furniture. It can usually be dated in the same way. Chairs were by far the most common pieces of furniture made for children. Items made in the 19th and 20th centuries tend to be more widely available, and consequently more affordable than that of the 17th and 18th centuries. Later children's chairs are attractive and functional and can be purchased for modest sums, although it should be noted that they no longer comply with EC safety regulations.

Walnut elbow chair, with vase splat back, scrolling arms, on cabriole legs, 18thC.
£180–210 / €270–310
$320–370 BWL 🔨

◄ **Victorian child's rosewood baronial chair,** decorated with woolwork crests, carved with foliate scrolls and cartouches.
£180–210 / €270–310
$320–370 FHF 🔨

To find out more about antique furniture see the full range of Miller's books at **www.millers.uk.com**

◀ **Mahogany elbow chair,** with upholstered seat, legs cut down, Dutch, 19thC. The value of this piece has been dramatically reduced by the shortening of its legs, which has ruined the scale of the chair. In original condition this chair would have been worth £300 / €450 / $530.
£200–240 / €300–360 $350–420 G(L) 🔨

Hepplewhite-style painted open armchair, stamped 'B. Harmer', 18thC. The distressed condition of the later paintwork has adversely affected the value of this armchair.
£200–240 / €300–360 $350–420 G(L) 🔨

Victorian mahogany spoon-back nursing chair. The upholstered back of this nursing chair adds to its value. Without this additional feature it would have been more affordable, but less comfortable.
£200–240 / €300–360 $350–420 WW 🔨

George IV mahogany open armchair, stamped 'J. C. J.'. The presence of the maker's stamp is always beneficial, as it adds to the value of furniture.
£200–240 / €300–360 $350–420 WW 🔨

◀ **Pair of Victorian Gothic-style mahogany hall chairs.** The Gothic style is currently fashionable and therefore collectable.
£210–250 / €310–370 $370–440 B(Kn) 🔨

Child's oak Windsor armchair, 19thC. Fewer chairs of this type from the early 19thC have survived, making this child's chair rarer than those of the mid- to late-19thC. However, they are still affordable today.
£230–270 / €340–400 $410–480 LAY 🔨

Locate the source

The source of each illustration in Miller's can be found by checking the code letters below each caption with the Key to Illustrations, pages 286–290.

Pair of mahogany open armchairs, with scrolling arms, early 20thC. Pairs of chairs are worth proportionally more than individual chairs.
£240–290 / €360–430
$420–500 FHF

Oak rocking chair, with a spindle back and rush seat, restored, North Country, early 19thC. The quality of restoration has a big effect on the price of an item. A bad restoration can greatly detract from the value, while good, sympathetic restoration is acceptable.
£220–250 / €330–370
$390–440 CHAC

Pair of early Victorian mahogany hall chairs.
£250–300 / €370–440
$440–520 SWO

▶ **Child's ash, beech and elm Oxford chair,** c1840. The patination on a piece of furniture can greatly influence its value. The good colour of this chair has been acquired by years of polishing and waxing to achieve a deep, soft sheen that is pleasing to the eye and touch.
£260–290 / €390–430
$460–510 F&F

Chippendale-style mahogany elbow chair, with carved decoration, pierced splat and tapestry seat, late 19thC. Although this chair is of good quality, the style has become less popular of late, possibly due to the heaviness of the design.
£280–330 / €420–490
$500–580 SWO

Three Regency *faux-bamboo* painted ash chairs, comprising one open armchair and two side chairs, with rush seats, one distressed. Chairs sold in lots of two or four are preferable to the purchaser as they make balanced sets, and therefore command a higher price. This group of three chairs is a good buy.
£300–360 / €450–540
$530–640 WW ⚒

Child's armchair, with rush seat, Continental, c1850. The unusual Continental style of this child's chair makes it desirable to collectors in the UK.
£270–300 / €400–450
$480–530 F&F ⊞

Beech rocking chair, c1880. Rocking chairs are rarer and generally more expensive than those without rockers. The good patina of the wood is another desirable element of this piece.
£270–300 / €400–450
$480–530 COF ⊞

▶ **Pair of Regency painted side chairs.** These chairs would have been more desirable had they not been painted. Plain mahogany or rosewood would be preferable.
£300–360
€450–540
$530–640 B(Kn) ⚒

◀ **Victorian child's mahogany chair,** c1860.
£340–380
€510–570
$600–670 TIM ⊞

Child's ash and elm Windsor armchair, c1830. Dark patinas are preferable, but they should not be too black in colour. This chair has a rich colour and patina making it an attractive buy.
£310–350 / €460–520
$550–620 F&F ⊞

Ash Windsor rocking chair, with crinoline stretcher and rockers, part stripped, West Country, 19thC. In good condition, this chair could have been worth £100 / €150 / $180 more. The cost of restoration should always be considered when buying a piece of furniture.
**£350–420 / €520–620
$630–740 WW** ⚱

Regency mahogany bergère, with caned back and sides, 1800–25. Bergère chairs are not popular in the USA. In the UK they sell for between £1,000–3,000 / €1,500–4,500 / $1,800–5,300, depending on quality and condition. Had this chair sold in the UK, it could have made in excess of £1,000 / €1,500 / $1,800.
**£350–420 / €520–630
$620–740 NOA** ⚱

Birch high/rocking chair, with lift-up tray, late 19thC, 36in (91.5cm) high.
**£360–400 / €540–600
$640–710 SAT** ⊞

◄ **Walnut correction/deportment chair,** with a cane seat, c1830. A correction chair was a high-backed chair on which children were taught to sit correctly.
**£360–400 / €540–600
$640–710 TIM** ⊞

Set of six Edwardian rosewood chairs, with carved backs and upholstered seats, c1880. These chairs are not of a strong structural design, making them more decorative than practical, hence their lower value.
**£380–450 / €570–670
$670–800 WilP** ⚱

George III mahogany carver chair, with rope-twist splat and scroll arms.
**£360–430 / €540–640
$640–760 L&E** ⚱

Find out more in

Miller's Buying Affordable Antiques, Miller's Publications, 2004

Child's ash and elm Windsor armchair, c1825.
£390–430 / €580–640
$690–760 F&F ⊞

Pair of Victorian oak Gothic-style hall chairs, with tracery backs and legs. This is a pair of good quality chairs at an affordable price.
£400–480 / €600–720
$710–850 SWO ⚒

Mahogany ladder-back dining chair, 18thC.
£410–490 / €610–730
$730–870 SWO ⚒

Mahogany swivel desk chair, the scrolled crest-rail mounted with a silver plaque inscribed 'presented to J. M. Bates 1904–1916', restored, early 20thC. Presentation plaques only add to the value of an item if the recipient is well known and of interest to the general public.
£420–500 / €630–750
$740–890 DN(BR) ⚒

◄ **Wing chair,** the spiral-twist frame with later upholstery, late 17thC. The colour of reupholstery can adversely affect the value of a chair, as in this case.
£450–540 / €670–800
$800–960 SWO ⚒

Child's ash primitive chair, with comb back, on three faceted legs, 19thC. Primitive designs are currently very popular with collectors of children's chairs.
£440–520 / €660–770
$780–920 WW ⚒

Sets/pairs

Unless otherwise stated, any description which refers to 'a set' or 'a pair' includes a guide price for the entire set or the pair, even though the illustration may show only a single item.

◀ **Pair of mahogany dining chairs,** with scroll backs, 19thC. Sets of dining chairs become devalued when split up.
£470–560
€700–830
$830–990 B(Kn) ⚒

Victorian giltwood Egyptian revival-style armchair. The opulent style of this armchair is of limited appeal to UK buyers. It could have achieved a higher price on the Continent, where such pieces are still desirable.
£470–560 / €700–830
$830–990 S(O) ⚒

The look without the price

Louis XV-style carved giltwood desk chair, c1860.
£480–570 / €720–850
$850–1,000 S(O) ⚒

Had this chair been a genuine Louis XV piece, it would have been worth at least 10 times as much. An original Louis XV chair would have been of a less flamboyant style.

Set of four Regency mahogany dining chairs, including a pair of open carvers, with inlaid and pierced mid-rails above leather upholstered seats, repaired and restored. In good condition these chairs would have been worth about £7,500 / €11,200 / $13,300. The repairs and restorations have detracted from the hammer price.
£480–580 / €720–860
$850–1,000 DN(BR) ⚒

Find out more in
Miller's Antiques Price Guide,
Miller's Publications, 2004

Beech grandfather chair, c1875.
£450–500 / €670–750
$800–890 COF ⊞

◀ **Carved oak armchair,** with a painted and embossed leather back and figural arm fronts, late 19thC. This style of armchair is more popular on the Continent, making furniture such as this a good buy in the UK.
£490–590 / €730–880
$870–1,050 SWO ⚒

Pair of Victorian mahogany revolving tub armchairs, with bobbin supports, stamped 'P' and the Patent registration mark for 7 December 1880, 25in (63.5cm) wide.
£520–620 / €770–920
$920–1,100 TRM 🔨

Set of six George III mahogany dining chairs.
£700–840 / €1,050–1,250
$1,250–1,500 L 🔨

Set of four Victorian carved walnut dining chairs, with stuff-over seats, on cabriole front legs.
£560–670 / €830–1,000
$1,000–1,200 AH 🔨

Figured woods

All woods have their own distinctive graining or figuring, some more so than others. This was often greatly enhanced by the way in which the wood was cut, and if used as a veneer, how the veneers were matched. Look out for distinctive burr cuts, particularly in walnut, oak and elm. Colour and patination can also add to the appeal of the figuring.

◄ **Set of eight late Victorian oak dining chairs,** including two carvers. Larger sets of dining chairs are very desirable.
£700–840 / €1,050–1,250
$1,250–1,500 PFK 🔨

Chests & Coffers

Stained fruitwood and pine mule chest, the panelled front above a long drawer, 18thC, 44in (112cm) wide. Chests made of fruitwood and pine are a cheaper alternative to those made of oak.
£150–180 / €230–270
$270–320 WW 🔨

Grain-decorated six board chest, with a moulded cover, cover split, American, 1800–50, 36½in (92.5cm) wide. This chest is of particular American appeal as it has New England-style decoration.
£190–220
€280–330
$340–390 JDJ 🔨

◄ **Panelled walnut blanket box,** with wrought-iron hinges, early 18thC, 48¼in (122.5cm) wide.
£190–220
€280–330
$340–390 JDJ 🔨

Elm mule chest, with bracket feet, 18thC, 48½in (123cm) wide. Elm chests are usually of plank rather than panel construction, making this one rather unusual.
£250–300 / €370–450
$440–530 B(Kn) 🔨

Miller's compares...

A. Oak coffer, with later carving, 17thC, 41¾in (106cm) wide.
£300–360 / €450–540
$530–640 B(Kn) 🔨

B. Oak chest, the hinged top above a frieze with carved arches and panels, early 18thC, 56¾in (144cm) wide.
£600–720 / €890–1,050
$1,050–1,250 DN 🔨

Item A has later carving, which has detracted from its value. It also has only three panels on the top and single panels to the sides. Item B, however, has four panels on the top and two to the sides, and has more elaborate decoration, making it a more desirable purchase.

Oak blanket box, the hinged top opening to reveal a candle box, the panelled front with a carved frieze, 18thC, 44in (112cm) wide. The simple decoration and small size of this box make it a desirable piece of furniture for today's smaller homes.
£320–380 / €480–570
$570–670 WL 🔨

Oak coffer, the front with moulded panels, late 17thC, 48in (122cm) wide.
£300–360 / €450–540
$530–640 PF 🔨

Oak and fruitwood chest, the panelled front applied with carved mermaids, inscribed 'Heidemans Anno 1798', damaged, south German, 1798, 29in (73.5cm) wide. The design and decoration of this chest appeals more to the Continental market than to that of the USA or UK, hence the lower price achieved.
£350–420 / €520–620
$620–740 S(Am) 🔨

Elm plank coffer, with moulded plinth, 18thC, 46½in (118cm) wide.
£350–420 / €520–620
$620–740 B(Kn) 🔨

Oak coffer, the moulded top opening to reveal a candle box, the panelled front with possibly later carved decoration, late 17thC, 50¼in (127.5cm) wide.
£360–430 / €540–640
$640–760 DN(Bri) 🔨

Pine blanket box, enclosing a candle box, East European, c1900, 42in (106.5cm) wide.
£450–500 / €670–750
$800–890 COF ⊞

Oak and marquetry coffer, the top with two moulded panels inlaid with star motifs, the frieze with four cushion-moulded marquetry-framed panels, inlaid with stylized tulips and birds, on a moulded plinth, north European, 18thC, 59in (150cm) wide.
£550–660 / €820–980
$970–1,150 HYD 🔨

Decoration

The decorative appeal of furniture is greatly enhanced by the use of features such as crossbanding, stringing and marquetry. Probably originating from Holland, marquetry was first used to a significant extent in Britain during the William and Mary period when naturalistic designs of birds, flowers and leaves were used. During the Adam and Sheraton periods a more refined, elegant style was favoured, using more restrained decoration in the form of stringing with plain or patterned line, or perhaps inlay in contrasting woods to the main veneer. These styles were revived during the late Victorian and Edwardian eras.

Pine blanket box, Continental, c1890, 45in (114.5cm) wide.
£530–600 / €790–890
$940–1,050 COF ⊞

Oak coffer, 17thC, 55½in (141cm) wide.
£590–700 / €880–1,050
$1,050–1,250 L 🔨

Oak plank chest, early 17thC, 44in (112cm) wide. The early date and good condition of this chest make it very desirable and accounts for the high price realized.
£590–700 / €880–1,050
$1,050–1,250 B(Kn) 🔨

Chests of Drawers & Commodes

Mahogany bowfronted commode,
the hinged top above a dummy drawer,
with ceramic liner, early 19thC,
28¼in (72cm) wide.
£200–240 / €300–360
$350–420 WW ⚹

To find out more about antique
furniture see the full range of
Miller's books at
www.millers.uk.com

Mahogany shop chest of seed drawers, c1890, 24in (61cm)
wide. The small size of this item makes it very desirable. It could
possibly be used in the kitchen for storing spices.
£200–220 / €300–330
$350–390 MIN ⊞

Miller's compares...

A. Late Georgian inlaid-mahogany bow-
fronted chest of drawers, 47¼in (120cm) wide.
£220–260 / €330–390
$390–460 WilP ⚹

B. Regency mahogany bowfronted chest of
drawers, 35¾in (91cm) wide.
£750–900 / €1,100–1,300
$1,350–1,600 B(Kn) ⚹

Item A has five drawers and an overhanging top, which is currently less fashionable with
buyers. Item B is a more elegant piece with four graduated drawers, a flush top and more
desirable handles, all of which have contributed to its value.

◄ **Victorian mahogany chest of drawers,** the moulded top above two short and three long graduated cockbeaded drawers, 42in (106.5cm) wide.
£230–250
€ **340–370**
$410–440 DD 🔨

George III mahogany chest of drawers, 36½in (92.5cm) wide.
£280–330 / € **420–490**
$500–580 B(Kn) 🔨

Mahogany chest of drawers, with two short and three long cockbeaded drawers flanked by baluster-turned columns, mid-19thC, 45in (114.5cm) wide. The heavy, ornate decoration of this chest is not popular at the moment. If this style appeals to you then now is the time to buy.
£280–330 / € **420–490**
$500–580 PF 🔨

George III-style mahogany chest of drawers, with two short over three long cockbeaded drawers, 30in (76cm) wide.
£280–330 / € **420–490**
$500–580 PF 🔨

Figured mahogany chest of drawers, with glass handles, Continental, probably German, 19thC, 41¾in (106cm) wide. This style of chest of drawers is currently unpopular, hence the low price.
£290–340 / € **430–510**
$510–600 DD 🔨

Victorian mahogany bowfronted chest of drawers, with two short over two long drawers, 40½in (103cm) wide.
£300–360 / € **450–540**
$530–640 SWO 🔨

► **Victorian mahogany bowfronted chest of drawers,** with two short over three long drawers, 43¾in (111cm) wide.
£350–420
€520–620
$620–740 B(Kn) 🔨

George IV mahogany-veneered barrel-front chest of drawers, with two short over three long drawers, stamped 'P. Jackson', losses to veneer, later handles, 42½in (108cm) wide. The later handles on this piece partially cover the locks on the top drawers, making them unusable. This, and the veneer losses have kept the price low.
£300–360 / €450–540
$530–640 WW 🔨

Georgian mahogany chest of drawers, with two short over three long drawers. The handles on this chest of drawers have been replaced. If restored to its original look, this item would be an attractive piece.
£360–400 / €540–600
$640–710 SV ⊞

◄ **George III mahogany chest-on-stand,** with three short over four long drawers, later stand, 56in (142cm) wide.
£380–450
€570–670
$670–800 SWO 🔨

Hardwoods

The nature of the various types of tropical hardwood used in furniture is such that many pieces are ideal for use in today's more urban-style properties. Items such as chairs, tables, cabinets and chests of drawers made of mahogany, satinwood and rosewood are particularly suitable and will blend with the current fashion for minimalism. The dramatic figuring of rosewood, the silky patina of satinwood and tight patterns of amboyna will have a premium over other woods – it is just a matter of personal taste.

George III mahogany chest of drawers, with two short over three long drawers, 37¾in (96cm) wide.
£380–450 / €570–670
$670–800 B(Kn) 🔨

Mahogany bowfronted chest of drawers, with two short over three long drawers, mid-19thC, 41in (104cm) wide.
£400–480 / € 600–720
$710–850 PF ⚒

◄ **Mahogany chest of drawers,** with four long drawers, French, 19thC, 40½in (103cm) wide.
£380–450 / € 570–670
$670–800 CHTR ⚒

George III mahogany bowfronted chest of drawers, 41½in (105.5cm) wide.
£420–500 / € 630–750
$740–890 L ⚒

▶ **George IV mahogany and satinwood-banded parquetry-strung night commode,** the hinged top above two cupboard doors enclosing a pull-out drawer, over a deep drawer, 18¾in (47.5cm) wide. This commode has good inlay and has been adapted to make it into a more useful piece of furniture. This may possibly have increased its value.
£440–520 / € 660–770
$780–920 WL ⚒

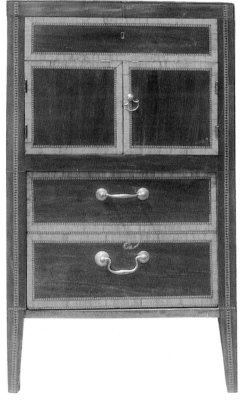

Mahogany bowfronted chest of drawers, with three long drawers, 1875–1900, 33½in (85cm) wide.
£450–540 / €670–800
$800–960 NOA ≫

George III oak chest of drawers, with two short over four long drawers flanked by brass-capped mahogany pilasters, North Country, 50½in (128cm) wide. The extra drawer in this chest of drawers denotes that it is of North Country origin.
£470–560 / €700–830
$830–990 WW ≫

Miller's compares...

A. Oak chest-on-chest, with two short over five long drawers, on bracket feet, back of top section replaced, early 19thC, 43¼in (110cm) wide.
£490–590 / €730–880
$870–1,050 SWO ≫

B. George III mahogany chest-on-chest, the upper section with two short over three long drawers, the lower section with fitted brushing slide above three graduated drawers, later handles and feet, 40¼in (102cm) wide.
£750–900 / €1,100–1,300
$1,350–1,600 FHF ≫

Although Item B has later handles and feet, the age, colour and design of the piece make it more desirable than the poorer quality workmanship of Item A.

Mahogany bowfronted chest of drawers, handles replaced, early 19thC, 34in (86.5cm) wide. Originally, this chest of drawers would have had either knob handles or plainer versions of the current handles. The replacement of the knobs has detracted from the price.
£600–720 / €890–1,050
$1,050–1,250 PF ≫

Georgian pine chest of drawers, 44in (112cm) wide.
£630–700 / €940–1,050
$1,100–1,250 TPC ⊞

Miller's compares...

A. Mahogany miniature apprentice chest of drawers, c1820, 10½in (26.5cm) wide.
£500–560 / €750–830
$890–990 F&F ⊞

B. Mahogany miniature bowfronted chest of drawers, c1820, 15in (38cm) high.
£700–780 / €1,050–1,200
$1,250–1,400 TIM ⊞

The bowfronted style, together with the quality of the workmanship of Item B is preferable to the more basic design of Item A. These factors account for the difference in price.

◄ **Victorian pine chest of drawers,** with two short over five long drawers, 63in (160cm) high.
£720–800
€1,050–1,200
$1,250–1,400
TPC ⊞

► **George III commode,** converted to a chest of drawers, 23¼in (59cm) wide. The conversion to a chest of drawers has made this item a much more practical piece and has probably increased its value.
£820–980
€1,200–1,450
$1,450–1,750
SWO ✎

Walnut and crossbanded chest of drawers, with two short over three long drawers, altered bracket feet, 18thC, 40¼in (102cm) wide. This item would have been worth over £1,000 / €1,500 / $1,800 more if it had not been altered and if the colour were deeper.
£620–740 / €920–1,100
$1,100–1,300 SWO ✎

Cupboards & Cabinets

Victorian walnut coal purdonium, 24in (61cm) high.
£55–65 / €80–95
$100–115 SV ⊞

Victorian ebonized and inlaid cabinet, with gilt mounts, 32¼in (82cm) high.
£280–330 / €420–490
$500–580 SWO ✎

Miller's compares...

A. Table cabinet, with six short drawers above two mahogany-fronted panelled doors, with turned bone handles, 21in (53.5cm) wide.
£150–180 / €230–270
$270–320 WW ✎

B. Victorian rosewood table cabinet, with nine drawers, c1850, 19¼in (49cm) wide.
£480–570 / €720–850
$850–1,000 S(O) ✎

Item B sold for a higher price than Item A because it is a better quality piece, has finer styling and is made of rosewood. It also has the advantage of a pair of doors enclosing all the drawers.

Lady's walnut work cabinet, the cover enclosing a painted and mother-of-pearl-embellished harbour scene on glass, opening to reveal sewing compartments, the lower section with cabinet doors enclosing three drawers, 19thC, 13½in (34.5cm) wide. This is an attractive piece, of small size, with the added interest of a painted scene inside the lid.
£280–330 / €420–490
$500–580 PFK ✎

◄ **Pine cupboard,** with two doors and a drawer, Irish, c1880, 55in (139.5cm) wide.
£280–310 / €420–470
$500–550 Byl ⊞

Edwardian mahogany demi-lune display cabinet, on four cluster-column legs, 35in (89cm) wide.
£300–360 / €490–540
$580–640 FHF ✎

Miller's compares...

A. George III oak wall hanging cupboard, the door inlaid with a conch shell, 43¼in (110cm) high.
£160–190 / €240–280
$280–330 SWO 🔨

B. Oak corner cupboard, with walnut banding, c1760, 36in (91.5cm) high.
£710–790 / €1,050–1,200
$1,250–1,400 F&F ⊞

Marquetry-inlaid rosewood cabinet, the two doors with bevelled mirror plates, labelled 'James Shoolbred & Co, London', c1900, 22in (56cm) wide.
£320–380 / €480–570
$570–670 NOA 🔨

The inlay on Item A could have been added at a later date. Item B is of a good colour, with dentil cornice decoration, walnut banding, and is in better condition than Item A and therefore sold for over four times as much.

Edwardian inlaid-mahogany table display cabinet, with four glazed doors, 26¼in (66.5cm) wide. The small size of this cabinet makes it practical for use in the modern home.
£380–450 / €570–670
$670–800 SWO 🔨

◀ **Edwardian inlaid-mahogany music cabinet,** with glazed door enclosing shelves above four drawers, 20in (51cm) wide. The elegance and narrow style of this cabinet makes it suitable as a multi-purpose storage cabinet.
£380–450 / €570–670
$670–800 PF 🔨

Victorian walnut sewing cabinet, the top with a fitted interior, the turned legs joined by a tier, 15¾in (40cm) high. The good walnut figuring on this sewing cabinet makes it very desirable.
£350–420 / €520–640
$620–740 L&E 🔨

To find out more about antique furniture see the full range of Miller's books at **www.millers.uk.com**

◄ **Walnut-veneered side cabinet,** the unglazed door with later silk enclosing shelves, with brass mounts, late 19thC, 32in (81.5cm) wide. Cabinets such as this one sometimes had a glass plate or a brass grille in the door panel.
£400–480
€600–720
$710–850 WW ⚒

Edwardian satinwood inlaid music cabinet, the six drawers with fall-fronts, 20¾in (52.5cm) wide.
£420–500 / €630–750
$740–890 SWO ⚒

► **Early Victorian mahogany side cabinet,** with two panelled doors, 33in (84cm) wide.
£450–540
€670–800
$800–960
B(Kn) ⚒

Find out more in

Miller's Pine & Country Furniture Buyer's Guide, Miller's Publications, 2001

Pine dresser, with glazed upper section, Irish, c1880, 49in (124.5cm) wide.
£380–430 / €570–640
$670–760 Byl ⊞

Pine dresser, with a glazed top, Irish, c1875, 47in (119.5cm) wide.
£380–430 / €570–640
$670–760 Byl ⊞

◄ **Pine cupboard,** with two doors over two drawers, Irish, c1875, 56in (142cm) wide.
£410–460 / €610–690
$730–810 Byl ⊞

George III oak bedside cabinet, inlaid with stringing, stars and fan quadrants, with cupboard flanked by small drawers, above recess and two long drawers, 22½in (57cm) wide.
£470–560 / €700–830
$830–990 L ✎

Miller's compares...

A. Oak clothes press, the two ogee panelled doors enclosing hanging space, over four short cockbeaded drawers, brackets missing from stile feet, Welsh, early 19thC, 50in (127cm) wide.
£470–560 / €700–830
$830–990 PF ✎

B. George III oak linen press, the moulded cornice above two crossbanded and panelled doors enclosing an interior with four slides, over two short and two long graduated drawers, on bracket feet, 49in (124.5cm) wide.
£880–1,050 / €1,300–1,550
$1,550–1,850 HYD ✎

Linen presses are currently less popular than in the past because of their large size. Item A is of poorer quality than Item B, which is of a better colour. Item B also has a more stylish, elongated design, which has contributed to its value.

Pine dresser, Irish, c1870, 48in (122cm) wide.
£510–570 / €760–850
$900–1,000 Byl ⊞

▶ **Oak armoire,** the two doors with serpentine inset panels, French, 19thC, 77in (195.5cm) high. The style of this French armoire is popular in the UK because it is not overly ornate and is of elegant proportions.
£560–580 / €830–860
$990–1,050 WW ✎

Late Victorian satinwood linen press, 49in (124.5cm) wide.
£580–650 / €860–970
$1,000–1,150 P&T ⊞

Hardwood display cabinet, with carved panels of branches and flowers, the open shelves above hinged doors, Chinese, c1890, 37¾in (96cm) wide. This is an unusual, quality piece in good condition.
£600–720 / €890–1,050
$1,050–1,250 SWO ⚲

Oak armoire, with two geometrically moulded doors above a panelled base, 18thC, 50in (127cm) wide.
£680–810 / €1,000–1,200
$1,200–1,450 WW ⚲

The look without the price

Charles II-style oak wall cupboard, 19thC, 37in (94cm) wide.
£660–790 / €980–1,150
$1,150–1,350 S(O) ⚲

This cupboard is very decorative but the low price reflects the late date. An original Charles II cupboard would cost £1,200–1,500 / €1,800–2,250 / $2,100–2,650.

◄ **Victorian mahogany linen press,** the two panelled doors enclosing four slides, above two short over two long drawers, late 18thC, 46¾in (119cm) wide.
£680–810 / €1,000–1,200
$1,200–1,450 CHTR ⚲

► **George III oak breakfront house-keeper's cupboard,** with later handles, 69¼in (176cm) wide. The Victorian handles on this piece of furniture detract a little from its value.
£880–1,050
€1,300–1,550
$1,550–1,850
L&E ⚲

Desks & Writing Tables

Miller's compares...

A. Late Victorian walnut pedestal desk, the turned gallery with two drawers, leather skiver and nine further drawers, 48in (122cm) wide.
£200–240 / €300–360
$350–420 DN(EH) ⚒

B. Victorian mahogany pedestal desk, the upper section with gallery above a writing slope, 54¼in (138cm) wide.
£910–1,100 / €1,350–1,600
$1,600–1,900 B(Kn) ⚒

Item A, despite being made from walnut, is significantly more affordable than Item B. Item B is not only of an earlier date, but is also better in terms of quality, has good colour and visual appeal which accounts for it having sold for over four times as much as Item A.

Victorian oak pedestal desk, 47½in (120.5cm) wide.
£300–360 / €450–540
$530–640 SWO ⚒

Locate the source

The source of each illustration in Miller's can be found by checking the code letters below each caption with the Key to Illustrations, pages 286–290.

Oak clerk's desk-on-stand, the fall-front opening to reveal a fitted interior, early 19thC, 19¼in (49cm) high. The poor colour of this desk has contributed to its low price. Professional restoration to the faded wood could increase its value.
£320–380 / €480–570
$570–670 SWO ⚒

Miller's compares...

A. George III mahogany bureau, the fall-front enclosing a fitted interior, above four long drawers, 39in (99cm) wide.
£280–330 / €420–490
$500–580 PF ✎

B. Walnut bureau, with fitted interior, mid-18thC, 39in (99cm) wide.
£680–810 / €1,000–1,200
$1,200–1,450 B(Kn) ✎

Item A is later in date than Item B and is made from mahogany, whereas Item B is made from walnut which is a more sought after wood. These factors contributed to Item A being less desirable and consequently fetching a lower price than Item B.

Boulle and ebonized bureau de dame, mid-19thC, 29in (73.5cm) wide. This style of furniture was popular in the 19thC and Edwardian period. It is less likely to fit into a contemporary home so can be obtained at an affordable price.
£400–480 / €600–720
$710–850 B(Kn) ✎

The look without the price

▶ **George III oak bureau,** the fitted interior with a secret drawer above four further drawers, 35¾in (91cm) wide.
£440–520
€660–770
$780–920 SWO ✎

Brass-bound oak military secretaire chest, the central fitted drawer surrounded by four short and three long drawers, 19thC, 48in (122cm) wide.
£420–500 / €630–750
$740–890 BWL ✎

This oak secretaire chest is a practical and attractive piece at an affordable price. However, if it had been made of mahogany its value would be doubled.

Mahogany pedestal desk, late 19thC, 61in (155cm) wide.
£440–520 / €660–770
$780–920 B(Kn) ✎

Find out more in

Miller's Collecting Furniture: The Facts At Your Fingertips, Miller's Publications, 1998

Victorian George III-style mahogany pedestal desk, 56¾in (144cm) wide. Pedestal desks were made in a variety of sizes. They are attractive and practical pieces of furniture for use in an office or study, having the added bonus that, unlike bureaux, they are able to accommodate computers.
£520–620 / €**770–920**
$920–1,100 B(Kn) 🔨

Victorian carved oak Wellington chest/secretaire, the frieze drawer above a fitted interior and four drawers, 31in (78.5cm) wide.
£450–540 / €**670–800**
$800–960 BWL 🔨

◀ **Edwardian mahogany cylinder bureau,** with satinwood stringing, the roll-top enclosing a fitted interior and writing slide, 30in (76cm) wide.
£610–730
€**910–1,100**
$1,100–1,300
B(Kn) 🔨

Find out more in

Miller's Furniture Antiques Checklist, Miller's Publications, 2001

George III mahogany kneehole desk, the crossbanded top above a slide and eight drawers, with a recessed cupboard, 35¾in (91cm) wide. This desk is a high-quality piece of furniture with an attractive colour and design, plus the additional benefit of a writing slide. These factors account for its higher value.
£700–840 / €**1,050–1,250**
$1,250–1,500 HYD 🔨

▶ **Victorian rosewood and marquetry davenport,** 21¾in (55.5cm) wide. This davenport is attractive and unusual, as it does not have the usual drawers to the base. Davenports are not practical for use in modern homes as they cannot accommodate a computer and, as a result, have fallen in value over recent years.
£700–840
€**1,050–1,250**
$1,250–1,500
B(Kn) 🔨

Mirrors & Frames

Victorian oak mantel and mirror,
American, 19thC, 62in (157.5cm) wide.
This style of mantel and over mirror is
popular in the USA and would have
achieved significantly less if sold in the UK.
£170–200 / €250–300
$300–350 DuM 🔨

**Mid-Georgian mahogany
fretwork wall mirror,**
with a moulded surround,
15in (38cm) wide.
£135–160 / €200–240
$240–280 DN(Bri) 🔨

Bronze shaving mirror,
with bevelled glass, 19thC,
14½in (37cm) high.
£160–190 / €240–280
$280–340 JAA 🔨

◄ **Wall mirror,** in
a Dutch-style ebony
frame applied with
gilt-brass cartouches
and cherubs, 19thC,
30½in (77.5cm)
wide. Ebony frames
with baroque-style
motifs were popular
in Holland, giving
rise to the term
'Dutch-style'.
£200–240
€300–360
$350–420 NSal 🔨

Skeleton mirror, c1750, 15¾in (40cm)
high. 'Skeleton' is used to describe a mirror
with a plain frame that does not have
drawers to the base.
£210–240 / €310–360
$370–420 F&F ⊞

◄ **Mahogany toilet mirror,**
with reeded supports, 1830–37,
24in (61cm) high. The reeded,
carved columns are a good
indication that it was made
during the reign of William IV.
£220–260 / €330–390
$390–460 G(L) 🔨

► **Regency mahogany
dressing mirror,** 25in (63.5cm)
high. The barrel front and style of
turning on this mirror are common
features of Regency design.
£230–270 / €340–400
$410–480 BWL 🔨

◄ **George III mahogany dressing mirror,** with three drawers, 21in (53.5cm) wide. This mirror was put up for sale by the Rothschild Estate. The provenance of this item has added to its value.
£250–290
€370–430
$440–510 LHA ⚒

Gilt wall mirror, with carved and pierced cresting, the base with three candle holders, 19thC, 45½in (115.5cm) high. It is advisable to check ornate mirror frames very carefully before purchase, as they are more susceptible to damage, which can be costly to repair.
£300–360 / €450–540
$530–640 FHF ⚒

Miller's compares...

B. Gilt and ebonized mirror, applied with faceted glass buttons, Irish, mid-19thC, 32¼in (82cm) wide.
£520–620 / €770–920
$920–1,100 B(Kn) ⚒

A. Cast-gilt wall mirror, moulded with trailing flowers and poppy-heads, 19thC, 33½in (85cm) high.
£280–330 / €420–490
$500–580 SWO ⚒

Item A is a good-quality mirror within an ornate frame. Item B, however, has a plainer, beaded frame which is popular at the moment, making the mirror more suitable in today's home and contributing to its higher price.

Edwardian inlaid-rosewood wall mirror, with two candle-stands, 27½in (70cm) high.
£300–360 / €450–540
$530–640 SWO ⚒

► **Carved-giltwood girandole,** with fixing for missing candelabra, Venetian, late 19thC, 32¼in (82cm) wide. The missing candelabra brackets have reduced the price of this girandole by approximately £200 / €300 / $350.
£320–380 / €480–570
$570–670 B(Kn) ⚒

Walnut wall mirror, with carved and turned decoration, 19thC, 49¼in (125cm) wide. This is a good quality mirror, which is reflected in the price.
£350–420 / €520–620
$620–740 SWO ✂

George III mahogany bowfronted toilet mirror, with three drawers, on bracket feet, 18in (45.5cm) wide. The attractive shield shape makes this mirror more distinctive and enhances the price.
£320–380 / €480–570
$570–670 G(L) ✂

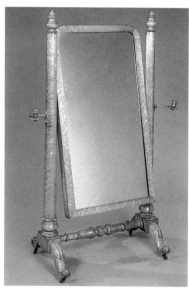

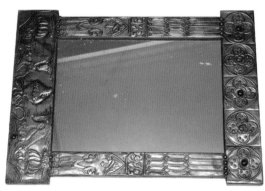

Gothic revival brass mirror, c1875. The workmanship and extravagant design of the frame account for the high price of this mirror. All old mirror plates will have deteriorated to some extent and will have non-reflective spots. Be suspicious of any mirror in perfect condition.
£450–500 / €670–750
$800–890 TDG ⊞

Early Victorian bird's-eye maple cheval mirror, with tapered pillars and brass candle arms, on lotus-carved cabriole legs, 31½in (80cm) wide. This mirror has many desirable features such as well-figured bird's-eye maple, good-quality carving and the intact candle sconces which all contribute to its value.
£650–780 / €970–1,150
$1,150–1,400 TEN ✂

► **Walnut cushion-framed wall mirror,** with later plate, c1695, 22¾in (58cm) wide. This William and Mary mirror would have been worth £1,500 / €2,250 / $2,650 had the plate been original.
£960–1,150
€1,450–1,700
$1,700–2,000
S(O) ✂

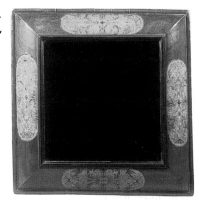

Sofas & Settees

Rococo revival rosewood sofa, with later velvet upholstery, worn and in need of repair, American, 1850–75, 72in (183cm) wide. This sofa would make an ideal restoration project and was therefore a good buy for a purchaser willing to undertake the repair work.
£160–190 / €240–280
$280–340 NOA 🔨

Pine settle bed, Irish, c1875, 72in (183cm) wide. The base of this settle pulls out to reveal a crude bed. These items are mostly used today as an extra storage facility.
£340–380 / €510–570
$600–670 Byl ⊞

Oak settle, with panelled back, on bobbin-turned legs and stretchers, with later upholstered seat, 18thC, 73½in (186.5cm) wide. This style of settle is currently unpopular, which is why this piece sold for a very reasonable price.
£500–600 / €750–890
$890–1,050 SWO 🔨

Edwardian mahogany bergère settee, with turned front legs and loose cushions, 55½in (141cm) wide.
£400–480 / €600–720
$710–850 SWO 🔨

Edwardian inlaid-mahogany comb-back two-seater settee, with upholstered seat and turned legs, 48½in (123cm) wide.
£590–700 / €880–1,050
$1,050–1,250 WilP 🔨

Louis XVI-style painted and parcel-gilt salon suite, comprising a canapé and two *fauteuils*, restored, late 19thC.
£800–960 / €1,200–1,450
$1,400–1,700 B(Kn) 🔨

Stands

George III mahogany washstand, the folding top above a single drawer, 15¾in (40cm) wide.
£120–140 / €180–220 $210–260 WilP ⚒

Pine plant stand, c1900, 11in (28cm) wide. The current popularity of furniture from the Arts and Crafts movement accounts for the high price of this plant stand.
£310–350 / €460–520 $550–620 COF ⊞

Victorian mahogany wash basin and stand, 21in (53.5cm) wide. Freestanding wash basins tended to be a novelty item in the Victorian period.
£175–210 / €260–310 $310–370 B(Kn) ⚒

Victorian mahogany washstand, with a tiled back, 43½in (110.5cm) wide.
£280–330 / €420–490 $500–580 FHF ⚒

The look without the price

Robert Adam-style pedestal/plant stand, c1900, 41½in (105.5cm) high.
£240–280 / €360–420 $420–500 NOA ⚒

A genuine Robert Adam plant stand would have been worth £8,000–10,000 / €12,000–15,000 / $14,000–17,500, but this piece gives you the same look, as well as being functional, at a substantially lower price.

◀ **Walnut hall stand,** the mirror and five tiles above a marble-topped drawer flanked by two umbrella stands with drip trays, late 19thC, 36in (91.5cm) wide. The Aesthetic style of this hall stand is currently popular and therefore adds to its value.
£340–400 / €510–600 $600–710 PF ⚒

Miller's compares...

A. Mahogany boot and whip stand, with brass handle, early 19thC, 26in (66cm) wide.
£380–450 / €570–670
$670–800 WW ⚘

B. Mahogany boot and whip stand, c1840, 37in (94cm) high.
£700–840 / €1,050–1,250
$1,250–1,500 S(O) ⚘

Item A is an earlier example of a mahogany boot stand than Item B, and this would normally make it the more valuable of the two. However, in this case the design and quality of Item B is superior, making it more valuable than Item A.

Mahogany candlestand, with turned stem, 1830–37, 35½in (90cm) high.
£400–480 / €600–720
$710–850 NSal ⚘

The look without the price

Louis XV-style giltwood torchère, the top on three acanthus, shell and foliate garland-decorated scrolling supports with outswept scrolling legs, late 19thC, 35¾in (91cm) high.
£580–690 / €860–1,050
$1,050–1,200 B(Kn) ⚘

If this were a genuine Louis XV torchère it would have achieved 10 times this price. Moreover, if it had been attributed to a particular maker, it would have been even more valuable.

Mahogany urn stand, the moulded top above a drawer and open fret frieze, early 20thC, 21in (53.5cm) wide. It is unusual for an urn stand to have a drawer. However, this stand made twice its estimated value, suggesting that on the day of the auction there were at least two keen bidders for it.
£420–500 / €630–750
$740–890 PF ⚘

▶ **Mahogany washstand,** c1835, 55½in (141cm) wide. This good quality washstand has an adaptable design which could be usefully employed as a serving table in the modern home.
£600–720 / €890–1,050
$1,050–1,250 S(O) ⚘

Stools

▶ **Edwardian mahogany piano stool,** with upholstered seat and scroll handles, 23¼in (59cm) wide.
£90–105
€135–155
$160–185 DD ⚒

Ash and elm milking stool, Irish, c1880, 12in (30.5cm) high.
£30–34 / €45–50
$55–60 Byl ⊞

Victorian rosewood stool, with upholstered seat and spiral-turned legs, 16in (40.5cm) wide.
£100–120 / €150–180
$170–200 WW ⚒

Miller's compares...

A. Late Victorian fruitwood revolving piano stool, with three turned legs and centre pendant, 35½in (90cm) high.
£90–105 / €135–155
$160–185 PFK ⚒

B. Carved walnut adjustable piano stool, c1860, 21in (53.5cm) high.
£340–380 / €510–570
$600–670 MTay ⊞

Item B is made from walnut, which is more desirable than the fruitwood of Item A. This, together with the more elegant design of Item B, accounts for its higher price. An added factor in the price difference is that Item A is covered in an unsuitable material that has detracted from its value.

Edwardian mahogany and satinwood-inlaid piano stool, with rising seat and turned handles, 20½in (52cm) wide.
£170–200 / €250–300
$300–350 G(L) ⚒

▶ **Mahogany stool,** with later drop-in seat, 19thC, 19in (48.5cm) wide.
£180–210 / €270–310
$320–370 WW ⚒

If this footstool had been made of solid rosewood its value would have increased by £200 / €300 / $350.

Simulated rosewood footstool, worm damage, early 19thC, 15in (38cm) wide.
£110–130 / €165–195
$195–230 WW ✗

Victorian oak stool, the upholstered top above applied lion mouldings, on monopodia legs, 28in (71cm) wide. The unusual carved legs and feet on this item are very desirable and increase its value.
£280–330 / €420–490
$500–580 G(L) ✗

◄ **Victorian walnut stool,** with upholstered seat, on cabriole legs, 18in (45.5cm) wide. The use of walnut and the attractive legs of this stool have increased its value.
£320–380
€480–570
$570–670 WW ✗

Pair of horn footstools, with upholstered tops, late 19thC, 18in (45.5cm) wide. Horn footstools sell well in America, but are less popular in the UK.
£350–420 / €520–630
$620–740 NOA ✗

Chippendale revival-style stool, the seat with applied floral wool-work, late 19thC, 22in (56cm) wide.
£380–450 / €570–670
$670–800 NSal ✗

A stool of this type could be worth £1,500–2,000 / €2,200–3,000 / $2,250–3,500 if it were in good condition and a genuine Chippendale piece.

◄ **William IV mahogany stool,** the sides heavily carved with scrolling and foliate patterns, with leather upholstery, 35½in (90cm) wide.
£420–500 / €630–750
$740–890 NOA ✗

Tables & Side Furniture

Victorian oak side table, with frieze drawer, 28in (71cm) high. The simple design and poor condition of this table are reflected in its low price.
£65–75 / €95–110
$115–135 G(L) ✎

Mahogany Pembroke table, with a dummy and a real drawer, c1850, 39¼in (99.5cm) wide, together with a George III-style toilet mirror. This is a good illustration of how purchasing a multiple lot can provide you with a bargain. Here, the table probably accounted for 80 per cent of the overall price.
£95–110 / €140–165
$170–190 S(O) ✎

Oak side table, 18thC, 41¼in (105cm) wide.
£110–130 / €165–195
$195–230 CHTR ✎

◀ **George III oak tripod table,** with turned support, alterations, 30in (76cm) wide. There has been a modification to the top of the column of this table, which accounts for its low price.
£170–200
€250–300
$300–350 B(Kn) ✎

The look without the price

Regency mahogany Pembroke table, with associated base, 36¼in (92cm) wide.
£165–195 / €240–290
$290–340 B(Kn) ✎

The correct base for this table would have been a single column with either quadruple- or triple-splayed legs. In original condition this piece could have made £300–350 / €450–520 / $530–620.

George III mahogany tea table, with hinged leaf, damage and repairs, 33½in (85cm) wide. The price of this table reflects the fact that it is in poor condition. Sympathetic restoration could more than triple the value, but the cost of such work should be taken into account by the purchaser.
£180–210 / €270–310
$320–370 SWO

George III mahogany occasional table, alterations, 24in (61cm) high.
£190–220 / €280–330
$340–390 G(L)

▶ **Kingwood side table,** with a pierced brass gallery, the top with inlaid floral ribbon decoration, French, early 20thC, 23¼in (59cm) wide. Although missing a small piece of veneer and having slight water damage, this side table is made from inlaid kingwood which is both attractive and desirable. These small imperfections will not have detracted greatly from the value of the piece.
£210–250 / €310–370
$370–440 SWO

Mahogany reading table, the top with two easel panels, early 19thC, 36in (91.5cm) wide.
£190–220 / €280–330
$340–390 TRM

Edwardian mahogany work table, the frieze drawer above a work bag and undertier, 51in (129.5cm) wide.
£200–240 / €300–360
$350–420 SWO

Miller's compares...

Rosewood and walnut chiffonier, with two mirror-back tiers above panelled doors, 19thC, 41¾in (106cm) wide.
£220–260 / €330–390 $390–460 SWO

A. Victorian mahogany work table, with spindle-galleried wool cradle, alterations, 18in (45.5cm) wide.
£200–240 / €300–360 $350–420 TRM

B. Mahogany work table, with turned stem and wool cradle, 19thC, 21in (53.5cm) wide.
£620–740 / €920–1,100 $1,100–1,300 BWL

Item A is a standard work table that has undergone some adaptations, thus lowering its value. Item B has the advantage of a moulded edge to the top and an unusual column shape, which add to its desirability, hence increasing its value.

Early Victorian mahogany side table, with two frieze drawers, on turned legs, 44in (112cm) wide.
£240–280 / €360–420 $420–500 WilP

Find out more in

Miller's Antiques Pocket Fact File, Miller's Publications, 2001

George III tripod table, on a turned column, 18in (45.5cm) wide.
£230–270 / €340–400 $410–480 SWO

▶ **Renaissance-style walnut centre table,** with marble top, 19thC, 45¾in (116cm) wide.
£240–280 / €360–420 $420–500 S(Am)

Miller's compares...

A. Victorian mahogany card table, leg replaced, restorations, 35¾in (91cm) wide.
£260–310 / €390–460
$460–550 B(Kn) 🔨

B. William IV rosewood-veneered card table, with baize-lined swivel folding top, 36¼in (92cm) wide.
£400–480 / €600–720
$710–850 WW 🔨

Item A would have been worth £5,000–6,000 / €7,500–8,900 / $8,800–10,600 in its original condition. The low price here reflects the damage and repairs that have been undertaken. Item B, however, is made of rosewood, which is more desirable than mahogany, and it has a good quality base, thus making it the more valuable card table.

Late Regency mahogany Pembroke table, with a drawer, on spiral-turned legs, 42in (106.5cm) wide.
£300–360
€450–540
$530–640 E 🔨

Victorian rosewood work table, with chessboard top, 17in (43cm) high. The inlaid chessboard makes this a desirable piece and adds to its value.
£300–360 / €450–540
$530–640 G(L) 🔨

▶ **George III mahogany side table,** 34¼in (87cm) wide.
£300–360
€450–540
$530–640 B(Kn) 🔨

Cherrywood Sheraton drop-leaf dining table, on turned legs, some damage, c1820, 65½in (166.5cm) extended. Furniture made from cherrywood is currently very popular in the US.
£300–360 / €450–540
$530–640 JDJ ⚒

▶ **Walnut and satinwood side table,** with a frieze drawer, on tapering legs, Continental, 19thC, 23¼in (59cm) wide.
£300–360
€450–540
$530–640 B(Kn) ⚒

William IV mahogany coaching table, 33in (84cm) wide. First popular in the mid-late 19th century, coach tables are a variant of butlers' trays that could fold flat when not in use. They were used for picnics or when eating in trains or coaches. They are still very useful today.
£320–380 / €480–570
$570–670 B(Kn) ⚒

Mahogany bidet, with reeded legs, c1830, 23in (58.5cm) wide.
£320–360 / €480–540
$570–640 GBr ⊞

◀ **Victorian simulated-rosewood side table,** the later mahogany top above a frieze drawer, on twin lyre supports, 29½in (75cm) wide.
£340–400
€510–600
$600–710 WW ⚒

Edwardian mahogany side table, 26in (66cm) wide. This is an unusual design for a side table which has increased its value.
£340–380 / €510–570
$600–670 WAA ⊞

◀ **George III mahogany console table,** 49¼in (125cm) wide.
£350–420
€**520–630**
$620–740 L ✻

Victorian walnut needlework table, with fitted interior and bag, on turned end supports, 22in (56cm) wide.
£350–420 / €**520–630**
$620–740 AMB ✻

◀ **Mahogany kneehole side table,** with ebony stringing and three drawers, 19thC, 36¼in (92cm) wide.
£360–430 / €**540–640**
$640–760 SWO ✻

Victorian oak three-tier buffet, the two drawers moulded with lion masks, with spiral-turned supports, 45in (114.5cm) wide. The attractive colour and carving on this buffet are desirable and have increased its value.
£370–440 / €**550–660**
$650–780 PF ✻

Mahogany-veneered breakfast table, with lion-paw feet, 19thC, 46¾in (119cm) diam.
£370–440 / €**550–660**
$650–780 SWO ✻

◀ **Victorian mahogany side table,** with two frieze drawers. Frieze drawers are decorative dummy drawers usually opposite real drawers. They were used to balance the design of a piece of furniture.
£380–450 / €**570–670**
$670–800 B(Kn) ✻

The look without the price

Late Georgian-style mahogany sofa table, with satinwood crossbanding and cockbeaded frieze drawers, the downswept legs with brass paw caps and casters, early 20thC, 53½in (136cm) extended.
£370–440 / €550–660
$650–780 PFK ⚒

If this sofa table had been Georgian rather than early 20th-century, it could have been worth around £2,000 / €3,000 / $3,500.

George III mahogany bowfronted sideboard, on turned tapering legs, 54in (137cm) wide.
£380–450 / €570–670
$670–800 SWO ⚒

Victorian walnut boardroom table, with skiver-inset top, requires restoration, 122¾in (312cm) wide. Skiver is a form of vegetable-tanned sheep's or lambs' skin. This leather was once very popular as book bindings and table covering due to the variety of colours and textures available. The obvious damage to the skiver of this boardroom table has decreased its value since it will now be costly to replace.
£380–450 / €570–670
$670–800 PFK ⚒

Mahogany and marquetry tripod table, 19thC, 26¾in (68cm) wide.
£380–450 / €570–670
$670–800 S(O) ⚒

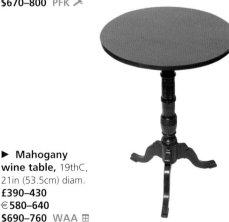

▶ **Mahogany wine table,** 19thC, 21in (53.5cm) diam.
£390–430
€580–640
$690–760 WAA ⊞

George IV mahogany breakfast table,
with hinged leaves and frieze drawer, on a
turned column, 35in (89cm) wide.
£400–480 / €600–720
$710–850 B(Kn) 🪓

**George III mahogany serpentine side
table,** 28¼in (72cm) wide. A serpentine top
generally indicates that a piece of furniture
is good quality, more so if it is made of
walnut, or mahogany as in this example.
£420–500 / €630–750
$740–890 B(Kn) 🪓

► **Victorian inlaid
figured walnut
Sutherland table,**
the drop leaves
decorated with
foliate panels,
30in (76cm) wide.
£410–490
€610–730
$730–870
DN(Bri) 🪓

Mahogany bowfronted sideboard, the frieze drawer flanked
by deep drawers, on tapering legs, early 19thC, 47¼in (120cm) wide.
£440–530 / €660–790
$780–940 CHTR 🪓

► **George III
mahogany
Pembroke table,**
with two frieze
drawers and two
opposing dummy
drawers, 19¾in
(50cm) wide.
£490–580
€730–860
$870–1,050
AMB 🪓

◄ **Edwardian
mahogany nest of
three tables,** with
satinwood banding
and stringing, largest
15in (38cm) wide.
£440–530
€660–790
$780–940 WW 🪓

The look without the price

Louis XVI-style kingwood side table, with a drawer and two slides, French, late 19thC, 32¼in (82cm) wide.
£490–580
€730–860
$870–1,050 S(O) ✎

A genuine Louis XVI side table could be worth twice as much as this example.

Late Victorian mahogany side table, the cleated plank top with brass screws above a frieze drawer, on a chamfered X-frame with a pierced star stretcher, 36in (91.5cm) wide. The unusual design of this side table has added to its value.
£590–710 / €880–1,050
$1,050–1,200 WW ✎

◀ **Victorian mahogany three-tier buffet,** with three-quarter gallery, turned finials and moulded tiers, on ring-turned supports, 48in (122cm) wide.
£770–920
€1,150–1,350
$1,350–1,650
DN(BR) ✎

Elm and fruitwood centre table, French, c1800, 78¾in (200cm) wide. The simple design and good grain on this table make it a desirable piece and therefore more valuable.
£790–940 / €1,200–1,400
$1,400–1,650 S(Am) ✎

Miller's compares...

A. Oak gateleg table, the frieze with one drawer, 17thC, 50½in (128.5cm) wide.
£680–810 / €1,000–1,200
$1,200–1,400 L ✎

B. Oak gateleg table, 17thC, 50in (127cm) wide.
£800–960 / €1,200–1,450
$1,400–1,700 L ✎

Although both Item A and Item B are made of oak, Item A is a plainer shape than Item B. Item B has better design features such as bobbin-turned legs and attractively-shaped aprons, which have enhanced its value over Item A.

Whatnots & Butlers' Trays

Victorian rosewood five-tier whatnot, with twist-turned supports and baluster feet, 48¾in (124cm) high.
£390–460 / €580–690
$690–810 Bea ✐

Miller's compares...

A. Victorian walnut three-tier whatnot, on spiral-turned supports, 23in (58.5cm) wide.
£400–480 / €600–720
$710–850 BWL ✐

B. Victorian walnut three-tier whatnot, the tiers veneered, with spiral-twist supports and a base drawer, slight damage, 26¼in (66.5cm) wide.
£880–1,050 / €1,300–1,550
$1,550–1,850 WW ✐

Item A is a basic design with unattractive colour. Item B, on the other hand, is not only better quality and colour, but has the addition of a drawer to the base, which makes it a more desirable piece, thus increasing the price.

Mahogany five-tier whatnot, with a central drawer, late 19thC, 16in (40.5cm) wide.
£480–570 / €720–850
$850–1,000 SWO ✐

Whatnots were fashionable in the Regency period and were generally built as free-standing or as corner shelves. They comprised four or five tiers and occasionally had a drawer. They were usually made of mahogany and used to display decorative objects. The value of a whatnot is determined by its condition and decorative appeal. Victorian examples were less robust and more susceptible to damage.

Mahogany butler's tray, on a stand, c1825, 25½in (65cm) wide. The good quality of the stand has increased the desirability of the piece and therefore its value.
£860–1,000 / €1,300–1,500
$1,500–1,800 S(O) ✐

Ceramics

Saturday mornings are usually one of the highlights of the week for me as this is when I view what is on offer at my local general auction. I am usually accompanied by some friends on whom my enthusiasm for rummaging through boxes in search of a bargain has rubbed off. Sometimes there are quite a few of us and the outing becomes something of a social event.

Unsurprisingly themes and patterns start to emerge during our searches, and slowly but surely we start to discover what we like, and then begin to collect it. This year Japanese works of art have become our primary concern, and we find that we are not the only ones who share this interest, for we are gradually having to pay more for our purchases. It is certainly an area of the market place that has become very popular in the past 12 months. The prices made for Asian works of art are increasing as the economic successes of countries such as China, Taiwan, Japan and Hong Kong are filtering through to our rural auctions. While strolling around the Summer Fine Art Fair at Olympia this year, it was obvious by the number of people dealing in Oriental works of art that they are regarded as a lucrative commodity. This year, some enthusiasts have expressed concerns that there are fewer bargains to be found, but I do not agree. Stories still pervade of a good find in the local car boot or yard sale. In one case a lucky purchaser eventually sold his lot at auction for nearly £600 / €900 / $1,050, and it had only cost him £15 / €22 / $26!

Art pottery has always been popular, with Royal Doulton, Moorcroft and other perennial favourites maintaining their status, but there has been a sharp rise in the prices for majolica and wares manufactured by Martin Brothers. Embracing all areas, there seems to be a strong desire to own rare novelty items. In the last few years there has been a great interest in the interior design programmes shown on television. The effect of this is that more people are now buying 'works of art' to display in their modern interiors. Sculptural ceramic art seems to be the most popular choice.

Generally, it is perceived by many that the past year has been a difficult one in the antiques market, but ceramics on the whole have remained a buoyant field. The interest is still high and increasing numbers of people are collecting ceramics.

This can be partly attributed to the revolutionary effect of the internet, where hundreds of items can be viewed in just a few minutes. Most auction rooms have embraced the modern technological internet revolution and offer good digital images and condition reports to help you find your lots. I am of the opinion that it has never been easier to source rare collectors' items than it is today.

I hope this edition of *Miller's Buying Affordable Antiques* aids you in your search for new purchases. Hard graft still pays off, so good luck and happy hunting to you all.

Hamish Wilson

Baskets & Boxes

Model of a basket, early 19thC,
2½in (6.5cm) high. This small basket would
be a good first piece for a collection.
**£40–45 / €60–65
$70–80** WW 🔨

The look without the price

This box has suffered an extensive amount of damage. If it had been in perfect condition it could have fetched £150–200 / €220–270 / $300–350. However, it would still make an attractive display piece.

Tin-glazed box and cover, the knop in the shape of a bird, painted with buildings, damaged, 18thC, 4½in (11.5cm) high.
**£70–80 / €105–120
$125–140** WW 🔨

Edwardian pottery money box,
European, 7in (18cm) high.
**£70–80 / €105–120
$125–140** HAL 🔨

▶ **Royal Worcester porcelain basket-weave vase,** 1909, 3in (7.5cm) high. Prices for Worcester items are currently stable.
**£95–110 / €140–165
$170–195** WAC ⊞

◀ **Ceramic trinket box,** decorated with roses, c1900, 3in (7.5cm) diam. Trinket boxes are a popular collecting area and they are generally low in price.
**£100–110
€150–160
$175–195** LBr ⊞

Porcelain casket, the cover with gilt-metal mounts and decorated with floral sprays and a metal rose branch, Continental, late 19thC, 7½in (19cm) high.
£100–120 / €150–180
$175–210 DD ✤

Meissen porcelain box and cover, painted and gilded with a gentleman playing a lute accompanied by his lady, blue crossed swords to base, lid as found, 19thC, 3in (7.5cm) wide. This box may have been used as a trinket, pill or patch box.
£150–180 / €220–270
$270–320 TMA ✤

Belleek Shamrock basket, three-strand, Irish, First Period, 1863–90, 5½in (14cm) wide. Belleek baskets made with three or more strands of clay are more desirable than those with just one strand. Prices for Belleek are currently stable, so now may be a good time to start a collection.
£200–240 / €300–360
$350–420 DN(Bri) ✤

The look without the price

Porcelain basket, moulded as overlapping leaves, applied with flowers, c1840, 13¼in (33.5cm) wide.
£160–190 / €240–280
$280–340 WW ✤

This attractive basket is in the style of Coalport. If it had actually been made by Coalport, and carried factory marks, it could have fetched £400–600 / €600–890 / $710–1,050. Moulded leaves and flowers are easy and relatively inexpensive to restore if damaged.

Canton enamelled basket and stand, with painted decoration and pierced borders, damaged, repaired, 19thC, stand 8½in (21.5cm) wide. Asian ceramics are achieving good prices at the moment, and although this basket is damaged, its rare shape makes it desirable.
£180–210 / €270–310
$320–370 G(L) ✤

Find out more in

Miller's Ceramics Buyers Guide, Miller's Publications, 2000

Candlesticks

Pair of Wedgwood jasper ware candlesticks, with relief-moulded decoration, impressed mark, late 19thC, 7¼in (18.5cm) high. Jasper ware is more popular in rarer colours such as duck egg, lilac, pale brown and green, rather than the usual dark and pale blue.
£75–90 / €110–135
$135–160 G(L) ✍

Pair of Royal Worcester figural candlesticks, each modelled as a putto holding a cornucopia shell, impressed marks, one restored, 19thC, 6¾in (17cm) high. Novelty and whimsical items such as these are very popular with buyers.
£240–280 / €360–420
$420–500 FHF ✍

Jasper ware

Wedgewood jasper ware has often been forged and reproduced due to its popularity. Many of the copies were cast from original pieces, with the result that they lack the crisp modelling of genuine pieces.

Bow candlestick, modelled as a young boy standing beside a flowering tree, c1770, 9¾in (25cm) high. This candlestick is by a good maker, is high quality, and could be worth as much as £400–500 / €600–750 / $710–890.
£280–330 / €420–490
$500–580 SWO ✍

Derby porcelain figural candlestick, modelled as a seated cherub, c1770, 6¾in (17cm) high. Although the rococo style of this item is not particularly fashionable at the moment, if you like it, now is a good time to buy.
£100–120 / €150–180
$175–210 SWO ✍

Staffordshire porcellaneous figural candlestick, c1835, 8in (20.5cm) high.
£520–580 / €770–860
$920–1,050 DAN ⊞

◄ **Chamberlain's Worcester chamberstick,** painted with a view of Malvern, with gilt decoration, title and painted script mark, slight wear, c1835, 3in (7.5cm) high. Items painted with named views are desirable, as are painted marks. Both these factors have contributed to the high price of this item.
£340–400 / €510–600
$600–710 WW ✍

Cups, Mugs & Tea Bowls

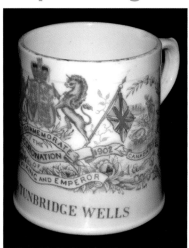

St John's pottery mug, commemorating the coronation of King Edward VII, inscribed 'St John's Tunbridge Wells', 1902, 3½in (9cm) high. Although commemorative ware is not particularly popular, this mug might appeal to buyers from the Tunbridge Wells area.
£30–35 / €45–50
$55–65   JMC ⊞

Victorian Ironstone china mug, transfer-printed and colour-washed with chinoiserie waterside pavilions and figures, marked 'hano', 5in (12.5cm) high.
£45–55 / €70–80
$80–95   PFK ⚒

> To find out more about antique ceramics see the full range of Miller's books at
> **www.millers.uk.com**

▶ **Regency bone china Derby-style mug,** painted with rose sprays, with gilt initials 'FE', 2½in (6.5cm) high. This affordable mug has a simple and attractive design and would make a good addition to a collection.
£35–40 / €50–60
$60–70   PFK ⚒

◀ **Gilt coffee can,** Nippon mark, 1900–20, 2in (5cm) diam. Japanese eggshell porcelain wares were initially cheap to produce – as a result prices have never been very high.
£40–45 / €60–70
$70–80   BAC ⊞

Victorian Burgess & Leigh breakfast cup and saucer, decorated with the farmers' arms, cup 4in (10cm) high. Burgess & Leigh items are becoming very collectable and therefore could be a good area to invest in.
£45–50 / €70–75
$80–90   JACK ⊞

Gaudy Welsh cup and saucer, decorated with Tulip pattern, c1865, 4in (10cm) diam. Gaudy Welsh pieces are highly collectable, especially those with 'lighter' decoration such as this.
£55–65 / €80–95
$100–115   TOP ⊞

◄ **MacIntyre bone china mug,** commemorating the coronation of King Edward VII, c1902, 3in (7.5cm) high.
£65–75 / €95–110
$115–130 H&G ⊞

Noritake cup and saucer, with gilt and jewel decoration, 1908–11, 3in (7.5cm) diam. Noritake is a good maker to look out for. It tends to be of a higher quality than most other Japanese eggshell ceramics and is currently rising in value.
£70–80 / €105–120
$120–140 BAC ⊞

◄ **Noritake coffee can and saucer,** with floral decoration, 1908–1911, 2in (5cm) diam.
£70–80 / €105–120
$120–140 BAC ⊞

Noritake coffee can and saucer, 1908–11, 2in (5cm) diam. Noritake wares are currently attracting higher prices so this item offers good value for money as it could be worth as much as £90 / €135 / $160.
£70–80 / €105–120
$120–140 BAC ⊞

Ceramic cup, commemorating Queen Victoria, 1897, 4in (10cm) high. This item appears to be crazed and has worn gilding which has lowered its value.
£70–80 / €105–120
$120–140 WAA ⊞

Miller's compares...

A. Royal Doulton beaker, commemorating the coronation of King Edward VII, 1902, 4in (10cm) high.
£70–80 / € 105–120
$120–140 H&G ⊞

B. Ceramic mug, commemorating Arthur Wellesley, 1893, 5in (12.5cm) high.
£220–250 / € 330–370
$390–440 POL ⊞

Both these mugs are commemorative ware. However, Item A is commemorating the Royal family, a fairly common subject for such wares, whereas Item B is commemorating a political figure. Rarer subjects such as politics, hunting and mythology command higher prices, which is why Item B sold for three times as much as Item A.

Chinese export *famille rose* tea bowl and saucer, c1770, saucer 5in (12.5cm) diam.
£75–85 / € 110–125
$135–150 DAN ⊞

Belleek Shamrock cup and saucer, Irish, Second Period, 1891–1926, 2½in (6.5cm) high. Harp-shaped handles on Belleek pieces are very sought after by collectors and can add as much as 10 per cent to the value of the item.
£80–90 / € 120–135
$140–160 MLa ⊞

Mottoware jug, inscribed 'God Bless You Tommy Atkins', c1900. Tommy was the traditional name for British Soldiers in WWI. The expression was made popular by Rudyard Kipling in his poem about Tommy Atkins, entitled 'Tommy'. This jug would appeal to collectors of military items as well as collectors of ceramics.
£85–100 / € 125–150
$150–175 AMB ✦

◀ **Doulton mug,** commemorating Paddington Station, London, dated 1887, 3½in (9cm) high. This mug is by a good maker and will attract collectors. The London reference also adds interest.
£85–95 / € 125–140
$150–170 WAA ⊞

Commemorative mugs

Items with regional interest are best sold in the region they are commemorating in order to achieve the highest price. Mugs commemorating battles or events are currently more popular than Coronation wares at present, and named factories such as Doulton can also increase value.

Satsuma cup and saucer, signed, Japanese, Meiji period, 1868–1911, 4in (10cm) diam. The gilding on this cup and saucer is in very good condition and this, together with the signature, account for its value.
£100–115 / €150–170
$175–200 BAC ⊞

◄ **Copper lustre cup,** mid-19thC, 5in (12.5cm) high. This cup has a very good shape, which has contributed to its value. However, lustreware is at present not commanding high prices.
£105–120
€155–180
$185–210 DAN ⊞

Cup and saucer, commemorating Queen Victoria, 1897, saucer 8in (20.5cm) diam. The large size of this cup and saucer adds to its appeal.
£105–120 / €155–180
$185–210 Ans ⊞

► **Child's pearlware mug,** decorated with children playing games, c1840, 3in (7.5cm) high. Pearlware is a good collecting area as there are many items available. Examples with humorous prints are very popular.
£110–125
€165–185
$195–220 RdV ⊞

Locate the source

The source of each illustration in Miller's can be found by checking the code letters below each caption with the Key to Illustrations, pages 286–290.

Miller's compares...

A. Imari lidded beaker and saucer, with floral decoration, minor damage, Japanese, early 18thC, saucer 6in (15cm) diam.
£120–140 / €180–220
$210–260 WW ⚒

B. Berlin cup, cover and saucer, painted with classical figures and a column, within gilt borders, inscribed 'Venus and Adonis', slight rubbing, blue sceptre marks, German, early 19thC.
£490–580 / €730–860
$870–1,050 WW ⚒

Although Item A is Imari, it is not as collectable as Item B, the Berlin cup and saucer. Also, Item B has finer decoration, including a titled scene – which always commands a premium – and this is why it sold for more than Item A.

Coffee cup and saucer, Chinese, c1760, 2¼in (5.5cm) diam. Good-quality decoration is important on Chinese ceramics.
£135–150 / €200–220
$240–270 DAN ⊞

Faïence mug, decorated with panels of flowers and diaper patterns, marked 'S', German, 1700–50, 6in (15cm) high.
£140–165 / €220–250
$260–290 WW ⚒

Imari tea bowl and saucer, decorated with panels of landscapes, marked, Japanese, early 18thC. Imari items with bold decoration are popular with today's buyers.
£140–165 / €220–250
$260–290 WW ⚒

Faïence & Delft

Faïence is the term used for tin-glazed earthenware made outside Italy, although, rather confusingly, it is named after the Italian town of Faenza. The same wares are called maiolica if they were actually made in Italy. Dutch tin-glazed earthenware is known as Delft, named after the town which was the principal production area. Small chips and fritting are to be expected on earthenware pieces due to the fragile nature of the medium, but large chips do decrease the value.

The look without the price

Vienna-style cup and saucer,
painted with panel entitled 'Paris and Helena', painted beehive and impressed marks, 19thC, saucer 4½in (11.5cm) diam.
£150–180 / €220–270
$270–320 G(L) ⚒

Although this cup and saucer are not authentic, they are still very attractive and would make very good display pieces. If they had actually been made at the Vienna porcelain factory the price would be nearer £200 / €300 / $350.

The look without the price

Porcelain mug, possibly Coalport, decorated with birds within gilt borders, some wear and small crack, c1810, 4in (10cm) high.
£160–190 / €240–280
$280–330 WW ✿

This mug is in good condition and has interesting decoration. It does not have a maker's mark although it could possibly have been made by Coalport. If it could definitely be attributed to the Coalport factory its value could be as high as £250 / €370 / $440.

◀ **Three Worcester coffee cups, a tea bowl and six saucers,** spiral moulded, decorated with gilt sprigs and borders, marked, c1790. Although decorated with a fairly common Worcester pattern, this is a large set and offers very good value for money.
£160–190 / €240–280
$280–330 WW ✿

Mandarin trio, slight wear to gilding, Chinese, c1770, saucer 5in (12.5cm) diam. Although there is some wear to the gilding, this attractive trio would appeal to collectors.
£160–180 / €240–270
$280–320 DAN ⊞

Derby porcelain porter mug, the central panel decorated with a basket of fruit, possibly by Brewer, crowned batons and 'D', minor damage, handle riveted, c1810, 5½in (14cm) high. The painted panel on this mug is of very high quality, and if it had been in perfect condition it could have achieved £300–400 / €450–600 / $530–710.
£160–190 / €240–280
$280–330 TEN ✿

▶ **Tin-glazed tankard,** the pewter lid with a globe thumbpiece, inscribed 'I.P.F. 1782', the body decorated with stylized flowers, with a pewter base, handle cracked, German, late 18thC, 10in (25.5cm) high.
£165–195 / €240–280
$280–330 PF ✿

Samson armorial mug, decorated with a coat-of-arms and the motto 'Insperata Floruit', Chinese, 19thC, 7in (18cm) high. Samson armorial wares are particularly popular. They have high-quality decoration and good pieces to collect and research.
£180–210 / €270–310
$320–370 WW ⚒

Worcester trio, painted with flower sprays, square seal marks, saucer cracked, c1770.
£200–240 / €300–360
$350–420 WW ⚒

Derby porter mug, decorated with foliage, slight wear, marked, c1820, 4½in (11.5cm) high. Porter mugs often have worn gilding and it is rare to find an example in good condition, such as this piece.
£200–240 / €300–360
$350–420 WW ⚒

Berlin porcelain cabinet cup and saucer, the cup painted with classical figures, the saucer titled 'L'Attellier d'Appollo', with gilt embellishments, blue painted marks, 19thC, saucer 5in (12.5cm) diam.
£180–210 / €270–310
$320–370 FHF ⚒

Creamware pint mug, printed with a harvesting scene entitled 'Autumn', late 18thC, 5in (15cm) high. Creamware is very popular. This mug is a reasonable price for an item that would be a good addition to a collection.
£190–220 / €280–330
$340–390 CGC ⚒

▶ **Derby porcelain porter mug,** decorated with classical figures and gilt borders, flaking to enamels, crowned batons and 'D' mark, c1810, 5in (12.5cm) high. The flaking on this mug has reduced its appeal and therefore its value. In perfect condition it could be worth about £300–400 / €450–600 / $530–710.
£200–240 / €300–360
$350–420 TEN ⚒

Sunderland Low Ford Pottery creamware mug, transfer-printed with a boat and figures on pedestals, inscribed 'Dawson Lowford' and motto, minor damage, 19thC, 4¾in (12cm) high. This mug's naval theme would appeal to collectors. It is showing signs of wear, but in perfect condition it could possibly achieve £250–300 / €370–450 / $440–530.
£190–220 / €280–330
$340–390 TRM ⚒

◄ **Chamberlain's Worcester cup and saucer,** decorated with Jabberwocky pattern, No. 275, mid-19thC, 4½in (11.5cm) diam. This is an unusual pattern and it has increased the appeal and the value of this cup and saucer.
£220–260 / €330–390
$390–460 WW ⚒

◄ **Meissen beaker and saucer,** painted *en camaieu* with lovers in landscape vignettes, c1760, beaker 4in (10cm) high. High-quality Meissen pieces are currently achieving good prices.
£230–270
€340–400
$410–480 G(L) ⚒

Meissen cup and saucer, painted after Rugendas with battle scenes, between gilt dentil rims, blue crossed swords mark, 18thC.
£240–280 / €360–420
$420–500 G(L) ⚒

Porcelain *trembleuse* chocolate cup and saucer, signed, Austrian, Vienna, 1765, 2¾in (7cm) high. *Trembleuse* cups and saucers are rare and as a result can command a premium.
£250–300 / €370–450
$440–530 DORO ⚒

Flight & Barr Worcester armorial teacup and saucer, enamelled with a peacock, rare script mark 'Manufacturers to their Majesties and Royal Family', saucer glue-repaired, 1792–1807. Flight & Barr Worcester pieces are currently very popular. Although it is damaged, this cup and saucer is very desirable – the peacock crest has added value and interest. In perfect condition it could be worth a further £100 / €150 / $175.
£280–330 / €420–490
$500–580 G(L) ⚒

Diana cargo tea bowl and saucer, decorated with a landscape and diving birds, 1817, saucer 6in (15cm) diam. If buying a piece of Chinese cargo ware, it as advisable to obtain the correct documentation in order to prove its authenticity.
£310–350 / €460–520
$550–620 RBA ⊞

Chamberlain's Worcester miniature cup and saucer, painted with flowers on a gilt ground, script mark, 1820–30, 3¾in (9.5cm) diam. This is a collectable and high-quality cup and saucer with an attractive and unusual handle which may explain its high value.
£360–430 / €540–640
$640–760 WW ⚒

◀ **Worcester mug,** printed with floral sprays, c1770, 6in (15cm) high. Although Worcester pieces are popular with buyers, prices are currently stable, so now may be a good time to invest.
£380–450
€570–670
$670–800 WW ⚒

Find out more in

Miller's Chinese & Japanese Buyers Guide, Miller's Publications, 2004

Stoneware mug, commemorating the marriage of Queen Victoria, 1840, 5¼in (13.5cm) high.
£330–390 / €490–580
$580–690 SAS ⚒

Worcester mug, transfer-printed with Natural Sprays Group pattern, later copied at Lowestoft, c1770, 6in (15cm) high. Transfer-printing – or bat printing – is a technique that uses gelatin to apply a design to the curved surfaces on ceramics.
£400–480 / €600–720
$710–850 G(L) ⚒

Pair of Bow coffee cans, applied with moulded prunus sprays, c1755, 3½in (9cm) high. These Bow coffee cans are of academic interest, which is why they achieved a high price.
£420–500 / €630–750
$740–890 SWO ⚒

Sunderland lustre frog mug, probably by Scott of Southwick, printed with 'The Sailor's Farewell', c1820, 5in (12.5cm) high.
£450–500 / €630–750
$740–890 WAA ⊞

Frog mugs

Frog mugs were drinking mugs with a small model of a frog on the inside, usually near the base. They were made at Leeds, Sunderland, Nottingham and other northern English potteries. They are currently very popular, especially with buyers in the UK.

◀ **Doulton Lambeth tyg,** by Frank Butler, the silver-mounted rim with beaded foliate decoration, above classical masks, 1878, 6in (15cm) high. Buyers should look for 'FB' incised in the decoration on Frank Butler pieces. Pieces signed or initialled by the artist command higher prices than unmarked examples.
£460–550 / €690–820
$810–970 G(L) ⚒

◀ **Creamware quart mug,** printed and painted with a cavalry skirmish, early 19thC, 6in (15cm) high.
£460–550 / €690–820
$810–970 CGC ⚒

▶ **Derby stoneware loving cup,** stamped and incised with flowers and inscription, Brampton or Chesterfield, 1834, 10in (25.5cm) high. This is a rare and typically English loving cup, and would appeal to collectors.
£780–940 / €1,150–1,400
$1,400–1,650 S(O) ⚒

Dishes & Bowls

Nippon porcelain bowl,
with hand-painted decoration,
c1900, 10in (25.5cm) diam.
£40–45 / €60–70
$70–80 DuM 🔨

**Tin-glazed earthenware
bowl,** decorated with birds and
flowers, Continental, late 18thC,
13½in (34.5cm) diam. This bowl
appears to be damaged, but
in perfect condition it could
achieve nearer £100–150 /
€150–220 / $175–270.
£45–55 / €70–80
$80–95 G(L) 🔨

MacIntyre dish, decorated
with a map of India, 1890,
4in (10cm) diam. Novelty dishes
are always collectable. The
map on this dish would appeal
to collectors of items with a
Colonial interest.
£45–50 / €65–75
$80–90 HO ⊞

Miller's compares...

**A. Red Cliff Ironstone
tureen,** American, late 19thC,
11½in (29cm) high.
£40–45 / €60–70
$70–80 DuM 🔨

**B. Leeds Pottery creamware
soup tureen and cover,** with
rope-twist handles, impressed
mark, finial missing, late 18thC,
13¾in (35cm) wide.
£330–390 / €490–580
$580–690 WW 🔨

Item A is made of Ironstone, which was mass-produced, and
is by a little-known maker. Item B is by a well-known pottery,
is made of creamware – a higher quality earthenware that
was made to imitate porcelain – and has attractive rope-
twist handles. It is these factors that combine to make
Item B a more pleasing and valuable piece than Item A.

◀ **Blue and white dish,**
Oriental, c1900, 12in (30.5cm)
diam. This dish appears to be
Japanese and with its attractive
shape and bold decoration it
could fetch almost twice as
much at auction.
£50–60 / €75–90
$90–105 FOX ⊞

▶ **Kutani dish,** decorated
with a water-front scene and
birds, signed, Japanese, late
Meiji period, 1868–1911,
9in (23cm) diam. Kutani
pieces have fallen from favour
recently and consequently
prices have dropped.
£55–65 / €80–95
$105–115 BAC ⊞

Miller's compares...

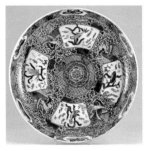

A. *Famille verte* saucer dish,
decorated with panels of fish
surrounded by phoenix, damaged
and restored, Kangxi period,
1662–1722, 10½in (26.5cm) diam.
£70–80 / €105–120
$120–140 WW ⚒

B. *Famille rose* saucer dish,
c1760, 6in (15cm) diam.
£150–170 / €220–250
$270–300 DAN ⊞

**Victorian jasper ware
stilton dish and cover,**
decorated with classical figures,
finial damaged, 10½in (26.5cm)
diam. This Wedgwood jasper
ware stilton dish has a finial that
is slightly damaged. In perfect
condition it could have achieved
£150 / €220 / $270.
£70–80 / €105–120
$120–140 TRM ⚒

Both Item A and Item B are Chinese porcelain pieces with
good-quality decoration. Item A, however, has been
damaged and this has lowered its value, despite it being a
larger size and of an earlier date. Item B, on the other hand,
is in very good condition and consequently sold for a higher
price than Item A.

Vung Tau cargo bowl,
Chinese, 1690–1700, 5in
(12.5cm) diam. If buying a
piece of Chinese cargo ware,
it as advisable to obtain the
correct documentation in order
to prove its authenticity.
£70–80 / €105–120
$120–140 McP ⊞

Famille rose bowl, decorated
with dragons and flaming pearls,
Jiaqing seal mark, restoration,
Chinese, 1796–1820,
7¾in (19.5cm) diam.
£70–80 / €105–120
$120–140 WW ⚒

Nanking cargo Imari bowl, pattern
missing, c1750, 8in (20.5cm) diam. This
bowl was once decorated but the pattern
has been removed by its long immersion in
the sea. However, it is a very good shape
and appears to be in good condition.
£75–85 / €110–125
$135–150 RBA ⊞

▶ **Three Dutch Delft
dishes,** painted with portraits
and fruit trees, initialled
'PV' and 'OR', early 20thC,
14¼in (36cm) wide.
£80–95 / €120–140
$140–165 SWO ⚒

◀ **Satsuma bowl,** decorated with flowers and golden pheasants, signed, Japanese, Meiji period, 1862–1911, 5in (12.5cm) diam.
£85–95
€ **135–140**
$150–170 BAC ⊞

Grainger's Worcester bowl, moulded as a shell, painted with flowers, painted mark, c1902, 7¼in (18.5cm) wide.
£90–105 / € **135–155**
$160–185 SAS ⚒

Grainger's Worcester

Thomas Grainger (1783–1839) was originally an apprentice at Robert Chamberlain's Worcester factory. In 1801 he established a rival porcelain company with his partner John Wood, and they soon gained a good reputation for both useful and ornamental wares. George Grainger succeeded his father as head of the company and embraced the neo-rococo style, producing a wide range of decorative vases, tea and dessert wares which are characterized by extravagant shapes, bright rich colours and scrolled gilding. After George's death in 1884, the company was sold to Royal Worcester who continued production until after 1902.

Dish, moulded as a fish, decorated with figures, Japanese, late 19thC, 16½in (42cm) long. Novelty dishes, although popular, are more desirable and can command higher prices if they are in good condition.
£90–105 / € **135–155**
$160–185 CHTR ⚒

Miller's compares...

A. Caughley moulded bowl, printed with Chinese figures on a bridge and in a pagoda, gilt rim rubbed, marked 'S', c1780, 6in (15cm) diam.
£90–105 / € **135–155**
$160–185 WW ⚒

B. Worcester bowl, printed with a Chinese landscape, disguised numeral mark, c1770, 4¾in (12cm) diam.
£170–200 / € **250–300**
$300–350 WW ⚒

Apart from being earlier, Item B is made by Worcester which is more widely collected than Caughley and more suited to blue and white collectors, which explains why it sold for twice the price of Item A.

Minton bowl, decorated with Tobacco Leaf pattern, 19thC, 9¼in (23.5cm) diam. Minton pieces are highly collectable. This bowl has an attractive pattern and is a good buy.
£100–120 / €150–180
$175–210 BWL 🏶

Dish, decorated with deer, chipped, Chinese, Qianlong period, 1736–95, 20¼in (51.5cm) wide. Rare patterns, such as this example, can command high prices. This dish could have fetched a further 50 per cent.
£95–110 / €140–165
$170–195 WW 🏶

▶ **Royal Worcester dish,** moulded as a leaf, shape No. 1404, painted with flowers, date code for 1898, 6½in (16.5cm) wide.
£100–120 / €150–180
$175–210 G(L) 🏶

Wedgwood cream skimmer, c1910, 19in (48.5cm) wide. Cream skimmers are unusual and this example would be particularly desirable to a collector of Wedgwood.
£105–120 / €155–180
$185–210 SMI ⊞

▶ **Chamberlain's Worcester sugar bowl and cover,** printed with huts and trees, 1790–1800, 5½in (14cm) high.
£110–130
€165–195
$195–230 WW 🏶

Imari *ecuelle* and cover, decorated with flowers and foliage, restored, Chinese, early 18thC, 10½in (26.5cm) wide. This *ecuelle* is an attractive piece, and a good buy, even though it has been restored.
£110–130 / €165–195
$195–230 WW ⚒

Meissen dish, the floral decoration moulded in high relief highlighted with gilt, gilding worn, crossed swords and decorator's mark, late 19thC, 11¼in (28.5cm) diam.
£110–130 / €165–195
$195–230 DN(BR) ⚒

Imari bowl, decorated with cherry blossom, mid-19thC, 6in (15cm) diam. This item has rather pale colouring. Items with stronger colours can command higher prices.
£110–125 / €165–185
$195–220 BAC ⊞

New Hall bowl, painted with Chinese figures, pattern No. 157, some wear, c1800, 6in (15.5cm) diam.
£120–140 / €180–210
$210–250 WW ⚒

The look without the price

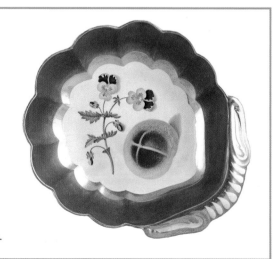

Porcelain dish, probably Derby, moulded as a scallop shell, painted with pansy and a peach, c1820, 9in (23cm) wide.
£120–140 / €180–210
$210–250 WW ⚒

This attractive and desirable botanical dish would make a fine display piece. It is thought to have been made at the Derby factory, but if it could be definitely attributed, it could be worth 40 per cent more than its current value.

Bowl, decorated with phoenix, flower mark, minor damage, 17thC, 6¾in (17cm) diam.
£130–155 / €195–230
$230–270 WW ⚒

▶ **Pair of Imari saucer dishes,** decorated with landscapes, Chinese, early 18thC, 9½in (24cm) diam.
£130–155 / €195–230
$230–270 WW ⚒

Creamware dish, painted with a botanical specimen 'Cape-Aitonia', hairline crack, 1800–10, 10½in (26.5cm) wide.
£130–155 / €195–230
$230–270 WW ⚒

***Famille verte* bowl,** decorated with phoenix, flowers and rockwork, the interior painted with birds, Chinese, Kangxi period, 1662–1722, 7¼in (18.5cm) wide.
£150–180 / €220–270
$270–320 WW ⚒

Botanical decoration

Botanical decoration became fashionable in the Victorian period, at a time when it was considered crucial that artists should depict their subjects as realistically as possible. Today it is a popular collecting area, and examples that have titles, and are by a good maker, command the highest prices.

◀ **John Rose sugar bowl and cover,** painted with gilt flowers and leaves, with ring handles, c1805, 5½in (14cm) high. The simple neo-classical decoration on this sugar bowl is currently very fashionable.
£150–180
€220–270
$270–320 WW ⚒

Caughley sugar bowl and cover, printed with landscapes, with gilt borders, 'Sx' mark, 1775–90, 4½in (11.5cm) high.
£160–190 / €240–280
$280–340 WW ⚒

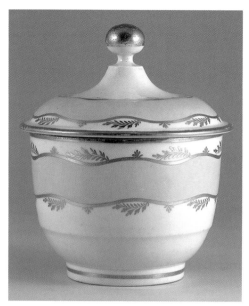

Bow dish, moulded with geometric diaper patterns, painted with flowers and insects, the reverse with four leaf trails, c1765, 7¾in (19.5cm) wide.
£170–200 / €250–300
$300–350 WW ⚖

Porcelain sugar bowl and cover, decorated with gilt foliage, with gilt ball finial, c1800, 6in (15cm) high.
£160–190 / €240–280
$280–340 WW ⚖

Dish, painted with lotus beneath a willow tree, with diaper border, Chinese, 18thC, 13¼in (33.5cm) wide. This dish would be attractive to collectors because it is an unusual shape and has well-painted decoration.
£170–200 / €250–300
$300–350 WW ⚖

Worcester bowl, printed with Birds in Branches pattern, with later clobbering, crescent mark, c1775 and later, 6¼in (16cm) wide. Clobber is the technique of applying enamel glazes over a blue and white underglaze.
£175–210 / €260–310
$310–370 SWO ⚖

▶ **Set of eight** *famille rose* **dishes,** decorated with insects and flowers, Chinese/Canton, mid-19thC, 9in (23cm) wide.
£190–220 / €280–330
$340–390 WW ⚖

◀ **Worcester sugar bowl and cover,** printed with flowers and a fence, with flower knop, crescent mark, c1770, 4¾in (12cm) high.
£180–210 / €270–310
$320–370 WW ⚖

Miller's compares...

A. *Famille rose* **punch bowl,** decorated with birds, flowers and insects, gilt-enriched, Cantonese, 19thC, 15in (38cm) wide.
£210–260 / €330–390
$390–460 PFK ⚒

B. Canton *famille rose* **bowl,** decorated with figures, birds, flowers and foliage, mid-19thC, 16in (40.5cm) diam.
£540–650 / €800–970
$960–1,150 WW ⚒

Item A and Item B are a similar size. The difference between them is that the finish and quality of decoration of Item B far exceeds that of Item A, which is why Item B sold for a much higher price.

Pair of Belleek oyster dishes, on shell feet, Irish, First Period, 1863–90, 5½in (14cm) wide.
£230–270 / €340–400
$410–480 G(L) ⚒

◀ **Charles Bourne bowl,** c1820, 6in (15cm) diam. This is a very reasonable price for an item with such a high-quality, heavily-gilded border.
£240–270
€360–400
$420–480 DAN ⊞

Doucai saucer dish, Chenghua mark, early 17thC, 8¾in (22cm) diam.
£250–300 / €380–450
$440–530 S(O) ⚒

Worcester butter boat, moulded as a leaf, painted with flowers, pseudo Chinese painter's mark, First period, 3¼in (8.5cm) wide.
£240–280 / €360–420
$420–500 L ⚒

▶ **Majolica dish,** modelled with a snake, a frog and a lizard, faint impressed mark, probably for Mafra, Portuguese, 1850–1900, 11¾in (30cm) diam. Majolica Mafra items are growing in popularity, and this dish could be expected to fetch a further 30 per cent.
£260–310 / €390–460
$460–550 WW ⚒

Vauxhall delft dish,
decorated with Bending
Chinaman pattern, repaired,
1720–30, 13in (33cm) diam.
This is a rare dish decorated in a
variety of colours and in good
condition, hence its high price.
£300–360 / €450–540
$530–640 WW

► **Andrew
Stevenson soup
tureen,** printed
with Netley Abbey
pattern, hair crack,
impressed maker's
mark, 1815–30,
13¾in (35cm) wide.
£330–390
€490–580
$580–690 DN

Worcester pickle dish,
moulded as a leaf, painted
with Pickle Leaf Daisy pattern,
painter's mark, c1758,
3¼in (8.5cm) wide.
£350–420 / €520–630
$620–740 G(L)

Saucer dish, with floral
decoration and diaper borders,
minor damage, 1735–45,
8in (20.5cm) diam. This piece is
Chinese porcelain decorated in
Europe for the western market.
It was part of the Bernard
Watney collection.
£350–420 / €520–630
$620–740 B

**Worcester Flight sucrier
and cover,** with painted
and gilt flowers, c1785,
6in (15cm) high.
£350–390 / €520–580
$620–690 JUP

► **Satsuma bowl,** enamelled
and gilded with a dragon and
seated figures, late 19thC,
8¾in (22cm) diam, on a pierced
hardwood stand.
£400–480 / €600–720
$710–850 G(L)

◄ **Worcester butter boat,** moulded as a leaf, painted with flowers, painter's three dot mark, First period, 3½in (9cm) wide.
£420–500 / €630–750
$740–890 L ⚒

Leeds Pottery creamware barber's bowl, with a feather-moulded border, impressed mark, 1790–1800, 12in (30.5cm) diam. This is a rare and unusual bowl, hence the high price.
£450–500 / €670–740
$800–880 KEY ⊞

Wedgwood jasper ware bowl, decorated with figures from the Domestic Employment designs by Lady Templetown, marked, 1780–90, 3in (7.5cm) diam. Early Wedgwood pieces by known designers such as John Flaxman and Lady Templetown are currently sought after.
£470–560 / €700–830
$830–990 B ⚒

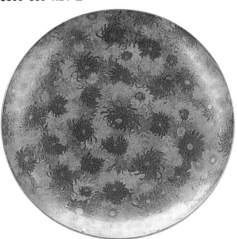

► **Satsuma earthenware dish,** painted in enamels and gilt with chrysanthemum flowerheads, signed 'Seizan', Meiji period, 1868–1911, 12⅝in (32cm) diam. Seizan is a well-known maker of Satsuma earthenware and the chrysanthemums have added appeal to this dish as they are the national flower of Japan.
£540–640 / €800–950
$950–1,100 S(O) ⚒

Auction or dealer?

All the pictures in our price guides originate from auction houses ⚒ and dealers ⊞. When buying at auction, prices can be lower than those of a dealer, but a buyer's premium and VAT will be added to the hammer price. Equally, when selling at auction, commission, tax and photography charges must be taken into account. Dealers will often restore pieces before putting them back on the market. Both dealers and auctioneers can provide professional advice, so it is worth researching both sources before buying or selling your antiques.

Imari bowl, the interior and exterior decorated in enamels and gilt with flowers and fruit, 1700–50, 6¼in (16cm) diam.
£600–720 / €890–1,050
$1,050–1,250 S(O) ⚒

Figures

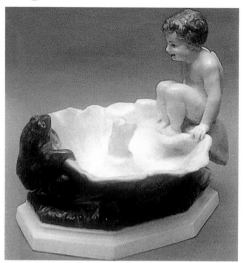

◄ **Derby porcelain figural group,** of a cherub and a toad sitting on toadstools, impressed factory marks, c1878. Cherubs are an appealing feature to collectors and novelty items are popular. This figural group has been modelled well and is a good buy.
£50–60 / €75–90
$90–105 AMB ⚒

The look without the price

Porcelain model of a hawk, some restoration, German, late 19thC, 9½in (24cm) high.
£55–65 / €80–95
$95–110 G(L) ⚒

In perfect, unrestored condition, this model of a hawk could have achieved between £150–200 / €220–330 / $270–390.

◄ **Bisque figure,** German, 1910, 4in (10cm) high. German bisque figures are not as popular as they once were so now is a good time to buy if you like them.
£65–75 / €95–110
$115–130 CCs ⊞

◄ **Two Hirado models of a cockerel and hen,** damaged, Japanese, 19thC, 5½in (14cm) high.
£70–80 / €100–120
$120–140 WW ⚒

Delft model of a bear, initialled 'AG', 19thC, 2¼in (5.5cm) high.
£90–105 / €135–155
$160–185 SWO ✍

▶ **Bisque perfume bottle,**
modelled as a doll, 1900,
3in (7.5cm) high. Perfume
bottles, especially novelty
examples, are highly sought after.
£105–120 / €155–175
$185–210 LBe ⊞

Pair of bisque figures, with hand-painted features and gilt accents, German, c1900, 16in (40.5cm) high.
£95–110 / €140–165
$170–195 JAA ✍

Set of three Dresden female figures,
painted scissor marks, late 19thC,
9¼in (23.5cm) high.
£110–130 / €165–195
$195–230 G(L) ✍

**Parian figure of a young
boy holding a butterfly net,**
19thC, 13in (33cm) high.
£120–140 / €180–210
$210–250 JAd ✍

◀ **Pair of porcelain figures,**
damaged, c1820, 4¾in (12cm)
high. The damage has
significantly reduced the value
of these figures. In perfect
condition they could be worth
£300–400 / €450–600 /
$530–710.
£120–140 / €180–210
$210–250 WW ✍

Majolica model of a chicken, 1900, 7in (18cm) high.
£150–170 / €220–250
$270–300 MLL ⊞

▶ **Staffordshire figure of a man,** probably Thomas Parr, wearing 18thC dress, c1870, 6½in (16.5cm) high. This rare Staffordshire figure has an attractive foliate base.
£150–165
€220–250
$270–300 DAN ⊞

Candle extinguishers

Collectors should be aware that in 1976 the Worcester factory decided to reproduce 14 extinguishers (or snuffers) using old moulds. These proved very successful with the public, who found them both charming and affordable, and they were produced for a period of 10 years. The Worcester factory stopped manufacturing extinguishers in 1986.

◀ **Royal Worcester snuffer,** modelled as a monk, c1908, 5in (12.5cm) high.
£150–165 / €220–250
$270–300 GGD ⊞

Staffordshire pottery figural group, entitled 'London 30 Miles', c1870, 10½in (26.5cm) high. Spill vase groups always appeal to collectors. Unusual or rare examples, such as this, can command significantly higher prices than spill vase groups more commonly found.
£180–210 / €270–310
$320–370 SWO ⚒

◀ **Salt-glazed stoneware flask,** in the form of a head in a nightcap, loop handle applied to back, with cork stopper, c1830, 10¾in (27.5cm) high. The large size and humorous nature of this flask account for its high value.
£160–190 / €240–280
$280–330 WW ⚒

◄ **Staffordshire figure of a fish seller,** c1860, 10in (25.5cm) high.
£240–270 / €360–400
$420–480 DAN ⊞

Kutani model of a cat, with gilt patches, late 19thC, 6in (15cm) high.
£220–260 / €330–390
$390–460 DN(Bri) ⚓

► **Meissen porcelain figure of a soldier,** modelled playing a bugle, instrument restored, crossed swords mark, late 19thC, 5¾in (14.5cm) high. The poor restoration to this figure has decreased its value by 100 per cent.
£300–360 / €450–540
$530–640 S(O) ⚓

◄ **Brown-Westhead, Moore & Co parian bust of Apollo,** impressed 'C Delpech regt. Published February 1st 1861 Art Union of London', c1861, 13in (33cm) high. The value of this bust is attributable to its large size, Art Union reference and Greek subject.
£330–390
€490–580
$580–690 SWO ⚓

► **Minton parian figure of Miranda,** by John Bell, 19thC, 15in (38cm) high.
£360–400
€540–600
$640–710 TMA ⊞

The look without the price

Porcelain Meissen-style model of a pug dog, incised 311, crossed swords mark, Continental, 1850–1900, 7in (18cm) high.
£380–450 / €570–670
$670–800 WW 🔨

This Meissen-style model would be a good addition to a collection of porcelain animals. However, had it been a genuine Meissen piece its value would be much higher at around £950 / €1,400 / $1,700.

◀ **Limbach figure of Autumn,** from the Four Seasons set, c1775, 6¾in (17cm) high.
£400–480 / €600–720
$710–850 G(L) 🔨

Samson porcelain figural scent, French, c1870, 3½in (9cm) high.
£390–430 / €580–640
$690–760 VK ⊞

◀ **Pair of Derby biscuit figures of a gardener and companion,** incised mark for Isaac Farnsworth, damaged, late 18thC, 5½in (14cm) high.
£400–450
€600–670
$710–800 TMA ⊞

▶ **Majolica pottery model of a lion,** c1870, 8½in (21.5cm) high. This model would be popular with the American market.
£450–540 / €670–800
$800–960 WL 🔨

Gardener biscuit porcelain figural group of a child and dog, impressed and stamped factory marks, late 19thC, 3in (7.5cm) high.
£480–570 / €700–850
$830–1,000 S(O) 🔨

Staffordshire porcellaneous figure of a man with a snake, c1840, 5in (12.5cm) high. It is the rarity of this Staffordshire figure that accounts for its high value.
£520–580 / €770–860
$920–1,050 DAN ⊞

Figure of a seated Buddha, impressed seal mark 'Zeng Longxing zao', 18thC, 4¼in (11cm) high.
£540–640 / €800–950
$960–1,150 S(O) 🔨

Miller's compares...

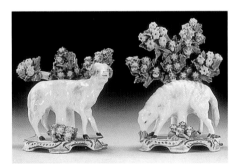

A. Pair of Bow models of sheep, each standing before a flowering tree, on a scroll-moulded base, minor damage and repairs, c1765, 4in (10cm) wide.
£540–640 / €800–950
$960–1,150 S(O) 🔨

B. Pair of Derby models of sheep, c1775, 3¼in (8.5cm) high.
£880–980 / €1,300–1,450
$1,550–1,750 AUC ⊞

Item A and Item B are by well-known makers of quality porcelain. Item A, however, has been damaged, and this has almost halved its value, whereas Item B is in very good condition and consequently sold for the higher price.

▶ **Pair of glazed pottery recumbent horses,** Chinese, early 20thC, 9in (23cm) wide, on wooden stands.
£590–700 / €880–1,050
$1,050–1,250 BUK 🔨

Miller's compares...

A. Pair of Dresden pugs, with gilded bells, Continental, c1870, 4½in (11.5cm) high.
£680–750 / €1,000–1,100
$1,200–1,350 RdeR ⊞

B. Meissen pug, crossed swords mark, c1870, 4in (10cm) high.
£850–950 / €1,250–1,400
$1,500–1,700 RdeR ⊞

Item A is a pair, and would be have been expected to command a higher price than an individual piece such as Item B. However, Item B has a more appealing face that will probably capture the attention of a buyer, and therefore it is valued at a higher price than Item A.

◀ **Royal Worcester figure of an Oriental man,** by James Hadley, from Countries of the World series, 1889, 7in (18cm) high.
£790–880
€1,200–1,350
$1,400–1,550
GGD ⊞

Meissen model of a Bolognese hound, with moulded shaggy coat, incised No. 335, front paws and tail chipped, crossed swords mark, German, c1850, 7½in (19cm) high. This hound has been modelled well and it is by a popular manufacturer. This is a very collectable piece which is reflected in its price.
£840–1,000 / €1,250–1,500
$1,500–1,750 B ⚘

◀ **Meissen desk paperweight,** painted with a titled view of Meissen and flower sprays, surmounted by a pug dog, minor restoration to pug, impressed and incised numerals, crossed swords mark, German, 1850–1900, 7½in (19cm) long. This paperweight is a rare form and is very good quality, hence its high price.
£900–1,050 / €1,350–1,550
$1,600–1,850 S(O) ⚘

Flatware

Miller's compares...

A. Cauldon plate, decorated with Rhine pattern, c1900, 10½in (26.5cm) diam.
£20–25 / €30–35
$35–40 FOX ⊞

B. Plate, by John & Richard Riley, depicting the King's cottage in Windsor Park, 1820–28, 6¾in (17cm) diam.
£165–185 / €240–270
$290–320 GRe ✎

Item A is a 20th-century copy of a 19th-century design, whereas Item B is an original 19th-century plate. This is why Item B sold for a much higher price than Item A.

Copeland pottery plate, commemorating Queen Victoria's Golden Jubilee, transfer-printed, 1887, 10in (25.5cm) diam.
£40–45 / €60–70
$70–80 GwR ⊞

For more examples of Commemorative Ware see Cups, Mugs & Tea Bowls (page 70)

Nippon plate, Japanese, early 1900s, 7in (18cm) diam.
£30–35 / €45–50
$55–65 BAC ⊞

► **Kutani plate,** decorated with birds and lotus, signed, Meiji period, 1868–1911, 9in (23cm) diam.
£50–60 / €75–90
$90–105 BAC 🔨

Nursery plate, the border moulded with the alphabet, printed with a scene entitled 'The Sheep Shearer', stained, c1840, 6¼in (16cm) diam.
£45–50 / €65–75
$80–90 SAS 🔨

► **Gaudy Welsh plate,** decorated with Feather pattern, c1860, 10in (25.5cm) diam.
£55–65 / €80–95
$95–110 TOP ⊞

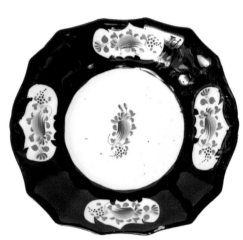

◄ **Cake plate,** by H. & R. Daniel, pattern No. 4678, c1830, 9in (23cm) diam.
£60–70 / €90–105
$105–125 TOP ⊞

◄ **Gaudy Welsh bread plate,** decorated with Tulip pattern, c1860, 9in (23cm) diam.
£60–70 / €90–105
$105–125 TOP ⊞

Plate, commemorating Sir Robert Peel, late 1880s, 7in (18cm) diam.
£75–85 / €110–125
$135–150 RCo ⊞

◄ **Linthorpe earthenware plate,** painted with chrysanthemums and monogrammed 'LH', c1900, 11½in (29cm) diam.
£75–90 / €110–130
$135–160 G(L) ✐

Linthorpe

The Linthorpe Art Pottery was established in 1879 by John Harrison, at the suggestion of the renowned designer Christopher Dresser. Linthorpe was the first company to use gas-fired kilns and employed a large number of people. Christopher Dresser, as Art Director, supplied many of the designs for the pottery and was one of the first European designers to visit Japan. He reproduced many Japanese-style and primitive South American designs, which though simple in shape, were considered avant-garde at the time. Although it only ran for 10 years, the pottery was very influential and Linthorpe pieces are avidly collected today.

◄ **Meissen porcelain saucer,** factory mark with two cancellation lines, 19thC.
£80–95 / €120–140
$140–165 SWO ✐

Cancellation lines

Meissen items with a mark crossed through with one line are factory seconds. However, items with a mark crossed through with two lines have been decorated outside the factory, possibly by a named artist. Faults that have occurred while in the factory do not decrease the value of an item as much as damage that has occurred later.

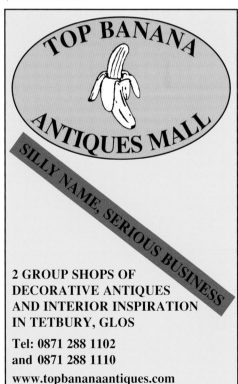

◄ **Royal Worcester plate,** decorated with a view of Pembroke Castle, signed 'Rushton', c1851, 10¾in (27.5cm) high.
£80–95
€120–140
$140–165 WW ✐

◄ **Child's pottery plate,** transfer-printed with a nursery rhyme, c1800, 5in (12.5cm) diam. Children's pottery plates are a popular collecting field and examples with nursery rhymes, which are also known as nursery plates, are very desirable.
£80–95 / €120–140
$140–165 AAN ⊞

The look without the price

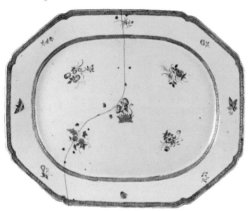

Famille rose **meat plate,** decorated with crest and flower sprigs, cracked, Chinese, Qianlong period, 1736–95, 20¼in (51.5cm) wide.
£90–105 / €135–155
$160–185 WW 🔨

Chinese *famille rose* pieces are very desirable and this is a particularly attractive plate. If it had been in perfect condition this meat plate could have achieved between £200–300 / €300–455 / $350–530.

Pair of Derby saucer dishes, painted with festoons of trailing flowers, one damaged, factory marks, late 18thC, 7in (18cm) diam.
£90–105 / €135–155
$160–185 WW 🔨

Chelsea dessert plate, painted with a butterfly and fruit, anchor mark, some restoration, mid-18thC, 8½in (21.5cm) diam. The enamel decoration on Chelsea pieces sits flush with the glaze instead of being slightly raised. This is because Chelsea used soft-paste porcelain for their wares.
£90–105 / €135–155
$160–185 G(L) 🔨

▶ **London delft plate,** painted with a figure and a bird, some restoration, c1740, 8¾in (22cm) diam. In good, unrestored condition this plate could have fetched a further £100 / €150 / $175.
£90–105
€135–155
$160–185 WW 🔨

Pair of delft plates, decorated with flowers, leaves and grasses, minor damage, 18thC, 8¾in (22cm) diam.
£100–120 / €150–180
$175–210 WW 🔨

Porcelain soup plate, from the Imperial service of Paul I, Emperor of Russia, decorated with a sepia landscape, incised '13', damaged, repaired, Russian, late 18thC, 9½in (24cm) diam. Despite the damage, the provenance of this soup plate has increased its value. It is important to have the correct documentation in order to confirm provenance.
£100–120 / €150–180
$175–210 WW ✹

Porcelain plate, commemorating Tsar Nicholas II, printed with a portrait, inscription and dated ribbon, French, c1896, 7in (18cm) diam. The Russian reference makes this plate a more unusual commemorative piece and adds to its value.
£110–130 / €165–195
$195–230 SAS ✹

▶ **Six ironstone plates,** possibly Spode, pattern No. 2147, heightened in gilt, 19thC, 8in (20.5cm) diam.
£100–120
€150–180
$175–210 SWO ✹

Bone china plate, commemorating the Golden Jubilee of Queen Victoria, 1889, 10in (25.5cm) diam.
£105–120 / €155–180
$185–210 H&G ⊞

English delft plate, probably Lambeth, painted with two figures and a landscape, cracked, mid-18thC, 8¾in (22cm) wide. This plate appears to be damaged. Had it been in better condition it could have achieved a further 60 per cent.
£110–130 / €165–195
$195–230 WW ✹

◀ **English delft plate,** painted with a stylized flower within a border of leaves, c1740, 9in (23cm) diam.
£120–140 / €180–210
$210–250 WW ✹

▶ **Nursery plate,** printed with a scene entitled 'The Farmyard', the border moulded with animals, c1840, 5in (12.5cm) diam.
£120–140 / €180–210
$210–250 SAS ✹

Worcester plate, printed with Pine Cone pattern, crescent mark, c1770, 6¼in (16cm) diam. Although this plate is decorated with a common Worcester pattern, it is in good condition and has achieved a good price.
£130–155 / €195–230
$230–270 WW ✗

Tea plate, decorated with grazing rabbits, c1820, 6½in (16.5cm) diam.
£135–150 / €200–220
$240–270 SCO ⊞

Set of six plates, transfer-printed with scenes depicting the production of bread, inscribed 'The Reaper' and 'The Progress of the Quartern Loaf', 19thC, 7in (18cm) diam.
£135–150 / €200–220
$240–270 AAN ⊞

The look without the price

Three Dutch Delft plates, painted with vases, damaged, 18thC, 10½in (26.5cm) diam.
£130–155 / €195–230
$230–270 SWO ✗

These matching plates would make an attractive and affordable display. If they had been in perfect condition this set of plates could have achieved a further £70 / €105 / $125.

Victorian majolica bread plate, moulded with wheat and leaves, the border inscribed 'Where reason rules the appetite obeys', 12½in (32cm) long.
£140–165 / €200–240
$240–290 DN(Bri) ✗

◀ **Lowestoft saucer,** painted with a peony and bamboo, c1770, 4¾in (12cm) diam. Lowestoft items are rare and very collectable. This example has decoration which is typical of the period and is very desirable.
£150–180 / €220–270 $270–320 WW 🔨

▶ **Royal Worcester plate,** commemorating Robert Baden Powell, c1900, 9in (23cm) diam. Pieces with a scouting theme are popular with collectors.
£155–175 €230–260 $270–310 H&G ⊞

Meat plate, decorated with Chinese Traders pattern, impressed '16', early 19thC, 6½in (16.5cm) wide. This plate offers very good value for money. It is decorated with a rare pattern and could have sold for £200–300 / €300–450 / $350–530.
£150–180 / €220–270 $270–320 G(L) 🔨

Porcelain charger, painted in the Imari palette with alternate panels of flowers, brocaded patterns and bamboo, the centre with peonies, early 20thC, 16in (40.5cm) diam.
£165–195 / €240–290 $290–350 PFK 🔨

Villeroy & Boch charger, 1870, 12in (30.5cm) diam. Villeroy & Boch are a well-respected German manufacturer and this charger may appeal to the American market where Victorian pieces are currently more popular.
£175–195 / €260–290 $310–350 CoCo ⊞

▶ **Bone china plate,** painted with a hunting scene, c1830, 10¼in (26cm) diam. Items depicting hunting scenes are popular with collectors.
£180–210 / €270–310 $320–370 WW 🔨

English delft plate, probably Bristol, decorated with a man and a woman beneath trees, repaired, 18thC, 9in (23cm) diam. The low price for this English delft plate is probably due to the fact that it has been repaired.
£190–220 / €280–330
$340–390 WW ⚘

Famille verte **plate,** decorated with crustaceans and shells, cracked, flowerhead mark, Chinese, Kangxi period, 1662–1722, 8¼in (21cm) diam.
£190–220 / €280–330
$340–390 WW ⚘

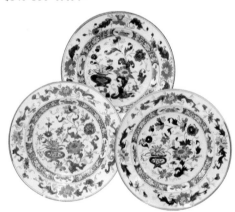

Set of three Imari plates, with floral decoration, Qianlong period, 1736–95, 9in (23cm) diam.
£190–220 / €280–330
$340–390 G(L) ⚘

Three Sèvres plates, painted with floral sprays, small rim chips, marked, 1760–70, 9¾in (25cm) diam. Despite having rim chips, these plates have achieved a high price. Sèvres items are currently very popular.
£200–240 / €300–360
$350–420 WW ⚘

◄ **Pair of Ridgway plates,** painted with panels of flowers, with gilt vines and a gilt edge, early 19thC, 9½in (24.5cm) diam. Ridgway items are currently selling well.
£210–250 / €310–370
$370–440 NSal ⚘

Famille rose plate, decorated with horses, flowers and butterflies, Chinese, mid-18thC, 9in (23cm) diam.
£230–270 / €340–400
$410–480 WW ⚒

Slipware plate, decorated with triangular panels, 18thC, 8¼in (21cm) diam. Slipware items, especially those with more decorative patterns, are currently sought after.
£220–260 / €330–390
$390–460 WW ⚒

▶ **Liverpool delft plate,** c1780, 9in (23cm) diam. Liverpool was an important pottery production centre from the mid-18thC. It is noted for its blue-painted delftware, which is eagerly collected. However, it is often difficult to identify as there are many similar pieces on the market.
£250–280 / €370–420
$440–500 KEY ⊞

Kutani wall plate, painted with a mythological dragon and princess, 19thC, 18in (45.5cm) wide. This plate would be attractive to collectors because it has a high-quality finish and is in good condition.
£240–280 / €360–420
$420–500 G(L) ⚒

18 Sèvres plates, the borders moulded with flowers and scrolls, damaged, 1770–80, 9½in (24cm) diam. This is a large set of plates, but their low price reflects the fact that they are damaged and of plain design.
£260–310 / €390–460
$460–550 WW ⚒

▶ **Chelsea plate,** with feather-scroll-moulded border, painted with flower sprays, brown anchor mark, c1760, 8¼in (21cm) diam. This is a good example of a Chelsea plate and would appeal to collectors.
£260–310
€390–460
$460–550 WW ⚒

◀ **Set of four Staffordshire plates,** moulded with geometric patterns and trellis borders, 1750–1800, 8in (20.5cm) diam. The rarity of the geometric moulding on these plates account for their high value.
£280–330
€420–490
$500–580 WW ➢

Vienna plate, decorated with a portrait of a young girl, edged in gilt, 19thC, 9½in (24cm) diam.
£280–330 / €420–490
$500–580 B(W) ➢

Pearlware meat platter, c1820, 14in (35.5cm) wide.
£290–320 / €430–480
$510–570 CoCo ⊞

Imari charger, gilt decoration rubbed, Japanese, late 19thC, 17¾in (45cm) diam.
£300–360 / €450–540
$530–640 SWO ➢

Basket plate, moulded with floral spray and butterflies, Chinese, 18thC, 9in (23cm) diam. Pierced rims are unusual and very desirable.
£300–360 / €450–540
$530–640 WW ➢

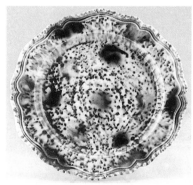

Pair of Whieldon-style plates, with gadrooned rims, one damaged, c1770, 9½in (24cm) diam. Whieldon ware items are popular and very collectable.
£300–360 / €450–540
$530–640 WW ➢

◄ **Delft lobed dish,** with Chinese transitional-style decoration, German, c1700, 8in (20.5cm) diam. Dutch Delft is more desirable, and has a larger group of collectors than German delft.
£310–350 / €460–520
$550–620 G&G ⊞

Delft dish, painted with a church and trees and sponged with manganese, c1740, 7¾in (19.5cm) diam. Manganese decoration can increase the value of a piece, especially when compared with a plain delftware example.
£300–360 / €450–540
$530–640 WW ⚹

Chinese export charger, with clobbered decoration, 18thC, 14in (35.5cm) diam.
£320–380 / €480–570
$570–670 G(L) ⚹

Delft meat plate, painted with peonies and bamboo, possibly Irish, c1760, 16in (40.5cm) wide.
£300–360 / €450–540
$530–640 WW ⚹

Clobbering

Clobbering is the technique of applying coloured enamel glazes over blue and white underglaze colours. It is a relatively rare technique.

Minton *pâte-sur-pâte* plate, decorated with three classical panels, signed 'A. Birks', gilt retailer's mark for Tiffany & Co, impressed factory marks, c1882, 8¾in (22cm) diam. Minton is synonymous with the *pâte-sur-pâte* technique and the Tiffany mark on this plate has made it highly desirable.
£360–430 / €540–640
$640–760 WW ⚹

English delft plate, possibly Bristol, painted with Arion II straddling a dolphin, damaged, mid-18thC, 8¾in (22cm) diam. Arion II, who lived in Corinth when the city was ruled by King Periander (625–585 BC), was the best citharist or lyre-player of his time, coming originally from Methymna, a city in the island of Lesbos. On his return from an artistic tour of Italy, he was robbed by the crew of his ship and forced to cast himself into the sea. Against all odds, however, he landed in Taenarum, in the southern Peloponnesian, riding on the back of a dolphin.
£340–400 / €510–600
$600–710 TEN ⚹

Delft plate, decorated with a swan and riverbank, c1740, 9in (23cm) diam.
£360–430 / €540–640
$640–760 WW ⚹

Pâte-sur-pâte

In 1870 the modeller Marc-Louis Solon introduced the *pâte-sur-pâte* technique, whereby white slip was built up and carved on a dark-coloured ground, such as pink, green or blue. The painstaking process often took several weeks to complete and was extremely costly, but the effect could be stunning.

Staffordshire salt-glazed stoneware plate, printed with a vignette of lovers in a garden, within a diaper-moulded border, 1760–70, 8¾in (22cm) diam. This very early plate has unusual decoration. It is very desirable and this accounts for its high price.
£400–480 / €600–720
$710–850 WW

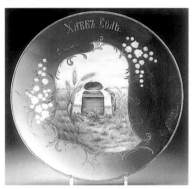

Porcelain dish, painted with a bread and salt dish in a field, the border inscribed in Russian 'bread, salt', late 19thC, 13in (33cm) diam. The Russian word for hospitality *khleb-sol*, translates literally as 'bread-salt'. This not only evokes the traditional Russian greeting for arriving guests – a presentation of bread and salt – but also underlines the importance of these two commodities to the Russian people.
£600–720 / €890–1,050
$1,050–1,250 S(O)

Sets/pairs

Unless otherwise stated, any description which refers to 'a set' or 'a pair' includes a guide price for the entire set or the pair, even though the illustration may show only a single item.

▶ **Majolica charger,** the centre decorated with a cavalier on a horse, the reverse with a mark for Monte Christo, Italian, Savona, late 19thC, 18in (45.5cm) diam. This charger would appeal to Italian collectors.
£470–560
€700–830
$830–990 B&L

English delft plate, probably London, decorated with a seated Chinaman by the sea with a rocky island and cliffs, c1770, 13¾in (35cm) diam.
£480–570 / €720–850
$850–1,000 S(O)

Minton dessert service, comprising two low stands and six plates, decorated with birds and flowers, one damaged, impressed marks, c1881, 9in (23cm) diam. Blue-edged pieces are a typical Minton feature. These examples also have pierced rims, making them a very attractive buy at this price.
£780–930 / €1,150–1,350
$1,400–1,650 WW

Jardinières

Miller's compares...

A. Burmantofts jardinière, with impressed geometric decoration, shape 2052A, impressed mark, c1890, 5½in (14cm) high.
£55–65 / €80–95 $95–110 G(L)

B. Burmantofts faïence jardinière, decorated in low relief with panels of flowers, on a moulded foot, shape 1857C, impressed mark, late 19thC, 11½in (29cm) high.
£300–360 / €450–540 $530–640 AH

The difference between Item A and Item B is their size. They are both made by the small art pottery Burmantofts and decorated in the Aesthetic taste, which is currently very popular. However, Item B is twice the size of Item A, and this is why it sold for a higher price.

Faïence jardinière, decorated with heraldic devices, flowers, insects and dragons, French, late 19thC, 17½in (44.5cm) wide. This jardinière is decorated with bold colours which would appeal to American collectors, and the heraldic devices also add interest. However, it is its large size that gives it its value.
£200–240 / €300–360 $350–420 NSal

▶ Wucai jardinière, decorated with dragons chasing pearls, restored, Chinese, late 17thC, 9in (23cm) diam. If it had been in original condition this item could have achieved £400–600 / €600–890 / $710–1,050.
£250–300 / €370–440 $440–530 B(Kn)

Watcombe Pottery jardinière, with incised decoration, late 19thC, 7¾in (19.5cm) high. The Egyptian-style decoration on this item is currently popular and has enhanced its value.
£85–100 / €125–150 $150–175 MAR

Pearlware flower pot, applied with floral swags hung from masks, hair cracks, c1800, 11½in (29cm) high. This is an interesting item, as flower pots are unusual, and it is also of an early date. These facts would account for its high price.
£180–210 / €270–310 $320–370 WW

Paris porcelain jardinière and stand, by Alexandre Moitte, marked, French, c1795, 8in (20.5cm) high.
£520–620 / €770–920 $920–1,100 S(P)

Jars & Canisters

◀ **Biscuit jar and cover,** with floral decoration, marked 'Imperial Austria', Austrian, c1900, 8in (20.5cm) long. Biscuit jars are very collectable in America, where this item was sold. It could be expected to achieve half this price in the UK.
£90–105 / €135–155
$160–185 JAA ➤

Watcombe Pottery biscuit barrel, with floral decoration, c1885, 7½in (19cm) high. The rare design on this piece has added to its value.
£140–160 / €210–240
$250–280 DPC ⊞

▶ **Crown Devon Cretian ware ginger jar,** with tube-lined decoration, impressed '27', early 20thC, 9½in (24cm) high, together with a matching pot with domed lid and finial.
£150–180
€220–270
$270–320 G(L) ➤

Willow pattern

The most recognizable of blue and white patterns, the Willow pattern was introduced by Spode in 1780 and depicts a Chinese love story in dark blue on a white ground. The Broseley pattern shows the same story but in a much paler blue and the pattern differs in that it shows two temples instead of one, the bridge appears on the right-hand side rather than the left and it has only two figures rather than three. However, not all Willow pattern items show the complete story, as larger transfers were often cut down to fit a variety of smaller items such as spoon rests.

Butter pot, with pierced cover, transfer-printed with Broseley pattern, 19thC, 6¼in (16cm) high.
£170–200 / €250–300
$300–350 TMA ➤

◀ **Porcelain tea canister,** painted with a panoramic landscape with figures, crowned crossed C's mark, Continental, probably 19thC, 4in (10cm) high. This canister appears to be missing its cover. If complete and in good condition it could have achieved £250 / €370 / $440.
£190–220 / €280–340
$330–390 WW ➤

▶ **Bargeware tobacco jar and cover,** inscribed 'Help Yourself', c1880, 7in (18cm) high.
£380–420 / €570–630
$670–740 JBL ⊞

Jugs & Ewers

◀ **Royal Doulton Toby jug,** entitled 'Old Charlie', c1850, 6in (15cm) high. Many of these jugs were reissued between 1934 and 1984, and were made using the original moulds. It is therefore advisable to check the marks very carefully on all Royal Doulton character jugs.
£45–50 / €65–75
$80–90 HarC ⊞

The look without the price

Majolica jug, relief-moulded with birds and leaves above a wicker effect band, Continental, 19thC, 9¼in (23.5cm) high.
£55–65 / €80–95
$95–110 G(L) ⚒

This unmarked but attractive majolica jug is a good example of how a well-known name can affect value. If this jug had been made by Wedgwood it could have achieved £200–300 / €300–450 / $350–530, and if it were made by Minton it could have been worth as much as £500–800 / €750–1,200 / $890–1,200.

Miller's compares...

A. Pair of Royal Doulton glazed stoneware ewers, gilded and moulded with flowers, early 20thC, 6¼in (16cm) high.
£35–40 / €50–60
$60–70 G(L) ⚒

B. Royal Doulton stoneware jug, with incised decoration of horses by Florence Barlow, impressed factory and artist's marks, dated 1874, 9in (23cm) high.
£400–480 / €600–720
$710–850 AMB ⚒

Although Item A is a pair of Royal Doulton ewers, they are not attributable to a particular artist. Item B, however, is a Royal Doulton jug decorated and signed by Florence Barlow, sister of Hannah Barlow, who are both desirable artists at the Royal Doulton factory. This makes Item B a more valuable, desirable and collectable jug than Item A.

Limoges porcelain cider pitcher, by W. Guerin & Co, with hand-painted decoration, French, c1910, 5½in (14cm) high. This item sold well on the American market where this style is popular. In the UK it might sell for only half this price.
£80–95 / €120–140 $140–165 DuM 🔨

Royal Worcester jug, moulded as a leaf, decorated with flowers and leaves, c1885, 5in (12.5cm) high. This attractively designed jug could have sold for £150–200 / €220–300 / $270–350 and was a good buy at auction for a lucky bidder.
£100–120 / €150–180 $175–210 WW 🔨

Treacle-glazed jug, commemorating the Corn Laws, painted with inscription 'Pancakes for All 1846', 6¼in (16cm) high.
£100–120 / €150–180 $175–210 SAS 🔨

Jug, transfer-printed with Sicilian pattern, mid-19thC, 9½in (24cm) high. This jug is an unusual shape with pretty decoration and would enhance any collection.
£130–155 / €195–230 $230–270 G(L) 🔨

The Corn Laws

The Corn Law Act was passed in Britain in 1815 as a measure to protect the interests of landowners when the highly-inflated prices for corn ceased at the end of the Napoleonic wars. This Act kept the price of corn and bread artificially high. Several protest groups arose during the early and mid-1800s to fight for repeal of the Corn Laws. The Anti-Corn Law League drew its members largely from middle-class merchants and manufacturers, whose aim was to loosen the restrictions on trade generally, so that they could sell more goods both at home and around the world.

Pair of Victorian Samuel Alcock & Sons porcelain water jugs, entitled 'Mortality and Immortality', decorated with classical figures, 10¼in (26cm) high.
£140–165 / €210–240 $250–300 DN(EH) 🔨

▶ **Caldas-style wine carrier,** with moulded decoration, the handle moulded as twisted vines, Portuguese, 19thC, 13in (33cm) high. This item is unusual in style and decoration. Wine carriers are more commonly decorated with serpents, but the applied bugs and frogs on this item are rarely found, which makes this a desirable and more valuable piece.
£150–180 / €220–270 $270–320 G(L) 🔨

Miller's compares...

A. Jug, with a pineapple-moulded body, with gilt cartouches enclosing hand-painted floral sprays, 19thC, 6¼in (16cm) high.
£165–195 / €240–290
$300–350 SWO ⚱

B. Jug, decorated with flowers and a landscape, inscribed 'James Parrot', 1847, 9in (23cm) high.
£430–480 / €640–720
$760–850 DAN ⊞

Item A and Item B are attractive hand-painted jugs. Item B, however, is a christening jug inscribed with the recipient's name. This makes Item B a very collectable piece and therefore more valuable than Item A.

Porcelain sauce boat, possibly Liverpool, decorated with floral sprays, c1760, 5in (12.5cm) long. This is an early porcelain piece and if it were confirmed to be from the Liverpool factory it would be rare and very sought after. The value, of course, would also increase.
£220–260 / €330–390
$390–460 WL ⚱

▶ **Pinxton milk jug,** painted with landscape scenes, gilt worn, c1820, 4½in (11.5cm) high. Pinxton items are very rare, which makes this jug a collectable and valuable item.
£220–260 / €330–390
$390–460 WW ⚱

Minton milk jug, moulded with vine leaves and grapes, painted with landscapes and buildings, 1820–30, 5½in (14cm) long.
£180–210 / €270–310
$320–370 WW ⚱

Mason's Ironstone ewer and basin, printed and painted with Imari pattern, printed mark, c1840, ewer 9¾in (25cm) high.
£220–260 / €330–390
$390–460 L&E ⚱

Lustre jug, transfer-printed with a hunting scene after George Morland, restored, early 19thC, 5¼in (13.5cm) high. This is probably a Sunderland piece. George Morland was a well-known painter and this connection has probably increased the appeal and value of the jug to collectors.
£220–260 / €330–390
$390–460 LHA ⚱

Miller's compares...

A. Sunderland lustre jug, printed with 'The Iron Bridge', *The Northumberland* and Masonic verse, chips, early 19thC, 9in (23cm) high.
£230–270 / €340–400 $410–480 G(L) ⚘

B. Sunderland lustre jug, printed with houses and trees, c1840, 6in (15cm) high.
£400–450 / €600–670 $710–800 WAA ⊞

Item A and Item B are both lustre jugs. However, Item B is painted with popular naive-style decoration, and this is what makes it more appealing and more valuable than Item A.

Mettlach pottery jug, No. 1562, painted with a portrait of The Trumpeter of Sackingen, and flanked by military trophies in low relief, late 19thC, 18½in (47cm) high. The Mettlach factory produced mainly dishes and tankards with historical themes. This item depicts the title character from Joseph Viktor Von Scheffel's epic love poem *The Trumpeter of Sackingen*.
£300–360 / €450–540 $530–640 AH ⚘

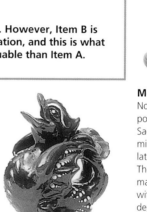

Leeds Pottery creamware sauce boat, c1770, 6in (15cm) long. This is an early example of Leeds creamware and has the deep cream colour associated with these pieces. Marked examples from this early period c1770 are extremely rare, but the flower and leaf terminals and the reeded, double-strap handle are all unmistakably Leeds. Sauce boats of this period were not always sold with a stand.
£260–290 / €390–430 $460–510 KEY ⊞

C. H. Brannam grotesque ewer, modelled as a winged dragon, minor damage, incised mark, 1891, 7¾in (19.5cm) high. Victorian grotesque art pottery is very collectable and is especially popular in America.
£290–340 / €430–510 $510–600 Bea ⚘

▶ **Pearlware armorial jug,** painted with a shield, three squirrels and flowers, spout damaged, c1790, 12¼in (31cm) high. This piece has many good features, is of a good shape and size and is pearlware with armorial decoration, all of which make it a desirable collector's piece.
£320–380 / €480–570 $570–670 WW ⚘

Hebe jug, North Country, c1830, 7in (18cm) high. This is a rare and collectable piece.
£310–350 / €460–520 $550–620 ML ⊞

Plaques

◀ **Sèvres Parian ware plaque,** commemorating the visit of Tsar Nicholas II and Empress Alexandra Romanova to the Sèvres factory, 1896, 3½in (9cm) diam.
£120–140
€**180–210**
$210–250 SWO ➴

▶ **Burmantofts faïence plaque,** relief-moulded with a coastal scene, impressed '1124', late 19thC, 17¾in (45cm) diam. There is a large chip on the rim of this plate that has detracted from its value.
£150–180
€**220–270**
$270–320 AH ➴

Royal Doulton earthenware plaque, painted with a mother and child, c1900, 9½in (24cm) high. This plate has been painted in a style that is currently unpopular, hence the low price of this item – a good buy if you like this style.
£150–180 / **€220–270**
$270–320 G(L) ➴

The look without the price

Pair of maiolica plaques, decorated with dancing figures and washerwomen, stamped 'Flli Bianchi, Napoli', 19thC, 6in (15cm) diam.
£180–210 / **€270–310**
$320–370 G(L) ➴

Eighteenth century maiolica plaques sell for four- and five-figure sums. Mythological or religious scenes and later versions are less valuable, so these 19th-century plaques would be an affordable starting point if you are intending to start a collection.

◄ **Porcelain plaque,** hand-painted with Beatrice Cenci, after Guido Reni, later frame, Continental, 19thC, 7½in (19cm) high.
£180–210
€270–310
$320–370 SWO ⚒

▶ **Porcelain plaque,** hand-painted with a young girl, later frame, Continental, 19thC, 8½in (21.5cm) high.
£200–240
€300–360
$350–420 SWO ⚒

◄ **Porcelain plaque,** printed and painted with Scottish figures in a landscape, in a glazed gilt frame, c1830, 6¾in (17cm) wide.
£260–310 / €390–460
$460–550 WW ⚒

Pair of porcelain plaques, one moulded with the Rape of the Sabines, each in a gilt-metal and ebonized wood frame set with hardstones, Italian, early 20thC, 14½in (37cm) high.
£420–500
€630–750
$740–890 SWO ⚒

◄ **Porcelain plaque,** hand-painted with a young lady, later frame, Continental, 19thC, 7½in (19cm) high. This pretty portrait appeals to buyers, thus making it desirable and adding to its value.
£440–520
€660–770
$780–920 SWO ⚒

***Famille rose* plaque,** decorated with children playing, 18thC, 8¾in (22cm) high, with fitted box.
£480–570 / €720–850
$850–1,000 S(O) ⚒

Services

Five pieces of Crown Derby, comprising two sauce tureens, two sauce boats and one tureen stand, decorated with Wilmot pattern, printed factory mark and impressed date 1885. Complete or part services are less fashionable than they were, but these items are still a good buy at this price.
£40–45 / €60–65
$70–80   AMB 🔨

Lustre tea service, comprising 24 pieces, painted with buildings and landscapes, c1820. While lustreware is collectable, this tea service is of a common design and pattern and this has kept the price low.
£65–75 / €95–110
$115–135   L&E 🔨

Mason's Ironstone part dinner service, comprising eight pieces, decorated with floral pattern, with gilt highlights, impressed marks, early 19thC. This is a good-quality tea service with an attractive pattern and border, making it a desirable purchase and greatly enhancing its value.
£120–140 / €180–210
$210–250   G(L) 🔨

The look without the price

Haviland & Co Limoges cabaret service, teapot cover missing and milk jug repaired, early 20thC.
£55–65 / €80–95
$95–110   G(L) 🔨

This style of tea service is currently unfashionable and as a result prices are low. However, this pretty and affordable service would still look very attractive in a display cabinet. If this had been an 18th- rather than 20th-century example of a Limoges tea service it could be worth substantially more, possibly as much as £1,000 / €1,500 / $1,800.

Dessert service, comprising eight pieces, each decorated with a named and painted Swiss or Alpine landscape view, 19thC, plates 9in (23cm) diam. Plates decorated with Continental scenes are less popular in the UK. If they had been painted with English views, these plates could have achieved £300–400 / €450–600 / $450–710.
£160–190 / €240–280
$280–340   TRM 🔨

Victorian bone china part tea service,
comprising 33 pieces, painted with flowers
and leaf-scroll borders. This attractive service
has sold for an affordable price because it is
unattributed to a particular maker.
£180–210 / €270–310
$320–370 G(L)

Copeland dinner service, comprising 45 pieces, with painted
decoration, some damage, 19thC.
£190–220 / €280–330
$340–390 SWO

Staffordshire pottery dinner service, comprising
38 pieces, printed with Pandora pattern, printed marks,
c1870, together with one Staffordshire plate decorated
with Willow pattern. Earthenware items with printed
decoration are less valuable than porcelain examples.
Nevertheless, this service is good value for money.
£230–270 / €340–400
$410–480 WL

Berlin part dinner service, comprising 12 pieces,
painted with passion flowers and gilded borders, minor
damage, pfennig and sceptre mark, 1840–60. This
service has particular appeal to Continental collectors
as it is marked for King Friedrich Wilhelm IV of Prussia,
giving it an interesting provenance. It has, however,
suffered some damage and this has kept the price low.
£250–300 / €370–450
$440–530 S(Am)

**Set of 12 Coalport porcelain dinner
plates,** retailer's mark, 1875–1900, 10¼in
(26cm) diam. This set of plates were sold at
auction in America. They would, however,
have more appeal in the UK where they
could be worth an additional 30 per cent.
£390–460 / €580–690
$690–810 NOA

Edwardian Royal Worcester coffee service, comprising
38 pieces, printed with floral sprays, painted marks, pattern
No. G3951, cake plate 9½in (24cm) diam, together with two
Grainger & Co tea cups. This is an unusually large service and
this has contributed to its value.
£610–730 / €910–1,100
$1,100–1,300 DN(BR)

Ceramic Stands

Bass & Co teapot stand, c1910, 7in (18cm) diam. Bass memorabilia is highly collectable.
£75–85 / €110–125
$135–150 MURR ⊞

Pair of pricket stands, modelled as crouching figures, Chinese, 19thC, 8¾in (22cm) high.
£260–310 / €390–460
$460–550 AMB ✦

Longquan celadon stand, pierced with six panels, Yuan/Ming Dynasty, 8½in (21.5cm) high. Celadon ware is very popular. This piece is particularly collectable because of its early date.
£720–860 / €1,050–1,300
$1,250–1,500 S(O) ✦

◄ **Faïence tazza,** decorated with floral motif and scrollwork borders, on a low foot, 18thC, 9¾in (25cm) diam. This item has glaze imperfections which have reduced the value. In good condition it could have achieved £100 / €150 / $175.
£75–90
€110–135
$135–160 SWO ✦

Miller's compares...

► **A. Chinese export teapot stand,** c1780, 5in (12.5cm) diam.
£145–165
€220–250
$260–290
DAN ⊞

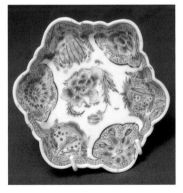

◄ **B. Chinese teapot stand,** c1760, 5in (12.5cm) diam.
£250–280
€370–420
$440–500
DAN ⊞

Item A is decorated in the well-known Willow pattern. Item B is of an earlier date and is decorated in the more desirable *famille rose* palette, and this is what makes it a more valuable stand than Item A.

Tea, Coffee & Chocolate Pots

◀ **Porcelain teapot and cover,** decorated in *famille verte* and *famille rose* colours, 1850–1900, Chinese, Canton, 6in (15cm) high. Cantonese ware is widely available, hence the low price of this item.
**£30–35 / €45–50
$55–65 MCA ⚒**

Miller's compares...

A. Measham bargeware teapot and cover, with teapot finial, inscribed 'Philip Willing Tibbs, Bachelors Tea Pot, Christmas 1893', at fault, 11½in (29cm) high.
**£90–105 / €135–155
$160–185 PF ⚒**

B. Bargeware teapot and cover, c1880, 14¼in (36cm) high.
**£540–600 / €800–890
$960–1,100 JBL ⊞**

Item A has the more usual colouring of pink, green and blue, it is damaged and it is rather small for a bargeware teapot. It does, however, have a finial in the form of a teapot which increases its appeal. Item B is more unusual as its colours are limited to pink and green and it features larger applied decorations of a lady and a dog, rather than the usual flowers and a motto. Item B also has two crowns which indicate that it is a commemorate piece. Size, condition, decoration and colouring all affect the desirability of bargeware items, and as Item B is superior to Item A on all four points, it is therefore the more valuable item.

Kutani coffee pot, with *Akae* decoration, signed, c1880, 8in (20.5cm) high. This item is of typical Kutani decoration but the unusual handle adds interest and therefore value.
**£35–40 / €50–60
$60–70 BAC ⊞**

Pearlware teapot and cover, moulded with bands of acanthus leaves and painted with flower sprays in *famille rose* style, some restoration, possibly Yorkshire, 1790–1800, 9¼in (23.5cm) high. In perfect condition, this unusual teapot could be worth two or three times this amount.
**£100–120 / €150–180
$175–210 WW ⚒**

Locate the source

The source of each illustration in Miller's can be found by checking the code letters below each caption with the Key to Illustrations, pages 286–290.

◀ **Belleek tridacna teapot,** with later cover, Irish, Second Period, 1891–1926, 8in (20.5cm) wide.
**£110–125 / €165–185
$195–220 WAA ⊞**

Minton teapot, decorated with Genevese pattern, c1880, 7in (18cm) wide. This teapot is undamaged and decorated with an attractive and widely-found pattern. This adds to its desirability as it would be easy to find further pieces with which to build a collection.
£115–130 / €170–195
$200–230 CoCo ⊞

Staffordshire teapot and cover, with bird finial and mask, on claw feet, some damages, c1750, 7¾in (19.5cm) high. This is a rare teapot which, despite being damaged, has sold at a reasonable price. In good condition it could have made £300–400 / €450–600 / $530–710.
£190–220 / €280–330
$340–390 WW ⚒

◄ **Worcester coffee pot and cover,** decorated with Japan pattern, knop restored, body cracked, square seal mark, c1770, 9½in (24cm) high. In good condition this teapot could have achieved £500–700 / €750–1,050 / $890–1,250.
£180–210
€270–310
$320–370 WW ⚒

Caughley teapot, cover and stand, decorated with gilt rose sprays and borders, slight wear, 1780–90, 6¾in (17cm) high. The value of this attractive teapot has been increased by its matching stand. Without the stand it could be worth only £150 / €220 / $270.
£220–260 / €330–390
$390–460 WW ⚒

> **For more examples of**
> Coffee & Teapots see Silver (pages 158–159)

Meissen coffee pot, decorated with panels of painted flowers and gilt scrolls, with rose finial, inside of cover damaged, marked, 19thC, 10in (25.5cm) high.
£210–250 / €310–370
$370–440 G(L) ⚒

Two _famille rose_ teapots, covers and stands, applied with flowerheads, damaged, Chinese, 18thC, 6½in (16.5cm) high. It is unusual to find a pair of teapots and stands. In undamaged condition they could have fetched £400–600 / €600–890 / $710–1,050.
£320–380 / €480–570
$570–670 WW ⚒

Worcester teapot, decorated with flower sprays, c1770, 5¼in (13.5cm) high. Teapots are often damaged with a chip on the knop or spout, or with scratched designs. This item is in good condition and this has increased its appeal and value.
£330–390 / €490–580
$580–690 SWO ⚒

Tiles

Miller's compares...

A. Ceramic tile, c1895, 6in (15cm) square.
£7–8 / €10–12
$12–14 SAT ⊞

B. Dutch Delft tile, 18thC, 5in (12.5cm) square.
£65–75 / €95–110
$110–130 JHo ⊞

Item A is a Victorian tile with printed decoration, whereas Item B is a hand-painted tile, which accounts for why it achieved a higher price than Item A.

Tile, with impressed decoration, c1885, 6in (15cm) square. This tile is unattributed to a manufacturer. Tiles by well-known makers such as Minton, Wedgwood or Moore & Co are much more valuable.
£5–9 / €8–14
$10–16 SAT ⊞

◀ **T. & R. Boote tile,** with embossed decoration, c1890, 6in (15cm) square.
£6–10 / €9–15
$10–18 SAT ⊞

▶ **Sherwin & Cotton tile,** with floral decoration, c1890, 6in (15cm) square.
£25–30 / €40–45
$45–55 C&W ⊞

Tile, with floral decoration within a geometric border, c1890, 6in (15cm) square. This tile is decorated with detailed moulding, making it more appealing to collectors.
£30–35 / €45–50
$55–65 C&W ⊞

◀ **Tile,** c1760, 4¾in (12cm) square. This tile is highly collectable due to the fact that it is English delft, and this has increased its value.
£35–40 / €50–60
$60–70 F&F ⊞

W. Godwin pottery tile, decorated with a lady, in the manner of Kate Greenaway or Thomas Allen, c1900, 6in (15cm) square. Items with decoration by Kate Greenaway, a well-known book illustrator, are very collectable.
£45–50 / €65–75
$80–90 PFK ⚒

▶ **Five Sherwin & Cotton tiles,** decorated with a flowering plant in a footed pot, framed, c1890, 30 x 6in (76 x 15cm).
£120–135 / €180–200
$210–240 SaH ⊞

Tile, probably by J. C. Edwards, decorated with two children, c1905, 8 x 6in (20.5 x 15cm). Decoration depicting young children always adds appeal and therefore value to a piece.
£155–175 / €230–260
$270–310 C&W ⊞

▶ **12 Minton tiles,** designed by J. Moyr Smith, depicting the fables, c1872, 6in (15cm) square. This is a highly desirable set of tiles with an appealing subject matter, hence the higher value of this item.
£560–670 / €830–1,000
$990–1,200 SWO ⚒

◀ **Tile,** c1730, 4¾in (12cm) square. This tile is possibly English which has added to its interest and value.
£55–65 / €80–95
$95–110 F&F ⊞

Liverpool delft tile, c1770, 5in (12.5cm) square. Liverpool delft is highly sought after and as a result the poor condition of this tile has not affected its value.
£55–65 / €80–95
$95–110 JHo ⊞

Four delft tiles, 18thC, 5¼in (13.5cm) square. The value of each tile is disproportionally increased by the number of tiles in a set.
£195–220 / €290–330
$350–390 AUC ⊞

Vases

Pottery vase, decorated with flowers, c1880, 12½in (32cm) high.
£25–30 / €40–45
$45–50 FOX ⊞

Belleek pot, Irish, Second Period, 1891–1926, 4in (10cm) diam. This is a common style of Belleek pot, hence its low price.
£40–45 / €60–70
$70–80 WAA ⊞

Salt-glazed vase, German, c1900, 8in (20.5cm) high. This vase would originally have been mass produced and this accounts for its current low value.
£45–50 / €65–75
$80–90 DSG ⊞

Spode chinoiserie two-handled pot/vase, decorated with chrysanthemums and pheasants, late 19thC, 8½in (21.5cm) high. This item has an unfashionable black background which reduces its value. The same item with a white background could be worth 35 per cent more.
£45–50 / €65–75
$80–90 G(L) ⚒

Pair of Satsuma vases, decorated with flying geese, slight damage, signed, Meiji period, 1868–1911, 8in (20.5cm) high. The quality of finish in Satsuma varies widely and these vases are of a lesser quality, hence the low price.
£65–75 / €95–110
$115–135 BAC ⊞

Porcelain spill vase, painted with panels of flowers and gilt, some wear, c1820, 4in (10cm) high. There is some wear to the gilding on this vase and this has lowered its value. However, it is still a good example of a porcelain spill vase and offers value for money.
£60–70 / €90–105
$105–125 WW 🔨

▶ **Branham ware vase,** with three wrythen handles, inscribed manufacturer's mark, 1899, 9in (23cm) high. This marked vase would appeal to collectors of Branham ware.
£80–95
€120–140
$140–170 AMB 🔨

Imari Fugakawa vase, decorated with Koi carp, small repair, signed, c1900, 4in (10cm) high. This is a good-quality vase that may become collectable in the future. It would be a good investment piece.
£65–75 / €95–110
$115–135 BAC ⊞

◀ **Spode pearlware vase and cover,** the body decorated with bamboo, chrysanthemums and rockwork, printed mark, c1820, 8¾in (22cm) high. This vase is possibly missing an outer cover. If complete, this item could be worth £150 / €220 / $270.
£90–105
€135–155
$160–185 WW 🔨

Pair of porcelain spill vases, decorated in the Sèvres style with panels of birds and gilt leaves, one cracked and worn, interlaced 'L's', marked, 19thC, 3in (7.5cm) high. One of these vases has suffered damage. Had it been in good condition, this pair could have achieved £200–300 / €300–450 / $350–530.
£100–120 / €150–180
$175–210 WW 🪶

A. C. Manzoni bottle vase, with incised decoration, inscribed 'hand drawn', 19thC, 7in (18cm) high.
£100–120 / €150–180
$175–210 SWO 🪶

▶ **Royal Worcester vase,** moulded with leaves, with three handles, c1900, 6¼in (16cm) wide.
£100–120
€150–180
$175–210 WW 🪶

Royal Worcester vase, painted with a robin on a gilt branch, 1900, 3¼in (8.5cm) diam. This attractive Royal Worcester vase is decorated with an appealing subject matter and is a good buy.
£110–130 / €165–195
$195–230 L 🪶

◀ **Victorian porcelain urn vase,** with classical decoration, converted to a table lamp, 13½in (34.5cm) high.
£100–120 / €150–180
$175–210 L&E 🪶

Doulton silicon vase, by Eliza Lupton, incised with flower trellis and scroll palmettes, 1885, 10½in (26.5cm) high. Although silicon ware is not particularly popular, this vase is an unusual shape which makes it more desirable. Plainer examples usually sell for around half this price.
£115–135 / €170–200
$200–240 DN(Bri) 🪶

Royal Worcester double-ended vase, moulded as bamboo, with gilt handle, 1884, 8¾in (22cm) high. This vase is attributed to the Aesthetic Movement of the late 19thC. It is currently a popular collecting area, which accounts for the high price of this item.
**£120–140 / €180–210
$210–250 WilP** ⚒

Pair of porcelain spill vases, painted with bands of roses and gilt borders, one foot with chip, c1820, 4¼in (11cm) high. These vases were a good buy. Even with the damage to one foot, this pair of vases would have been expected to fetch nearer £180 / €270 / $320.
**£120–140 / €180–210
$210–250 WW** ⚒

▶ **Minton porcelain vase,** decorated with sprigs of flowers, 1891–1902, 7¼in (18.5cm) high.
**£120–135 / €180–200
$210–240 FOX** ⊞

Miller's compares...

A. Royal Worcester nautilus shell vase, the rocky base moulded with shells, printed mark, c1898, 6¾in (17cm) high.
**£140–165 / €210–240
$250–290 WW** ⚒

B. Royal Worcester majolica nautilus shell vase, the shaped base applied with further shells and weed, impressed mark, 6¾in (17cm) high.
**£660–780 / €980–1,150
$1,150–1,350 S(O)** ⚒

Item A and Item B are both Royal Worcester nautilus shell vases. However, Item B is a majolica example, making it highly collectable. This explains why Item B sold for a much higher price than Item A.

Porcelain vase, painted with flowers on a gilt ground, two handles, mid-19thC, 11in (28cm) high.
**£150–180 / €220–260
$270–320 L&E** ⚒

◄ **Crackleware pillar vase,** decorated in *famille verte* colours, with pheasants, insects and foliage, with bands of Taoist symbols, Chinese, late 19thC, 24in (61cm) high. Chinese crackleware items are not particularly popular. However, this high-quality example is a large size and this may account for its high price.
£160–190 / €240–280
$280–330 NSal ⚒

► **Pair of Davenport potpourri vases and covers,** decorated in the Imari style, on dolphin supports, with pierced covers, faint hairline crack, printed mark, 1830–40, 6in (15cm) high. In prefect condition these vases could be expected to fetch £250–300 / €370–450 / $440–530.
£180–210 / €270–310
$320–370 WW ⚒

◄ **Pair of Canton *famille rose* vases,** painted with dignatories in various pursuits, with mask and ring handles, 19thC, 16in (40.5cm) high.
£280–330
€420–490
$500–580 G(L) ⚒

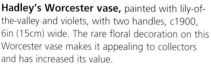

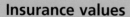

Hadley's Worcester vase, painted with lily-of-the-valley and violets, with two handles, c1900, 6in (15cm) wide. The rare floral decoration on this Worcester vase makes it appealing to collectors and has increased its value.
£280–330 / €420–490
$500–580 WW ⚒

Insurance values

Always insure your valuable antiques for the cost of replacing them with similar items, regardless of the original price paid. Both dealers and auctioneers can provide a valuation service for a fee.

► **Royal Worcester vase,** painted and gilded with flowers, 1890, 10½in (26.5cm) high.
£300–360
€450–540
$530–640 G(L) ⚒

◄ **Pair of *famille rose* vases,** painted with vases of flowers and floral borders, on later brass plinths, badly damaged, Chinese, Yongzhen period, 1723–35, 11½in (29cm) high. These vases are of a unusually early date. However, the damage has significantly reduced their value. In good condition they could be worth £1,000 / €1,500 / $1,800.
**£330–390 / €490–580
$580–690** DN(BR) ➘

Doulton stoneware vase, by George Hugo Tabor and Harriet E. Hibbut, the body decorated with a band of stylized foliage, impressed marks, dated 1884, 15in (38cm) high.
**£340–400 / €510–600
$600–710** Bea ➘

► **Vase,** painted with panels of figures, neck repaired, Chinese, 19thC, 24¾in (63cm) high. This is a large vase that is possibly from the early 19thC. It is painted in an interesting palette and offers very good value for money.
**£350–420 / €520–630
$620–740** WW ➘

Pair of Doulton Lambeth Art Union chine ware vases, applied with flowering plants, impressed factory marks, initialled 'FCR' for Florence C. Roberts, 1891–1902, 11in (28cm) high. These vases are a good example of Artist's pottery and were a good buy at auction.
**£420–500 / €630–750
$740–890** PF ➘

Pair of Paris porcelain Gothic-style vases, moulded in relief and gilded with strapwork, the handles in the shape of stylized dragons, one repaired, French, late 19thC, 16in (40.5cm) high. These high-quality vases are examples of exhibition-standard Paris porcelain and consequently sold for a high price.
**£420–500 / €630–750
$740–890** DN(BR) ➘

◄ **Pair of vases,** moulded with blossom and branches on a shaped tree trunk body, with European gilt-metal pierced bases, Chinese, 19thC, 13¾in (35cm) high. These vases are of a rare form and would appeal to collectors. The period stands have added 20 per cent to the value of the pair.
**£440–520 / €660–770
$780–920** DN ➘

Miscellaneous

Egg cup, commemorating Lord Kitchener and the Boer War, c1900, 2½in (6.5cm) high. Items with military interest are desirable and collectable and can command high prices.
£50–60 / €75–90
$90–105 H&G ⊞

Pair of porcelain scent bottles and stoppers, painted with floral friezes, Continental, 19thC, 6in (15cm) high. Although scent bottles are highly collectable, these examples have worn gilding and this has lowered their value. In good condition they could have fetched £80–100 / €120–150 / $140–175.
£55–65 / €80–95
$95–110 BWL 🔨

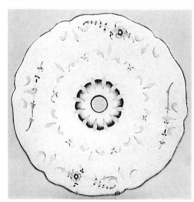

Creamware strainer, painted with flowers and tendrils, 'LB' monogram, 19thC, 13in (33cm) high. This item was a good buy at auction as it could have been expected to fetch £80 / €120 / $140.
£55–65 / €80–95
$95–110 WW 🔨

▶ **Stoneware scent bottle,** from the Hoi An hoard, Vietnamese, late 15thC, 2¾in (7cm) high. This item has a sticker with the name of the hoard and a bar code recording the item on a database. This provenance is important, without it this item would be worth half the price.
£70–80
€105–120
$125–140 AWI ⊞

The Hoi An hoard

In the 1990s, fishermen found a large cargo of 15th-century ceramics off the coast of Hoi An in Vietnam. The pieces were made in kilns in the northern province of Hai Duong and were being transported to markets in South East Asia.

Gouda ashtray, c1900, 4½in (11.5cm) diam.
£90–100 / €135–150
$160–180 DSG ⊞

Victorian majolica comport, moulded
in the shape of woven wicker,
12½in (32cm) wide.
£120–140 / €180–210
$210–250 G(L) ⚲

Miller's compares...

**A. Victorian Brownfields
cheese dome,** modelled
as a castle turret, with
hand-painted decoration,
on a turned wood base,
11in (28cm) high.
£100–120 / €150–180
$180–210 HOLL ⚲

**B. Brownfields majolica
cheese dome and
stand,** modelled as a
castle turret, impressed
marks, restored, c1870,
12½in (32cm) high.
£820–980
€1,200–1,450
$1,450–1,700 B ⚲

Item A and Item B are both Brownfields cheese
domes. Item A has a wooden stand that is
possibly of a later date whereas Item B, although
restored, is a high-quality example with a
matching ceramic stand. This is why Item B sold
for a higher price than Item A.

Two-piece faïence cruet and stand, late 19thC,
6in (15cm) high.
£120–140 / €180–210
$210–250 AMB ⚲

Spode scent bottle, decorated in raised gilt with
birds and trees, associated stopper, painted mark,
c1820, 3¼in (8.5cm) high.
£190–220 / €280–330
$340–390 WW ⚲

The look without the price

Meissen trencher salt, painted with panels of musicians, birds and fruit, cracked with one rivet, crossed swords mark with dot, German, c1760, 4in (10cm) wide.
£230–270 / €340–400
$410–480 WW ⚒

Although this salt has suffered damage, which has lowered its value, it is a marked Meissen piece that could command £300–500 / €450–750 / $530–890 if it was in good condition.

Kraak porselein kendi, decorated with panels of insects and flowers, neck repaired, Chinese, c1620, 9in (23cm) high. This would be a desirable item to collectors and in perfect condition it could be worth £1,000 / €1,500 / $1,800.
£280–330 / €420–490
$500–580 WW ⚒

Locate the source

The source of each illustration in Miller's can be found by checking the code letters below each caption with the Key to Illustrations, pages 286–290.

Cheese strainer, after a Worcester original, painted with fruit and flowers, Qianlong period, 1736–95, 7½in (19cm) diam. This is a rare attempt by a Chinese manufacturer to copy Worcester porcelain which adds value to the item.
£360–430 / €540–640
$640–760 S(O) ⚒

Porcelain scent bottle, probably Limoges, c1860, 4in (10cm) high. This is a good buy as it is a rare form of scent bottle and could have sold for £500–800 / €750–1,200 / $890–1,400.
£290–330 / €430–490
$510–580 VK ⊞

For more examples of
Scent Bottles see Glass (page 187)

Miller's compares...

A. Royal Worcester candle snuffer, modelled as Granny Snow, c1909, 3½in (9cm) high.
£240–270 / €360–400
$420–480 GGD ⊞

B. Royal Worcester candle snuffer, modelled as Granny Snow, c1903, 3in (7.5cm) high.
£360–400 / €540–600
$640–710 TH ⊞

Item A and Item B are Royal Worcester candle snuffers that are similar in date. However, the finish and quality of Item B far exceeds that of Item A, which is why Item B sold for a much higher price. According to Company legend, the figure of Granny Snow was inspired by a short-sighted lady who lived next to the Worcester factory. Each day she would stand in her garden to greet the pottery workers and if anybody startled her, she would throw up both hands to protect herself. Granny Snow first appeared in a Royal Worcester factory order book in 1868, when a coloured version was priced at one shilling.

Pair of porcelain wall brackets, applied with putti and flowers, symbolizing summer and winter, Continental, late 19thC, 11in (28cm) high. These wall brackets appear to have been damaged. In good condition they could be worth £500–800 / €750–1,200 / $890–1,400.
£400–480 / €600–720
$710–850 SWO ⚒

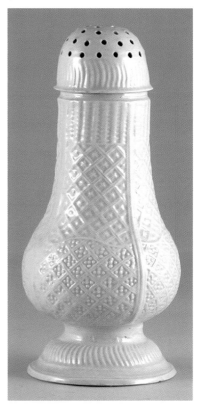

Pair of salts, decorated with a pagoda and boats, Chinese, Qianlong period, 1736–95, 3¼in (8.5cm) wide. It is rare to find this style of salt as a pair and this has subsequently doubled their individual value. Individually these salts could be worth around £150–200 / €220–300 / $270–350.
£630–700 / €890–1,050
$1,050–1,250 G&G ⊞

Staffordshire salt-glazed stoneware sugar sifter, moulded with diaper panels, c1760, 5in (12.5cm) high. This is an interesting and rare stoneware piece that is early in date. It has been well modelled into a shape that is more commonly associated with silver items of the period. This has made it collectable and enabled it to achieve a high price.
£730–870 / €1,100–1,300
$1,300–1,550 WW ⚒

Silver & Plate

The popularity of antiques has grown over the years and the media love to report the sales of rare and highly-priced pieces selling for six- and seven-figure sums, which of course is very exciting as we all hope to find a similar item knocking around our attics. However, this can give the false impression that all good quality antiques must cost tens of thousands and that we will never be able to own such a piece. Thankfully, this is not the case; in fact, with a budget of £1,000 / €1,500 / $1,800 there is a great deal of choice to be had, as this book demonstrates.

The last year has seen changes throughout the world of antique silver, with definite patterns starting to emerge. Specialist dealers and auctioneers selling good quality items seem to be going from strength to strength, increasing their business and clientele, whereas general sellers with less perfect stock are suffering, and many are leaving the business. One reason for the success of top dealers and auctioneers is that collectors and the general public who are thinking of purchasing their first antique are realizing that quality and rarity will always prove to be a wise investment; if you can combine the two, you are definitely onto a winner, even if you feel that you have paid over the odds. With the increase in range and availability of specialist publications covering all aspects of antiques, there is really no reason why the collector should not be well informed and hence make good decisions about purchases.

One particular area that has always been popular but has increased considerably over the last few years is collecting silver spoons. The aesthetic appeal of using a silver spoon has encouraged new collectors into this field, and with prices steadily increasing, investors are also combining their savings with this passion. At one time there were only specialist sales held by the top London auctioneers, but now sales occur regularly throughout the country. Another sign of the buoyancy of this market is the increase in collectors subscribing to The Silver Spoon Club of Great Britain, whose regular magazine, the *Finial*, encompasses all aspects of silver spoons, from the earliest apostles to souvenir examples. Every collector seems to have a different slant on what they collect. For example, some will go for a particular type of spoon, others may choose patterns, periods, makers or spoons with provincial hallmarks, for example Birmingham, Chester or Scotland, and this diversity gives a lot of scope for developing a comprehensive collection. A Victorian silver teaspoon with excellent hallmarks can easily be picked up at a market for as little as £15 / €20 / $25, a Queen Anne 1702 to 1713 Britannia silver Hanoverian Rattail tablespoon can be purchased for £250 / €370 / $440, and a 17th-century Lace-back Trefid spoon can be obtained for £750–1,000 / €1,100–1,500 / $1,350–1,800; all would be of good quality.

Whether you are at an auction house on viewing day or in a specialist silver shop, always ask questions about the piece you are looking at. Concentrate on any repairs, check to see if the hallmarks are legible, inquire whether the item is a good example of its type and find out about the history of the silversmith. Ask to handle the item – hold it with confidence, look at it carefully and if you have any doubts, listen to them, even if you do not know why!

Daniel Bexfield

Baskets, Bowls & Dishes

Silver sugar bowl, by R. Martin and E. Hall, chased with the signs of the Zodiac, London 1885, 4in (10cm) diam, 3oz. Many British silver companies used Indian-influenced designs such as this to decorate their work as it was a style popular with people returning from Colonial India.
£90–105 / €135–155
$160–185 WW 🔨

Pair of silver bonbon baskets, by H. Matthews, with lattice-pierced sides and floral embossing, Birmingham 1896, 7¼in (18.5cm) wide.
£110–130 / €165–195
$195–230 WW 🔨

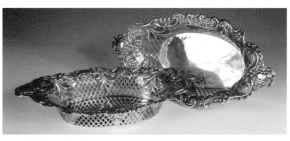

Pair of silver baskets, with pierced and embossed decoration, Birmingham, c1898, 10in (25.5cm) long.
£150–180 / €220–270
$270–320 SWO 🔨

Silver sugar bowl, by J. Jackson, decorated with punch-beading, on three feet, Irish, c1780, 5½in (14cm) diam. Irish silver continues to be popular with dealers and buyers alike, but pieces with legs such as these should be carefully checked for damage.
£130–155 / €195–230
$230–275 WW 🔨

◀ **Silver repoussé basket,** decorated with C-scrolls and floral motifs, with pierced swing handle, London 1774, 6½in (16.5cm) long, 4½oz.
£240–280
€360–420
$420–500 PF 🔨

Silver pedestal dish, probably by Perlington & Batty, with three handles, Chester 1904, 11in (28cm) wide, 30oz.
£240–280 / €360–420
$420–500 WW 🔨

▶ **Silver sugar bowl,** by Matthew West, embossed with stiff leaves and drapes, initialled, Irish, Dublin, c1780, 5¼in (13.5cm) diam, 6½oz.
£260–310 / €390–460
$460–550 WW 🔨

The look without the price

Pair of silver-plated entrée dishes and covers, with gadrooning and leaf and shell borders, c1810, 13¾in (35cm) long.
£270–320 / €400–480
$480–570 B(L) 🔨

These dishes would be worth £3,000–4,500 / €4,450–6,700 / $5,300–7,900 if they were made of silver.

Silver-plated dish cover, with a cast and chased handle, gadrooned moulding and horse-head crest, 19thC, 20in (51cm) wide. In 1970s America these dish covers were often cut in half and mounted on the wall to act as uplighters. This makes them harder to find in their complete state.
£280–330 / €420–490
$500–580 SWO 🔨

Silver assay bowl, monogrammed 'J. C. K.', Austrian, Vienna, 1872–1922, 12¾in (32.5cm) long, 668g.
£350–420 / €520–630
$620–740 DORO 🔨

Swing handles

Swing-handle baskets from the 18th century are usually cast, have decorative piercing and tend to be heavier than Regency examples. Before you buy always check the handle for part marks, which should be there if the piece is original, and examine the hinges for damage. Baskets with damaged or removed handles are always less desriable to collectors.

Silver cake basket, with gadrooned rim and swing handle, chased with foliate scrolls, marks rubbed, Sheffield, c1800, 12in (30.5cm) wide, 30oz. This silver cake basket would have made half as much again on the realized price if the marks were not rubbed.
£360–430 / €540–640
$640–760 G(L) 🔨

Find out more in

Miller's Silver & Plate Buyer's Guide, Miller's Publications, 2002

▶ **Silver basket,** by Emes & Barnard, with gadrooned border and reeded swing handle, London 1815, 13in (33cm) long, 36oz.
£840–1,000
€1,250–1,500
$1,500–1,750
S(O) 🔨

Boxes & Cases

Silver card case, engraved with a monogram and a crest, Birmingham 1864, 4in (10cm) long, 2oz. The engine-turned decoration on this card case is very crisp and could therefore have sold for at least twice this price.
£60–70 / €90–105
$105–125 DN(Bri) ♪

Miller's compares...

A. Silver vinaigrette, decorated with a flower, marks indistinct, early 19thC, 1in (2.5cm) long.
£35–40 / €50–60
$60–70 CHTR ♪

B. Silver snuff box, modelled as a book, with a flip-up cover and engraved sides, initialled 'MAD', maker's mark 'E', French or Dutch, 1810–14, 1½in (4cm) high, ½oz.
£140–165 / €210–240
$250–290 WW ♪

Despite the similar decoration of the tops of both Item A and Item B, Item B is more desirable as the book shape is more collectable than the simpler vinaigrette and it has clear marks that date it to a four-year period, unlike the indistinct marks on Item A.

Silver box, decorated with scenes and figures, Dutch, Schoonhoven 1887, 1¼in (3cm) high, ½oz.
£65–75 / €95–110
$115–135 WW ♪

▶ **Silver box,** decorated in relief with putti astride lions, marked for Chester, Continental, 1905, 3½in (9cm) long.
£70–80 / €105–120
$125–140 WW ♪

◀ **Silver box,** modelled as a violin, with gilt interior, import marks for London, Continental, c1894, 3½in (9cm) long. Although this silver box looks damaged, it has clear hallmarks and could have sold for £120–140 / €180–210 / $210–240.
£80–95
€120–140
$140–170 WW ♪

Silver and gilt powder box, by ISG, Birmingham 1907, 2½in (6.5cm) diam.
£90–105 / €135–155
$160–185 WAC ⊞

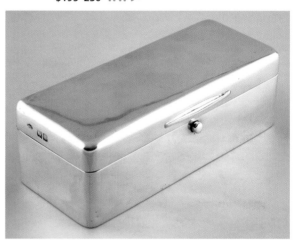

Silver dressing table box and cover, by F. Brasted, embossed with a shepherdess, within crimped borders, London 1879, 3¼in (8.5cm) diam, 3oz.
£110–130 / €165–195
$195–230 WW ⚘

Silver box, by G. Nathan, embossed with putti playing with a puppet, the sides with festoons of drapery, gilt interior, Chester 1900, 2¾in (7cm) diam, 2¼oz.
£110–130 / €165–195
$195–230 WW ⚘

Silver dressing table box and cover, engraved with crest and motto 'Fortes Fortuna Juvant', maker's mark 'IR', probably Irish or Scottish, c1800, 1½in (4cm) high.
£130–155 / €195–230
$230–270 WW ⚘

Silver box, by William Comyns, the button-operated cover enclosing a fitted and lined interior, London 1904, 5in (12.5cm) long.
£150–180 / €220–270
$270–320 WW ⚘

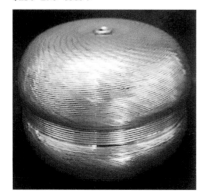

◀ **Silver string dispenser,** by HBA, modelled as a ball of string, with gilt interior, London 1904, 3in (7.5cm) diam. This unusual shape could have sold for £300–400 / €440–590 / $530–700.
£165–195
€240–290
$290–340 PFK ⚘

Silver vinaigrette, by Samuel Pemberton, the cover interior with gilt wirework, initialled 'MS', Birmingham 1803, 1½in (3.5cm) long, ½oz.
£165–195 / €240–290
$290–340 PFK ⚘

Miller's compares...

A. Silver snuff box, with a hardstone base and cover, probably German, 1740–60, 3in (7.5cm) long.
£160–190 / €240–280
$280–340 WW ⚒

B. Silver snuff box, by Henry Flavelle, the lid inset with marble, Irish, Dublin 1823, 2in (5cm) wide.
£660–790 / €980–1,200
$1,150–1,400 G(L) ⚒

While Item A is earlier and an elaborate shape, it is unmarked and has a less appealing colour stone than Item B. The red marble inset, attractive shape, named maker and Irish origin combine to make Item B a very attractive piece for collectors and therefore of a higher value.

▶ **Silver snuff box,** with engine-turned decoration, set with rubies, gilt interior, French, c1900, 2½in (6.5cm) long, 2oz. Although the rubies themselves do not add value, if any of them were missing it would detract from the overall desirability of the box.
£190–220 / €280–330
$340–390 WW ⚒

Silver tea caddy, retailed by Whytock & Sons, Dundee, on four paw feet, crested, London, c1904, 3½in (9cm) high.
£165–195 / €240–290
$290–340 SWO ⚒

◀ **Silver snuff box,** decorated in enamel with a capercaillie, with gilt interior, presentation inscription, marked 'Ku.W' for Kurzer and Wolf, Austrian, Vienna, 1872–1922, 4in (10cm) long, 143g. The price of this snuff box would be significantly affected if the enamel were chipped.
£210–250 / €310–370
$370–440 DORO ⚒

▶ **Silver box,** embossed with scenes of courting couples and putti, with hinged lid and gilt interior, import marks for London, French, Paris, 19thC, 8in (20.5cm) long.
£220–260 / €330–390
$390–460 DN(BR) ⚒

Silver snuff box, by Thomas Phipps and Edward Robinson, with engraved borders and gilt interior, initialled 'JP', London 1786, 3½in (9cm) long, 3oz.
£220–260 / €330–390
$390–460 WW ⚒

Silver and niello tobacco box, decorated with a riverside town, Russian 1872, 4½in (11.5cm) long.
£230–270 / €340–400
$410–480 G(L) ⚒

▶ **Silver snuff box,** by Nathanial Mills, mounted with mammoth-tooth ivory, Birmingham 1842, 3in (7.5cm) long.
£260–310
€390–460
$460–550 WW ⚒

Silver cigarette case, by Omar Ramsden and Alwyn Carr, chased with flowerheads and flames, Birmingham 1908, 3½in (9cm) long, 3oz. This cigarette case was made in the transitional period between Arts & Crafts and Art Nouveau. It should be insured for £2,200 / €3,300 / $3,900 as it was made by Omar Ramsden and therefore is very collectable.
£230–270 / €340–400
$410–480 WW ⚒

Niello

Niello is a decorating technique used on silver and occasionally on gold alloys, which involves filling depressions in a pattern crested by etching or engraving. The result is a block inlay decoration which has been popular since the Middle Ages. The technique is hazardous, however, due to the high lead content and noxious gases produced and is rarely used in modern production.

Silver card case, decorated with a view of Windsor Castle, maker's initials 'D. P.', Birmingham 1855, 4in (10cm) long.
£300–360 / €450–540
$530–640 G(L) ⚒

◀ **Silver snuff box,** with raised vine-leaf and grape borders, the gilt panel with a coat-of-arms and 'Treasure Our Inheritance', marked 'ID', London, c1813, 8¼in (21cm) long.
£320–380 / €480–570
$570–670 SWO ⚒

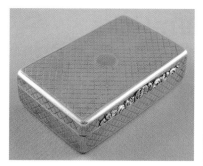

Silver-gilt snuff box, by Thomas Edwards, with engine-turned trelliswork, the applied thumbpiece chased with shells and scrolls, London 1851, 3¼in (8.5cm) long, 4¼oz.
£320–380 / €480–570
$570–670 WW ↗

Engine turning

Introduced at the end of the 18th century, engine turning used machine lathes to cut parallel lines into the silver surface to create a regular textured effect. It was mostly used to decorate small objects such as snuff boxes, card cases and vinaigrettes. The textured surface can be covered with transparent enamelling, called guilloché enamelling and it has been popular since the end of the 18th century.

▶ **William IV silver vinaigrette,** by Thomas Shaw, 1in (2.5cm) long.
£350–390
€520–580
$620–690 BEX ▦

◀ **George III silver patch box,** the cover inset with a miniature of a lady beneath a reverse-painted glass dome, 1in (2.5cm) high.
£370–440
€550–660
$650–780 G(L) ↗

Silver-gilt vinaigrette, by Joseph Wilmore, modelled as a watch, with engine-turned decoration, Birmingham 1834, 1½in (4cm) diam.
£420–500 / €630–750
$740–890 G(L) ↗

Silver-gilt pendant vinaigrette, modelled as a book, French 1845, 1in (2.5cm) long.
£430–480 / €640–720
$760–850 LBr ▦

▶ **Silver snuff box,** engraved with a floral and stiff-leaf decoration, gilt interior, marked 'IH', Austrian, Vienna 1816, 3¼in (8.5cm) long, 98g.
£460–550 / €690–820
$810–970 DORO ↗

Candlesticks & Chambersticks

Two wax jacks, one old Sheffield plate and modelled as a wirework globe, the other electroplated with conical snuffer, c1800. Although wax jacks were primarily used for sealing letters they could also have been used as a lighting source as they would have been positioned on the desk.
£90–105 / €135–155
$160–185 WW 🔨

Pair of Victorian electroplated candelabra, the fluted columns with foliate capitals, 23in (58cm) high.
£280–330 / €420–490
$500–580 WW 🔨

▶ **Pair of old Sheffield plate telescopic candlesticks,** probably by J. Watson & Son, c1835, 10¼in (26cm) extended.
£160–190
€240–280
$280–340 WW 🔨

The look without the price

George IV silver chamberstick, with detachable nozzle and associated snuffer, 5½in (14cm) diam, 9oz.
£260–310 / €390–460
$460–550 WW 🔨

With the matching snuffer this chamberstick would be worth double the price, but with matching wick trimmers it would be worth £12,000 / €17,900 / $21,200.

◀ **Pair of silver chambersticks,** by Mappin & Webb, with pierced rims and loop handles, 1897, 5in (12.5cm) diam.
£300–360
€450–540
$530–640 G(L) 🔨

Sets/pairs

Unless otherwise stated, any description which refers to 'a set' or 'a pair' includes a guide price for the entire set or the pair, even though the illustration may show only a single item.

Miller's compares...

A. Pair of dwarf candlesticks, modelled as Corinthian columns, 1896, 5¾in (14.5cm) high.
£280–330 / €420–490
$500–580 G(L) ⚖

B. Pair of silver candlesticks, modelled as Corinthian columns, marked 'H. H.', Sheffield 1892, 11in (28cm) high.
£750–900 / €1,100–1,350
$1,350–1,600 G(B) ⚖

Pair of silver candlesticks, the half-fluted stem with swags and shell-embossed scroll capitals, London 1908, 11¾in (30cm) high.
£300–360 / €450–540
$530–640 AH ⚖

Item B is a more suitable height for a dining table than Item A, which is quite short in comparison. The decoration on Item B is crisp and clear compared with Item A, making it more desirable .

▶ **Silver-plated tree-branch candelabra,** mounted with three putti playing musical instruments, 19thC, 17¾in (45cm) high. Sometimes these included glass dishes so they could be used as a centrepiece.
£520–620 / €770–920
$920–1,100 Bea ⚖

Silver chamberstick and matchbox, by Samuel Jacob, London 1897, 4in (10cm) long, 3½oz.
£430–480 / €640–720
$760–850 BEX ⊞

Find out more in

Miller's Silver & Sheffield Plate Marks Pocket Fact File, Miller's Publications, 2001

◀ **Pair of silver candlesticks,** by J. Davies & Son, with studded decoration and loaded bases, Sheffield 1905, 9in (23cm) high. This type of Arts & Crafts candlestick is hard to find and very desirable, hence the good price.
£750–900 / €1,100–1,350
$1,350–1,600 L ⚖

Condiments

The look without the price

Pair of silver salts, by Thomas Hayes, on claw-and-ball feet, Birmingham 1903, 3in (7.5cm) high.
£80–95 / €120–140
$140–170 WW ⚲

George III-style pierced silver was popular during the Victorian and Edwardian periods and can often be found for a fraction of the price of true George III items. These could be worth £250–300 / €370–440 / $440–770 if they were authentic George III.

Miller's compares...

A. Silver pepper pot, Birmingham 1898, 4in (10cm) high.
£90–100 / €135–150
$160–175 FOX ▦

B. Silver pepper pot, with detachable pierced cover, London mark, c1750, 6¾in (17cm) high.
£430–510 / €640–760
$760–900 Mit ⚲

Pair of silver pepper pots, Chester 1909, 3¼in (8.5cm) high.
£100–110 / €150–165
$175–195 FOX ▦

Item A is smaller and of a more modern design than Item B, which, although the maker's mark is unclear, has a clear assay mark for London. This, along with the early date, typical baluster form and excellent quality explains why Item B is more desirable to collectors and therefore more valuable.

Silver salt, by Gorham & Co, modelled as a mussel shell on a clam-shell foot, with gilt interior, American, c1880, 2½in (6.5cm) long, ½oz.
£120–140 / €180–210
$210–250 WW ⚲

The look without the price

George III-style silver pepper pot, by Charles Stuart Harris, London 1887, 4¾in (12cm) high.
£110–130 / €165–195 $195–230 DN(BR) 🔨

This is a good example of Victorian silver, however, if this pepper pot were George III rather than Victorian it could be worth between double and triple its current value.

Silver mustard pot, by C. Reilly and G. Storer, the hinged cover enclosing a gilt interior and spoon aperture, the base inscribed 'Exhibition 1851', London 1850, 3½in (9cm) high, 3½oz. This mustard pot could have sold for £200–300 / €300–440 / $350–530 as it is by a popular maker.
£130–155 / €195–230 $230–270 WW 🔨

◄ **Pair of silver salts,** by John Le Gallais, with later glass liners, London 1861, 3¼in (8.5cm) diam. Originally these salts would have had gilded interiors, but liners are still popular.
£140–165 €210–240 $250–290 WW 🔨

Silver cruet set, Chester 1857, 7¼in (18.5cm) long, in a fitted case.
£175–195 / €260–290 $310–350 LaF ⊞

Miller's compares...

A. Set of four silver pepper pots, modelled as teddy bears, damaged, maker's mark 'R. P.', Birmingham 1909, 1½in (4cm) high.
£190–210 / €280–310 $340–370 DN(BR) 🔨

B. Pair of silver pepper pots, modelled as teddy bears, Birmingham 1909, 1½in (4cm) high.
£450–500 / €670–750 $800–890 BLm ⊞

The contrast in price between these identical pepper pots demonstrates the importance of condition on value. Although there are four pots in Item A, they are all badly damaged, whereas the pots in Item B are in excellent condition making them worth over double the amount. Go for quality rather than quantity on novelty items.

Set of four silver salts, by Rupert Favell, with gilt interiors, London 1887, 3in (7.5cm) diam.
£180–210 / €270–310
$320–370 WW ✗

Miller's compares...

A. Silver mustard pot, by Arthur Sibley, with beaded borders and glass liner, crested, London 1859, 3in (7.5cm) high, 4oz.
£200–240 / €300–360
$350–420 WW ✗

B. Silver mustard pot, by George John Richards, with pierced decoration, London 1852, 2½in (6.5cm) long, 4½oz.
£450–500 / €670–750
$800–890 BLm ⊞

The ornate decoration and the intricate pierced bodywork makes Item B more desirable and valuable than Item A.

Silver pepper pot, by C. Saunders and F. Shepherd, modelled as a toy horse on four wheels, with detachable head, with incuse registered design number, Chester 1900, 2in (5cm) high.
£220–260 / €330–390
$390–460 WW ✗

Victorian silver-plated condiment stand, containing six cut-glass bottles, 12½in (32cm) high.
£290–340 / €430–510
$510–600 SWO ✗

◄ **George II-style silver sugar caster,** by Charles Fox II, the detachable cover with wrythen piercing and a knop finial, crested, London 1823, 9½in (24cm) high, 15oz.
£400–480 / €600–720
$710–850 WW ✗

Silver-plated cruet frame, with engraved decoration on cannonball feet, c1865, 8½in (21.5cm) high.
£300–360 / €450–540
$530–640 WW ✗

Locate the source

The source of each illustration in Miller's can be found by checking the code letters below each caption with the Key to Illustrations, pages 286–290.

Silver mustard pot, modelled as a barrel, 1874, 3in (7.5cm) high.
£410–490 / €610–730
$730–870 G(L) 🔨

Sampson Mordan & Co

Sampson Mordan (1790–1843) was one of the more desirable silver makers from London. He entered into the working world with an apprenticeship to John Bramah, who was a mechanic and inventor of the Bramah patent lock. It was here that he would have learned about precision-made machinery which stood him in good stead for his future. He entered his first mark 'SM' at the Goldsmiths Hall on 26th June 1823.

Upon his death two of his sons, Augustus and Sampson II, continued the business. In 1870 Edmund George Johnson bought into the firm to become a partner and in 1881 he became head of the company. Between 1822 and 1941 the company produced a wide range of products including smaller novelty items such as mechanical pencils, bookmarks, menu holders and card cases, as well as larger items such as pepper grinders.

George III silver cruet, containing five bottles, with bright-cut decoration, on a wooden base, 7¾in (19.5cm) diam, 18oz.
£440–520 / €660–770
$780–920 SWO 🔨

◀ **Pair of silver pepperettes,** possibly by Alfred Fuller, modelled as gavels, London 1891, 3in (7.5cm) long, 1oz.
£540–640
€800–950
$960–1,150 Bea 🔨

Silver pepper grinder, by Sampson Mordan & Co, crested and initialled, London 1880, 5½in (14cm) high.
£450–540 / €670–800
$800–960 S(O) 🔨

◀ **Pair of silver salts,** by A. Jaschinov, Russian, St Petersburg, 1795–1825, 4in (10cm) long.
£570–680 / €850–1,000
$1,000–1,200 BUK 🔨

Cups, Mugs & Tankards

Silver-mounted glass, marked for Messrs Hutton, London 1902, 5¼in (13.5cm) high.
£80–95 / €120–140
$140–170 WW

18thC-style silver-gilt two-handled cup, with embossed foliate decoration, Birmingham 1905, 3¾in (9.5cm) high.
£90–105 / €135–155
$160–185 GAK

Tazzas

Tazzas are a particular form of Venetian serving dish first popular in the 15th and 16th centuries, although they enjoyed a revival in the mid-19th century. A tazza will always have a shallow dish or bowl on a stemmed foot. Examples can be made of glass, silver or ceramic.

Miller's compares...

A. Silver beaker, with engraved and tooled decoration, the foot with a tongue-and-dart border, maker's mark distorted, French, Paris, 1819–38, 4½in (11.5cm) high, 3½oz.
£110–130 / €165–195
$195–230 WW

B. Silver beaker, by Lars Anders Hahnstedt, Finnish, Oulu 1775, 3¼in (8.5cm) high.
£530–630 / €790–940
$940–1,100 BUK

Item A is later and more elaborately decorated than Item B but the maker's mark is unclear, which reduces desirability. Item B is by a Finnish maker and is of particular interest to Finnish collectors. Had Item B been auctioned outside Scandinavia it may not have achieved this price.

◄ **Silver-gilt-mounted rock-crystal tazza,** engraved maker's mark 'IR', probably German or European, 1850–1900, 7in (18cm) high.
£220–260 / €330–390
$390–460 WW

The look without the price

Pair of silver beakers, by G. Nathan and R. Hayes, inset with coins, Chester 1896, taller 5in (12.5cm) high.
£220–260 / €330–390
$390–460 WW ⚒

Popular in the 17th century, coin-inset beakers and tankards are very rare. These Victorian copies, although still unusual, are a much more affordable alternative, as 17th-century examples could be ten or twenty times the price of these Victorian ones.

Silver two-handled cup, possibly by Joseph Lock, with applied girdle and gilt interior, London 1777, 6in (15cm) high, 16oz.
£300–360 / €450–540
$530–640 FHF ⚒

▶ **Silver mug,** by John Swift, with a leaf-capped scroll handle, London 1731, 4¾in (12cm) high, 12oz.
£360–430 / €540–640
$640–760 S(O) ⚒

Silver vodka cup, maker's mark 'SF', Russian, Moscow 1783, 1½in (4cm) high, 1oz.
£260–310 / €390–460
$460–550 WW ⚒

Silver christening mug, by George Angell, chased with a frontiersman and his tracker, also initialled 'TC to RHB', London 1856, 5¼in (13.5cm) high, 6oz.
£260–310 / €390–460
$460–550 S(O) ⚒

◄ **Silver mug,** by James Betham, later embossed with a pastoral scene, London 1766, 5¼in (13.5cm) high, 12½oz. This mug would originally have been plain and the embossed decoration added at a later date. Without the addition it could be worth twice as much but the pastoral scene is attractive to some collectors.
£360–430 / €540–640
$640–760 WW 🔨

Silver beaker, maker's mark 'GG', Russian, Moscow 1740, 3¼in (8.5cm) high.
£470–560 / €700–830
$830–990 BUK 🔨

Silver cup, with beaded scroll handles, inscribed 'MH To EH', marks indistinct, struck with 'TH' monogram, probably West Country, 1670–90, 3¼in (8.5cm) diam, 2oz.
£480–570 / €720–850
$850–1,000 WW 🔨

Russian silver

While Russian silver has always been a popular collecting field, it is currently even more so due to the fact that many Russians have started buying back pieces by the best makers such as Fabergé. This has had a knock-on effect across the market, increasing popularity.

Silver beaker, by Joseph Walley, modelled as a barrel, crested, maker's mark, Liverpool, 1777–78, 2¾in (7cm) high, 3½oz. Novelty barrel beakers such as this are popular with collectors and are an interesting addition to a collection. The fact that it is by a Liverpool silversmith and not a London one makes this item rare.
£800–960 / €1,200–1,450
$1,400–1,700 WW 🔨

Silver and niello tankard, with simulated coopering and double-scroll handle, Russian, St Petersburg 1866, 4¾in (12cm) high, 15oz.
£900–1,050 / €1,350–1,550
$1,600–1,850 PF 🔨

Cutlery & Serving Implements

Victorian silver butter knife, with a mother-of-pearl handle, 7¼in (18.5cm) long.
£18–20 / €26–30
$32–36 TASV ⊞

Silver sugar sifter spoon, with a plated bowl, Sheffield 1908, 7in (18cm) long.
£30–35 / €45–50
$55–65 CoCo ⊞

Victorian silver-plated pickle fork, 6in (15cm) long.
£30–35 / €45–50
$55–65 CoCo ⊞

Victorian silver-plated pickle fork, with a bone handle, 8in (20.5cm) long.
£35–40 / €50–60
$60–70 CoCo ⊞

▶ **Silver-plated fish servers,**
with ivory handles, c1900, in a fitted case, 5 x 13in (12.5 x 33cm).
£35–40 / €50–60
$60–70 CCO ⊞

◀ **Silver scroll-back teaspoon,** by James Tokey, London, c1750, 4¾in (12cm) long.
£40–45 / €60–65
$70–80 BEX ⊞

Silver preserve spoon, by Tiffany & Co, decorated with spiders and webs, initialled, American, c1900, 6in (15cm) long, 1oz. Individual spoons are an affordable way to add some good quality pieces by named makers to a collection. Pieces by Tiffany & Co appeal particularly to the American market and lots of patterns are collected.
£40–50 / €60–70
$70–80 WW ⚒

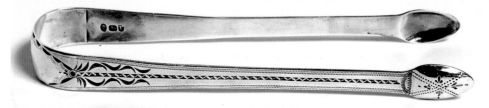

Silver bright-cut tongs, by George Winkle, repaired, London 1792, 5½in (14cm) long.
£50–55 / €75–85
$90–100 GRe ⊞

◀ **Set of three silver Scottish Fiddle pattern teaspoons,** initialled 'B' and numbered, inscribed 'AR', 1760–70, ¾oz.
£50–60 / €75–90
$90–105 WW ⚒

Silver bread fork, Sheffield 1904, 8in (20.5cm) long.
£50–60 / €75–90
$90–105 FOX ⊞

▶ **Silver sugar tongs,**
by Peter and Anne Bateman,
London 1798, 6in (15cm) long.
£50–60 / €75–90
$90–105 WAC ⊞

Pair of silver sugar tongs, by Bateman, London 1800,
5½in (14cm) long.
£50–60 / €75–90
$90–105 WAC ⊞

▶ **Pair of silver spoons, with** pierced bowls, import marks for Sheffield, Continental, 1901, 5½in (14cm) long, 4½oz.
£60–70 / €90–105
$105–125 WW ⚒

Sugar tongs

Prior to 1770 sugar nips were used to break sugar off the cone, but later tongs were used. These usually had bright-cut decoration and were large in size, but as sugar became more refined smaller tongs were produced, and sugar bowls followed suit. Examples with bright-cut decoration are particularly popular with collectors. Be aware, however, that cracks at the arch can reduce value and examples should always be checked for damage.

Silver Old English pattern tablespoon, by John Lampfort, London 1759, 8in (20.5cm) long.
£65–75 / €95–110
$115–135 CoHA ⊞

◀ **Silver folding prune fork,** with a mother-of-pearl handle, Sheffield 1878, 2½in (6.5cm) long.
£65–75 / €95–110
$115–135 CoHA ⊞

Auction or dealer?

All the pictures in our price guides originate from auction houses ⚒ and dealers ⊞. When buying at auction, prices can be lower than those of a dealer, but a buyer's premium and VAT will be added to the hammer price. Equally, when selling at auction, commission, tax and photography charges must be taken into account. Dealers will often restore pieces before putting them back on the market. Both dealers and auctioneers can provide professional advice, so it is worth researching both sources before buying or selling your antiques.

Silver toddy ladle, by George Adams, with a twisted stem, London 1858, 7¼in (18.5cm) long, 1oz.
£70–80 / €105–120
$125–140 WW ⚒

Silver tablespoons, by G. W., London 1906, 9in (23cm) long.
£70–80 / €105–120
$125–140 WAC ⊞

Miller's compares...

A. Silver Fiddle pattern caddy spoon, by William Chawner, with a gilt bowl, London 1827, 3¾in (9.5cm) long, ½oz.
£80–95 / €120–140
$140–165 WW ✣

B. Silver Fiddle pattern caddy spoon, by Joseph Wilmore, with a hollow stem, the bowl engraved with a fruiting plant, initialled 'H', Birmingham 1831, 3in (7.5cm) long.
£170–200 / €250–300
$300–350 WW ✣

Item A has a more common pattern, a gilt bowl and is visibly pitted from use. Item B is a more interesting shape, has an unusual hollow handle and is engraved making it the more desirable of the two spoons.

Pair of silver fish servers, by W. & J. Barnard, with pierced decoration and ivory cannon handles, crested, London 1880, cased. As fish dishes are becoming more popular, related items are becoming more collectable, so now is a good time to buy such items as their price is on the increase.
£90–105 / €135–155
$160–185 WW ✣

▶ **Sterling silver and steel table knife,** Japanese, c1900, 11in (28cm) long.
£135–155 / €200–230
$240–270 BEX ⊞

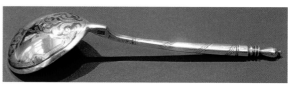

Silver niello spoon, Russian, Moscow, c1880, 6¼in (16cm) long, 1½oz.
£110–125 / €165–185
$195–220 BEX ⊞

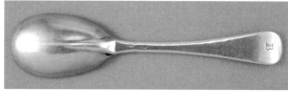

Silver Hanoverian pattern mustard spoon, with moulded rattail, initialled 'B', mark unclear, London 1720, 3½in (9cm) long.
£120–140 / €180–210
$210–250 WW ✣

◀ **Silver bright-cut tablespoon,** by J. Langlands and J. Robertson I, Newcastle, c1790, 9in (23cm) long, 2¼oz.
£160–180 / €240–270
$280–320 BEX ⊞

Miller's compares...

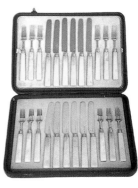

A. Set of 18 pairs of Victorian silver-plated fish knives and forks, with carved ivory handles and engraved blades and tines, cased. If this set was made of silver it could have sold for £2,000–2,400 / €3,000–3,600 / $3,500–4,250.
£170–200 / €250–300
$300–350 WW 🔨

B. Part set of silver Old English pattern flatware, comprising eight tablespoons, eight dessert spoons, four teaspoons and two sugar tongs, Sheffield 1896, in an oak case, 12 x 14in (30.5 x 35.5cm).
£370–440 / €550–660
$650–780 GAK 🔨

Set of 12 silver dessert knives and forks, by Unite & Hilliard, with ivory handles, Birmingham 1831, in a leather-covered case.
£175–210 / €260–310
$310–370 PF 🔨

Although Item B is incomplete, it is still more desirable than Item A as it is more practical for everyday use. Additionally, the ivory handles of Item A are prone to cracking and separating from the blades. Finally, the Old English pattern is one that continues to be produced today and is still very popular, making Item B more desirable.

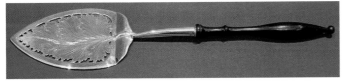

Silver 'leaf' slice, Continental, c1870, 8½in (21.5cm) long.
£230–260 / €340–390
$410–460 BEX ▦

Silver butter knife, bread fork and jam spoon, with mother-of-pearl handles, Birmingham 1899, 8½in (21.5cm) long.
£240–270 / €360–400
$420–480 BLm ▦

Three-piece silver-gilt christening set, by Lias Brothers, comprising knife, fork and spoon, cast with grape and vine decoration, London 1846–50. The unusual pattern would make this item very collectable.
£250–300 / €370–450
$440–530 B(NW) 🔨

◀ **Set of 12 silver-gilt and niello teaspoons,** the handles and bowls engraved with stylized flowers, Russian, Moscow 1836, 5½in (14cm) long.
£480–570 / €720–850
$850–1,000 S(O) 🔨

Jugs & Sauce Boats

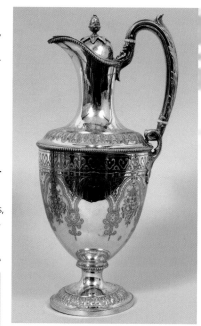

◀ **Silver ewer,** with chased borders, 1875–1900, 8in (20.5cm) high, 18oz. If this ewer was marked it could have sold for £350–400 / €520–590 / $610–700.
£45–50 / €65–75 $80–90 WW 🔨

▶ **Victorian silver-plated jug,** the body decorated with strapwork and flowers, with pineapple finial, 12¼in (31cm) high.
£60–70 / €90–105 $105–125 CHTR 🔨

Miller's compares...

A. Plate-mounted cut-glass claret jug, c1900, 8in (20.5cm) high.
£80–95 / €120–140 $140–170 WW 🔨

B. Silver-mounted cut-glass claret jug, by Elkington & Co, Birmingham 1896, 11in (28cm) high.
£910–1,100 €1,350–1,600 $1,600–1,900 AH 🔨

Claret jugs were very popular with the Victorians and examples were made to suit every budget. Item A is a simple design with a plated mount rather than silver, which would have originally been the more affordable option. Item B features a more decorative shaped bottle, with an elaborate silver mount by a quality maker and would have been a more expensive item when first purchased.

Pair of silver sauce boats, by Charles Stuart Harris, with swirl ribbing, capped scroll handles and moulded feet, London 1904, 4½in (11.5cm) long, 9oz.
£190–210 / €280–330 $340–390 NSal 🔨

Silver cream jug, by Alfred Griffiths, Birmingham 1902, 4¼in (11cm) long, 2½oz.
£210–240 / €310–360 $370–420 BEX ⊞

◄ **Silver cream jug,** decorated with bright-cut floral swags, Sheffield 1793, 4in (10cm) high. This cream jug is an unusual shape, making it attractive to some collectors.
£210–250
€310–370
$370–440 SWO ⚒

► **Silver cream jug,** by H. Matthews, Birmingham 1893, 3¼in (8.5cm) high, 2¾oz.
£310–350
€460–520
$550–620 BEX ⊞

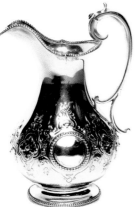

Silver cream jug, London 1859, 6½in (16.5cm) high.
£360–400 / €540–600
$640–710 BLm ⊞

Silver-mounted glass claret jug, by RFHE, with a hinged cover, London 1888, 8in (20.5cm) high.
£480–570 / €720–850
$850–1,000 HYD ⚒

Silver cream jug, by Charles Marsh, the rims cast with hounds, masks and fruiting vines, the sides embossed with various figures, architecture and two vacant cartouches, on floral paw feet, Irish, Dublin 1830, 25oz, with a matching sugar bowl.
£520–620 / €770–920
$920–1,100 WW ⚒

Find out more in

Miller's Silver & Plate Antiques Checklist, Miller's Publications, 2001

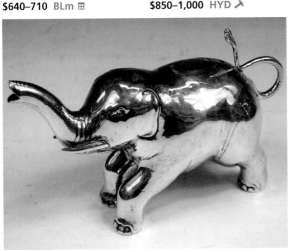

◄ **Silver cream jug,** modelled as an elephant, marked for Berthold Müller, Continental, import marks for 1904, 6¾in (17cm) long.
£730–870 / €1,100–1,300
$1,300–1,550 SWO ⚒

Salvers & Trays

Silver-plated salver, with engraved and beaded decoration, on shell and bracket feet, c1870, 19¼in (49cm) diam.
£90–105 / €135–155
$160–185 WW ✎

◀ **Silver pin tray,** by Walker & Hall, chased with repoussé portraits of a lady, with scrolling borders and raised sides, Sheffield 1901, 7in (18cm) high, 3oz.
£70–80 / €105–120
$125–140 NSal ✎

Condition

Silver-plated pieces often suffer from unsightly wear to the plate from usage or over-zealous cleaning. Unlike silver, polishing can wear away the top surface, reducing the value of the item. However, value can increase again if the item is replated well. Plated pieces can also be damaged around the feet; these are often weak points on cast pieces and should be carefully examined before purchasing.

Silver-plated and oak tray, with pierced gallery and inset silver plaque, on ball feet, London 1903, 24in (61cm) long.
£100–120 / €150–180
$175–210 G(L) ✎

◀ **Silver salver,** by SH, the floral-engraved centre with C-scroll diapers, within a shell and leaf-cast border, on triple cast paw feet, London 1829, 9in (23cm) diam, 16½oz.
£140–145
€210–240
$250–290 HYD ✎

Silver salver, by John Round, Sheffield 1900, 7½in (19cm) diam.
£145–160 / €220–240
$260–280 GRe ⊞

Miller's compares...

A. Silver salver, with shell border, on paw feet, Sheffield 1902, 10½in (26.5cm) diam, 18oz.
£230–270 / €340–400
$410–480 DN(EH) 🔨

B. Silver salver, by Ebenezer Coker, with an engraved armorial, on three feet, London, c1773, 12½in (32cm) diam, 25oz.
£630–750 / €940–1,100
$1,100–1,350 SWO 🔨

Silver salver, by Martin Hall & Co, with bright-cut foliate engraving, 1881, 7½in (19cm) diam, 13oz, with a fitted leather case.
£240–280 / €360–420
$420–500 G(L) 🔨

Despite the obvious similarities between these two salvers, Item B is over 100 years older than Item A. The high quality finish, respectable maker and larger size of Item B all contribute to the desirability of this example and add to its value. Hallmarks on pieces such as these are an important source of information for prospective buyers.

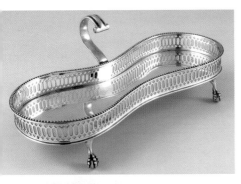

◀ **Silver snuffer's tray,** by R. Morton & Co, with pierced gallery, S-scroll handle, on claw-and-ball feet, Sheffield 1775, 7½in (19cm) long, 5½oz.
£260–310
€390–460
$460–550 WW 🔨

Parcel-gilt table centrepiece, by Joseph Angell, the centre engraved with a coat-of-arms and inscribed 'Sigillum Henrici Morten Cotton Armiger', London 1856, 9½in (24cm) diam.
£300–360 / €450–540
$530–640 WW 🔨

For more examples of
Snuff items see Boxes & Cases (pages 135–139)

◀ **Silver salver,** by Martin Hall & Co, engraved with a wreath of oak leaves and acorns, within a pierced rim embossed with festoons and floral medallions, London 1876, 10½in (26.5cm) diam.
£360–430
€540–640
$640–760 RTo 🔨

Silver teapot stand, by William Davie, on four hoof feet, Edinburgh 1774, 8in (20.5cm) wide, 6½oz.
£500–600 / €750–890
$890–1,050 WW 🔨

Tea, Coffee & Chocolate Pots

The look without the price

Silver-plated three-piece tea service,
maker's mark 'F. E. T. & Co', c1870.
£90–105 / €135–155
$160–185 WW 🔨

The intrinsic value of silver resides in the
material from which it is made. Despite
the ornate appearance of these items, the
fact that they are silver-plated will keep
the price down. If this tea service had been
silver rather than silver-plate it would have
cost £600–700 / €890–1,050 / $1,050–1,250.

Silver four-piece tea service, by Elkington & Co,
comprising tea kettle-on-stand, teapot, milk jug and
sugar pot, early 20thC.
£100–120 / €150–180
$175–210 WL 🔨

Silver teapot, by Charles Stuart Harris, with demi-fluted
decoration, London 1888, 5in (12.5cm) high, 16oz. This
is a beautiful teapot at a reasonable price.
£120–140 / €180–210
$210–250 G(L) 🔨

Silver teapot, by James Wakely and Frank Wheeler, pierced foliate
scrolling border above a spirally-fluted body, with hinged cover and
ebonized handle and knop, London 1894, 6¼in (16cm) high, 23oz.
£150–180 / €220–270
$270–320 L&E 🔨

▶ **Silver hot water pot,** by Charles Stuart Harris, with a wooden
handle and demi-fluted spiral decoration, London 1898, 8in (20.5cm)
high, 15oz. Charles Stuart Harris is now being recognized for high
quality and his use of thick gauge silver. As a consequent of this his
work is becoming very collectable and prices may rise.
£170–200 / €250–300
$300–350 G(L) 🔨

▶ **Silver coffee pot,** cast with a band of stiff leaves, with a hinged cover and scroll handle, London 1829, 8¾in (22cm) high.
£340–400
€**510–600**
$600–710 L&E ⚒

Silver coffee pot, marked 'J. C. K.' for J. C. Klinkosch, Austrian, Vienna, 1872–1922, 7½in (19cm) high, 15oz.
£260–310 / €**390–460**
$460–550 DORO ⚒

Silver teapot, by William Eley II, the hinged cover with cast flower finial, London 1824, 9in (23cm) long, 28oz.
£400–480 / €**600–720**
$710–850 NSal ⚒

Silver teapot, by Edward Hutton, London 1892, 7in (18cm) long, 7½oz. Silver usually sells best in its country of origin. English hallmarks can be particularly interesting to collectors as there are comprehensive records, which make it easier to research the origin of a piece, maker and date.
£450–500 / €**670–750**
$800–890 BEX ⊞

◀ **Silver coffee pot,** by Elder & Co, the cover with flower finial, the body with embossed decoration, Edinburgh 1833, 10¼in (26cm) high.
£600–720
€**890–1,050**
$1,050–1,250
WW ⚒

Writing Equipment

Silver inkwell, modelled as a bell, with inscription, Birmingham 1910, 4in (10cm) high.
£85–100 / €125–150
$150–175 DN(EH) ✐

The look without the price

Silver on these capstan inkwells tends to be thin and prone to damage, but this example is in excellent condition. They can range in size up to 12in (30.5cm) wide, and if this inkwell was of that size it would be worth **£500–600 / €740–890 / $880–1,050.**

Silver capstan inkwell, by A. & J. Zimmerman, the cover with a pen rest, with glass liner, loaded, Birmingham 1905, 5½in (14cm) diam.
£100–120 / €150–180
$175–210 WW ✐

Late Victorian silver-plate-mounted cut-glass inkstand, with a hinged cover, 9in (23cm) wide.
£135–160 / €200–240
$240–280 TMA ✐

Collecting writing equipment

Writing equipment is a popular collecting area with a wide variety of objects to choose from. As well as various sizes and styles of inkwells, there are pens, pencils, dip pens, *porte* crayons, paper clips, pounce pots, rulers, stamp holders and seals produced in silver. Many of the smaller, cheaper items tend not to be illustrated in auction catalogues, so always look through the captions and mixed lots for interesting pieces. Makers to look out for include Gorham Manufacturing Co, Tiffany & Co, Hicks of New York, Henri Aumont, Vales & Co and Sampson Mordan & Co.

◀ **Silver-mounted cut-glass inkwell,** crest indistinct, with retailer's stamp for Aspreys, London 1875, 3¾in (9.5cm) high.
£140–165
€210–240
$250–290 PFK ✐

▶ **Silver paper clip,** London 1900, 3in (7.5cm) long.
£200–230
€300–340
$350–410 BLm ⊞

Silver letter opener and penknife, by Sampson Mordan & Co, London 1897, 6in (15cm) long.
£220–250 / €330–370
$390–440 BLm ⊞

◀ **Silver inkwell,** by A. & J. Zimmerman, modelled as a bell, Birmingham 1908, 4¼in (11cm) high.
£260–290
€390–430
$460–570 GRe ⊞

Silver inkstand, comprising inkwell, wax compartment, pounce pot, pen stand and taper holder, with repoussé covers, 19thC, 6½in (16.5cm) long.
£230–270 / €340–400
$410–480 NSal ↗

Silver and ivory pencil, c1860, 4in (10cm) long.
£270–300 / €400–450
$480–530 BEX ⊞

◀ **Silver three-colour pencil,** by Sampson Mordan & Co, c1900, 4in (10cm) extended.
£320–360 / €480–540
$570–640 BEX ⊞

Silver inkstand, by Richard Morton, containing silver-mounted cut-glass pots, Sheffield 1808, 9in (23cm) long, 14oz.
£620–740 / €920–1,100
$1,100–1,300 S(O) ↗

◀ **Silver blotter,** by Vasili Ivanovich Andreyev, engraved with a winter landscape, hallmarked, Russian, Moscow, c1900.
£750–900
€1,100–1,350
$1,350–1,600
BWL ↗

Miscellaneous

Silver brush, by L&S, Birmingham 1902, 5in (12.5cm) long. This type of item is now rarely used as originally intended, which reduces the appeal to collectors who wish to display rather than use their pieces.
£25–30 / €35–45
$45–55 WAC ⊞

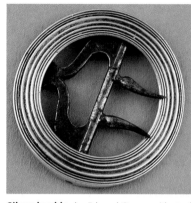

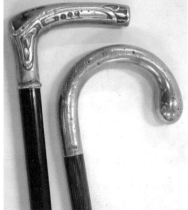

◀ **Two Edwardian silver-mounted walking sticks,** 36in (91.5cm) long.
£55–65 / €80–95
$95–115 G(L) 🔨

Silver buckle, by Edward Owen, with steel clasp, London, c1800, 1½in (4cm) diam, ¼oz. This piece would appeal to costume collectors as well as silver collectors.
£50–60 / €75–90
$90–105 WW 🔨

Silver buckle, by Robert Pringle, with pierced decoration, Chester, c1903, 3½in (9cm) long.
£60–70 / €80–105
$95–125 WW 🔨

Silver-mounted umbrella, c1890, 13in (33cm) long.
£70–80 / €105–120
$125–140 GBr ⊞

Silver-mounted glass scent bottle, with faceted glass body, engraved with monogram, maker's mark 'L&S', Birmingham 1910, 3½in (9cm) diam.
£60–70 / €80–105
$95–125 FHF 🔨

▶ **Silver-plated magazine rack,** c1880, 14in (35.5cm) wide.
£70–80
€105–120
$125–140 AL ⊞

Silver-mounted porcelain vase, by Samson, decorated with panels of Chinese *famille verte* floral decoration, red swastika mark, French, 19thC, 4¾in (12cm) high.
**£85–100 / €125–150
$150–175** DN(EH) ♪

To find out more about antique silver see the full range of Miller's books at
www.millers.uk.com

Silver thimble, with carved decoration, French, 19thC, 1in (2.5cm) high.
**£85–100 / €125–150
$150–175** RdeR ⊞

Old Sheffield plate egg frame, comprising six egg cups, with swing handle, c1800, 8½in (21.5cm) wide.
**£140–165 / €210–240
$250–290** WW ♪

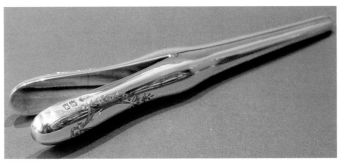

Silver glove stretchers, by C. J. D., London 1917, 7in (18cm) long, 2½oz. Small silver items, such as these glove stretchers, can be an affordable way to start a collection and learn about hallmarks.
**£145–165 / €220–250
$260–290** BEX ⊞

Silver hat pin stand, by Adie & Lovekin, Birmingham 1907, 3½in (9cm) high.
**£155–175 / €230–260
$270–310** BEX ⊞

Silver rococo-style christening set, by Lee & Wigfull, comprising mug, knife, fork, spoon and napkin ring, all with engraved initials, Sheffield 1898, 1899 and 1904, mug 4¾in (12cm) high, in a leather fitted case.
**£180–210 / €270–310
$320–370** PF ♪

Art Nouveau silver-mounted oak photograph frame, decorated with bluebells, Birmingham 1905, 8in (20.5cm) high. Art Nouveau pieces are always popular with collectors.
**£200–240 / €300–350
$360–420** G(L) ♪

Miller's compares...

A. Silver brandy saucepan, with a turned wood handle, maker's mark worn, London 1728, 3½in (9cm) diam, 3¾oz.
£230–270 / €340–400
$410–480 G(L) ✣

B. Queen Anne silver brandy saucepan, by William Fleming, with a turned wood handle, marked 'EG', initialled 'AP', London 1712, bowl 3¼in (8.5cm) diam, 3¾oz.
£660–790 / €980–1,200
$1,150–1,400 WW ✣

The flared shape, excellent condition and clear hallmarks make Item B more valuable than Item A, which is simpler and shows visible signs of wear. When purchasing items that require restoration, one must always include the cost of such repairs to the final value of the piece. What might seem like a good buy at the time may not be once these charges have been included.

Art Nouveau silver photograph frame, Birmingham 1903, 8in (20.5cm) high.
£230–270 / €340–400
$410–480 G(L) ✣

Silver photograph frame, by Marshall & Rutter, with gadrooning and central shield, Birmingham 1891, 8 x 6in (20.5 x 15cm).
£270–300 / €400–450
$480–530 RICC ⊞

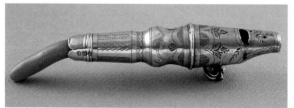

◄ **Child's silver whistle,** by John Touliet, with coral teether, London 1806, 4½in (11.5cm) long.
£330–390
€490–580
$580–690 WW ✣

Silver opium pipe, Chinese, c1900, 5in (12.5cm) long, 1¼oz.
£290–325
€430–490
$510–580 BEX ⊞

Silver pin cushion, by Addie & Lovekin, modelled as a duck, with set gem eyes and original lining, Birmingham 1909, 2½in (6.5cm) long.
£340–400 / €510–600
$600–710   FHF ⚖

Scent bottle, by Joseph Taylor, in an engraved silver case, 1802.
£330–370 / €490–550
$580–650   VK ⊞

Pin cushions

Pin cushions are a popular and affordable collecting area. Pig-shaped pin cushions are quite common and are worth less than more unusual shapes such as rats. As a general rule, smaller examples are more desirable and replaced cushions can lower the value.

Pair of silver pin cushions, by Mordaunt & Co, modelled as chicks, inscribed 'Enoch Lodge April 10th 1907', Chester 1906, 2in (5cm) wide.
£380–450 / €570–670
$670–800   S(O) ⚖

◀ **Silver tea caddy,** by John East, with sliding cover, London 1726, 3½in (9cm) high.
£460–550 / €690–820
$810–970   HYD ⚖

▶ **Pair of silver and enamel napkin rings,** Russian, Moscow 1880, 2in (5cm) diam, 3½oz.
£500–600 / €750–890
$890–1,050   DORO ⚖

▶ **Silver-gilt and cloisonné enamel** *kovsh*, by Ivan Khlebnikov, Russian, Moscow 1883, 3½in (9cm) wide.
£570–680 / €850–1,000
$1,000–1,200   S(O) ⚖

Glass

Glass, which has long been the Cinderella of the antiques world, is enjoying a remarkable renaissance. At a time when dealers in many of the traditional categories are struggling to find customers, an increasing number of stands devoted to glass are appearing at British antiques fairs. Refreshingly, the items on offer are growing ever more varied.

Those areas of greatest interest to glass collectors have traditionally been 18th-century drinking glasses, 19th-century coloured glass and, increasingly, 20th-century glass, particularly examples by leading designers, all of which continue to perform strongly. Typically, the recent dispersal of two important collections of drinking glasses generated high prices, especially for examples with unusual characteristics. One of the collections, which sold this year, comprised 80 pieces and fetched a total of £96,000 / €143,000 / $170,000, an average of £1,200 / €1,800 / $2,100 per glass.

Yet despite the boom in such top-of-the-range finery, the vast majority of glass sold in Britain changes hands for pennies rather than pounds. This is mainly because its owners fail to recognize what they have in their possession, whatever their nationality. Indeed, earlier this year an American woman offered for sale on eBay what she thought to be a worthless piece of glass. It was, in fact, a piece of Depression glass, made c1900 by Harry Northwood, which eventually sold for over £5,600 / €8,400 / $10,000. Only recently I bought 30 items of varied and generally dirty glassware, most dating from the 19th and 20th centuries, for a total of about £20 / €30 / $35. They included a huge, amber-tinted Art Nouveau vase signed by Thomas Webb, c1900 to 1910, for £1 / €1.49 / $1.77, and an equally large Victorian lead-crystal pressed-glass fruit bowl on a pedestal stand, c1860 to 1870, for the same sum. Such items are neither sufficiently rare or sought after to be displayed at a leading museum, nor will they make the grade at a top-ranking auction. Yet both are sufficiently bold and decorative to command the interest of the average collector, and represent just the tip of a colossal iceberg.

The key to acquiring such bargains lies in two critical factors: being in the right place at the right time, and in the collector's ability to recognize what he or she is looking at. There is little the individual can do to alter the fundamental laws of physics and become ever-present at every market stall. However, there is a great deal they can do to improve their knowledge and understanding of their particular speciality. Glass is a vast subject, so it is important for the beginner to concentrate, at least to begin with, on a small, specific area, of which there are literally hundreds to choose. It might be a particular colour, or engraved Victorian glasses, for example, Georgian rummers, or the products of an individual glassworks.

The number of books, television programmes and lectures devoted to all aspects of antiques is greater than ever before. However, a little knowledge can be a dangerous thing, and no-one would urge collectors to go in with all guns blazing based on information gleaned from one magazine article or a 30-second slot on a TV show. The knack is to learn gradually: talk to fellow collectors and to specialist dealers, handle as many pieces as possible and read as much as you can. Do remember, though, that all that glistens is not necessarily gold.

Andy McConnell

Baskets, Bowls & Dishes

Glass bowl, with acid-etched oak-leaf decoration, c1900, 7½in (19cm) diam. This piece is probably Bohemian and is a quality hand-made item. Although 'frilly' glass is currently unfashionable, this example still demonstrates that good-quality antique glass can be inexpensive.
£20–25 / €30–35
$35–40 JAA

Pitkin & Brooks cut-glass celery dish, signed, early 20thC, 12in (30.5cm) long. American cut-glass produced after 1900 is not as collectable as earlier pieces. This is because the pattern was pressed onto the bodies of 'figured blanks'. The cutters then only had to deepen and sharpen the design on their wheels.
£60–70 / €90–105
$100–110 JAA

Find out more in

Miller's Popular Glass of the 19th & 20th Centuries: A Collector's Guide, Miller's Publications, 2000

Glass footed bowl, with a frill rim and spiral decoration, c1890, 9in (23cm) diam.
£100–120 / €150–180
$175–210 DN(EH)

▶ **Amberina glass finger bowl and plate,** c1900, 6in (15cm) diam. The colours are achieved by reheating the finished pieces. Red examples are more popular than yellow ones.
£30–35 / €45–50
$55–65 JAA

Pair of cut-glass rinsers, decorated with bands of diamonds, c1820, 5½in (14cm) diam.
£80–95 / €120–140
$140–170 JAd

Victorian cranberry glass bowl, with applied crimped rim and border, silver-plated frame and carrying handle, 8in (20.5cm) high. This cranberry glass bowl represents good value for money.
£120–140 / €180–210
$210–250 FHF

Glass rinsers

Water-filled rinsers were used by diners for the purpose of washing their wine glasses between the courses of a meal, as the type of wine changed with every course. Glass rinsers first appeared in the 1770s, when small-bowled drinking glasses were replaced by the more generous rummers that remained on the table throughout the meal. Decorated to suit prevailing fashions, they were produced in colourless, blue, green and amethyst glass until the 1830s. Fine-quality reproduction rinsers made between 1910 and 1930 are more common than genuine pieces.

Thomas Webb & Sons Queen's Burmese ware glass sugar bowl, c1890, 4in (10cm) diam.
£130–155 / €190–220
$230–270 JAA ⚒

Burmese glass

Burmese glassware was invented and patented in 1885 by Frederick Shirley of the Mount Washington Glass Co, Massachusetts. In the same year, it was produced under licence by Thomas Webb & Sons, Stourbridge, under the name 'Queen's Burmese' after it was admired by Queen Victoria. The colour, which graduates from a lime-yellow at the base to a bold rose-pink at the top, was achieved by using uranium oxide and selective reheating. The piece was then acid-dipped to leave a satin finish and often applied with coloured enamel decoration.

Libbey cut-glass bowl, with diamond point bands and etched floral decoration, signed, c1910, 9in (23cm) diam. Libbey is a large American glassmaker based in Toledo, Ohio. During the 1893 Chicago World Fair it exhibited its wares on a stand manned by 130 blowers and cutters, who demonstrated their skills on specially-installed equipment. This type of glass is more popular with American, than with British or European, collectors.
£145–175 / €220–260
$260–310 JAA ⚒

Cranberry glass preserve dish, with silver cover, c1905, 4in (10cm) high. Cranberry glass is very popular and the presence of a hallmarked silver cover, as opposed to a silver-plated one, adds to the desirability of this item.
£175–195 / €260–290
$310–350 GRI ▦

Late Victorian glass Masonic bowl, engraved with 'The Ladder of Life', sun, moon and other emblems, on a knopped stem, 9in (23cm) high. Antique Masonic glass is avidly collected by modern Masons, hence the relatively high prices for these items. This piece was probably used as a punchbowl at meetings.
£280–330 / €420–490
$500–580 DN(EH) ⚒

The look without the price

Thomas Webb & Sons cameo glass salad bowl, carved with honeysuckle sprays and a butterfly, with a silver rim, foot rim chipped, marked, c1900, 9¼in (23.5cm) diam.
£530–630 / €790–940
$940–1,100 B ⚒

This bowl would make a very attractive display piece. If it were in perfect condition it could be worth an additional £1,000 / €1,500 / $1,750.

Bottles & Decanters

Lewis & Towers glass poison bottle, 1910, 9in (23cm) high. Blue was the most popular colour used for poison bottles, followed by green. These bottles remain quite common, largely because of the recent practice of excavating old rubbish tips, and as a result they can be purchased for relatively low amounts.
£14–18 / €20–28
$25–32 OIA ⊞

Dr Soules hop bitters glass bottle, 1872, 17in (43cm) high.
£16–20 / €20–30
$25–35 OIA ⊞

Victorian glass smelling salts bottle, with original dipper, 2½in (6.5cm) high. This bottle has retained its original stopper, without which its value would be about half this amount.
£18–22 / €30–35
$35–40 TASV ⊞

Brooke Bath glass codd bottle, c1880, 9in (23cm) high. When collecting bottles, condition and the name on the bottle are the most important factors. Rare or amusing names can increase the value tenfold.
£20–24 / €30–35
$35–40 OIA ⊞

▶ **Glass wine bottle,** late 18thC, 11in (28cm) high. This bottle was recovered from the sea and is covered with barnacles. Evidence of degradation from burial on land or at sea is detrimental to value. This bottle could possibly have fetched £300 / €450 / $530 if it had been in better condition.
£35–40 / €50–60
$60–70 OIA ⊞

Antique bottles

Antique glass bottles are a specialist collecting area, with values ranging from pennies to five-figure sums, according to rarity and condition. One example dating from the 1660s recently sold for £20,000 / €29,800 / $35,400. Dating from the 1650s, the practice of sealing bottles with initials, crests and dates enabled owners to identify their property and date the vintage of the contents. Seals continued to be applied to wine bottles even after the introduction of standard-sized bottle moulds in 1821, and their presence can boost values by ten times. However, the majority of Victorian embossed bottles can be found relatively cheaply and in all kinds of shapes, sizes and colours including amber, green, blue and amethyst.

Glass wine bottle, with seal for Trinity College Common Room, c1860, 12in (30.5cm) high. This bottle was blown from a Rickets mould, patented in 1821, and would have been refilled many times. In this particular case, the seal has doubled the value of this bottle.
£90–100 / €135–150
$160–180   OIA ⊞

The look without the price

Pair of Victorian silver-mounted glass bottles, stoppers missing, silver mount Birmingham 1844, 13in (33cm) high.
£160–190 / €240–280
$280–340   DN(EH) ⚒

These attractive silver-mounted bottles would originally have been sold as a set of three, contained in a silver-plated stand and fitted with cork stoppers with silver finials. The complete set would be worth around £500–600 / €750–890 / $890–1,050.

◀ **Glass bottle,** with gilded inscription for Pale Ale, c1880, 21in (53.5cm) high.
£165–180 / €240–270
$290–320   YT ⊞

▶ **Glass decanter,** hand-enamelled with medieval busts, with associated stopper, French, 1850–60, 5¼in (13.5cm) high, cased. This decanter would have sold for a higher price if the stopper had been original.
£175–210 / €260–310
$310–370   SWO ⚒

The look without the price

At first glance this appears to be a pair of decanters, worth three times more than a single example. When examined more closely, however, small differences, such as the diameter of their pouring rings, the height of their necks and the way their stoppers are seated, indicate that although similar, they are not a pair. Decanters of this shape and style were produced from around 1780 to bring style to the dining table and to improve the taste of red wine by allowing it to breathe. These handsome pieces are around 200 years old, yet sold at a price lower than that of a modern crystal decanter. They will not only retain their value but continue to enhance the pleasure of wine as originally intended.

Late Regency glass decanters, the necks with triple rings, with cut-glass stoppers, 9½in (24cm) high.
£175–210 / €260–310
$310–370   DN(Bri) ⚘

◀ **Glass decanter,** with ribbed and wrythen decoration, probably 1840–65, 11½in (29cm) high. This decanter was formed by blowing into a mould incorporating vertical pillars, then twisted into a spiral while the glass was still malleable. Its value would be increased if it still had its original cork stopper, which would have been mounted with a silver or silver-plated bunch of grapes.
£200–230 / €300–340
$350–410   GS ⊞

Glass wine bottle, 18thC, 11in (28cm) high. This bottle would make a very attractive lamp base. However, drilling it for a lamp flex would more than halve its value.
£220–260 / €330–390
$390–460   SWO ⚘

◀ **Acid-etched glass decanter,** probably Bohemian, decorated with Berainesque grotesques and strapwork, c1900, 11in (28cm) high.
£270–300 / €400–450
$480–530   HTE ⊞

The look without the price

The tantalus was the trademark of luxury goods maker George Betjemann & Sons, founded in London in 1851. When patented in 1880, the tantalus was defined as a 'stand for decanters, bottles and jars, to prevent surreptitious withdrawal'. This example, in carved oak with brass fittings and dating from around 1900, was produced by a lesser maker and contains moulded decanters that were later polished to create the effect of cut glass. It now shows signs of wear, but with tender loving care, including vigorous waxing and polishing, could easily be restored to almost original condition, a process that would significantly enhance its value.

Victorian oak tantalus, fitted with three glass bottles, with plated mounts and carrying handles, 13¾in (35cm) wide.
£200–240 / €300–360
$350–420 CHTR ✦

Onion-shaped glass wine bottle,
1710–15, 6¼in (16cm) high. The first English wine bottles, dating from the 1650s, had rounded bodies and were therefore unstable. They gradually evolved into the more stable onion shape by around 1700.
£310–370 / €460–550
$550–650 BBR ✦

Pair of Prussian-shaped glass decanters, cut with vertical prisms, diamonds and horizontal prisms, c1820, 10½in (26.5cm) high.
£720–800 / €1,050–1,200
$1,250–1,400 Del ⊞

◄ **Set of three glass decanters and stoppers,** inscribed 'Brandy', 'Holland' and 'Rum', possibly early 19thC, 9¾in (25cm) high.
£730–880 / €1,100–1,300
$1,300–1,550 WW ✦

Edwardian cut-glass brandy dispenser and cover, engraved with a figure playing a musical instrument, inscribed 'T. & J. Minns, Carlisle, Special old Cognac Brandy', with brass tap, 28in (71cm) high. The fact that this brandy dispenser can be traced to a pub in Carlisle, Cumbria has added to its value.
£730–880 / €1,100–1,300
$1,300–1,550 TRM ✦

Drinking Glasses

The look without the price

Fashions for coloured glass have changed over the years. Green, amethyst, blue and green were popular during the late 18th century and ruby-red, the most difficult to make, was perfected around 1840. Cranberry pink, developed around 1880, and blue remain the most popular colours, but green has recently fallen from its previous peak. These 200-year-old hand-made glasses, intended for drinking white wine, are great value at just £15 / €22 / $28 each.

Pair of wine glasses, c1800, 5in (12.5cm) high.
£25–30 / €35–40
$45–50 HTE ⊞

Deceptive wine glass, with a knopped stem and a plain foot, c1825, 4¼in (11cm) high.
£35–40 / €50–55
$60–70 Som ⊞

Miniature wine glass, with drawn trumpet bowl, c1760, 3in (7.5cm) high. Small glasses are not a very popular collecting field, although really tiny glasses do sell better than slightly larger ones. They were designed to hold a single shot of gin, which would have been sold in pubs or dram shops.
£65–75 / €95–110
$110–125 BrW ⊞

Glass rummer, the bowl with a petal-moulded base, 1790–1810, 4½in (11.5cm) high. Unlike mid-18th-century glasses that had tiny bowls, rummers like this can be used for everyday drinking.
£65–75 / €95–110
$115–135 Som ⊞

Wine glass, the wheel-engraved bowl with dot borders and waterlilies, on an inverted baluster stem and star-cut base, c1870, 7in (18cm) high. This is a practical glass with attractive engraving.
£75–85 / €110–125
$135–150 GGD ⊞

Miller's compares...

A. Bohemian ruby-flashed glass beaker, engraved with panels of architectural views, on a star-cut base, 1850–60, 5in (12.5cm) high.
£80–95 / €120–140
$140–170 DN(BR)

B. Silver-mounted glass beaker, by D. N. Dubinin, depicting four views of Helsinki, Russian, St Petersburg, c1850, 6in (15cm) high.
£420–500 / €630–750
$750–890 BUK

Bohemian glass goblet, engraved with a hunting scene and foliage, on a faceted stem and rosette-shaped foot, 19thC, 9¼in (23.5cm) high.
£100–120 / €150–180
$175–210 G(L)

Beakers were always an important component of the European glassmaker's repertoire and examples were commonly engraved with scenes of towns where they were retailed as souvenirs. These superficially similar pieces sold recently for widely different prices and important differences divide them. Item A is fairly average, with a traditional view framed by ruby-flashed decoration. Item B, however, is considerably superior on several counts. While it is also ruby-flashed, its foot and bowl are cased in a further layer of white glass and it is fitted with ornate Gothic-revival silver mounts marked by the Russian silversmith D. N. Dubinin, who worked in St Petersburg between 1849 and 1854. These features helped Item B achieve a much higher price than item A.

Find out more in

Miller's Glass Antiques Checklist, Miller's Publications, 2001

Pair of glass rummers, each engraved with a band of scrolling foliage, 19thC, 6in (15cm) high.
£110–130 / €165–195
$195–230 FHF

▶ **Bohemian glass goblet,** on a faceted stem and square base, 1890–1900, 8¾in (22cm) high. This goblet was hand-painted with enamels, each colour being fired onto the glass individually and at different temperatures. It was made in the *Historismus* style, so-called because it reflected a style that was popular about 100 years before this piece was actually made. The best examples bear the signature of Viennese retailer J. & L. Lobmeyr.
£120–140 / €180–210
$210–250 G(L)

Cordial or wine glass?

Mid-18th-century wine glasses are often mistakenly described as cordial glasses because modern observers cannot understand how wine could be consumed from vessels with such small bowls. However, before the 1770s, wine was consumed according to a strict social etiquette that demanded that the contents of each glass be emptied before being returned to the sideboard for refilling. Cordials (the contemporary name for liqueurs) were far stronger than wine and consumed from glasses with even smaller bowls, mostly by ladies in drawing rooms after dinner. It was not until the advent of more robust dining manners during the 1770s that the small-bowled wine glass gave way to the more generously-proportioned rummer drinking glass.

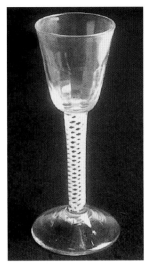

Glass, on a multiple opaque-twist stem and a conical foot, 18thC, 5½in (14cm) high. This is a very reasonable price for this style of glass.
£130–155 / €195–230 $230–270 LAY ✎

◄ **Glass rummer,** engraved with an egg-and-tulip band, on a moulded and stepped stem, early 19thC, 5¾in (14.5cm) high. It is currently believed that moulded square feet (including lemon-squeezer feet), and stoppers were made in Birmingham and sold wholesale to glassmakers, who then fitted them onto their products. When inspected under ultraviolet light, both feet and stoppers can show a widely differing degree of fluorescence, which does indeed suggest that the vessels they were fitted to were made elsewhere.
£130–155 / €195–230 $230–270 DN ✎

Lemon-squeezer feet

Moulded lemon-squeezer feet were fitted to numerous rummers and some decanters and candlesticks between 1770 and 1820. They were formed by pouring molten glass into a rigid mould made of carved wood or cast metal, then manually squeezed into its crevices with a hand-held plunger shaped like the common juice squeezer from which they take their name. The resulting ribbed dome made the foot lighter and generated reflected light.

Glass rummer, petal-moulded and engraved with branches and leaves, on a pedestal lemon-squeezer foot, c1810, 5½in (14cm) high.
£135–150 / €200–220 $240–270 GS ⊞

Wine glass, the funnel bowl above an air-twist stem, 18thC, 5¾in (14.5cm) high.
£140–165 / €210–240 $250–290 G(L) ✎

▶ **Glass rummer,** engraved with swags and stars, on a moulded pedestal lemon-squeezer foot, c1775, 5½in (14cm) high.
£140–160 / €210–240
$250–280 GS ⊞

Glass goblet, engraved with a galleon and a lighthouse, c1890, 5¼in (13.5cm) high. This goblet has attractive engraving and ships are always a popular collecting theme.
£140–160 / €210–240
$250–280 JAS ⊞

Bohemian overlaid glass goblet, engraved with a woodland scene, 19thC, 6in (15cm) high. If it had been overlaid in ruby, the value of this goblet would increase by about 20 per cent.
£150–180 / €220–270
$270–320 G(L) 🪓

Glass rummer, engraved with 'EMG' and a rose and thistle sprig, on a capstan stem and conical foot, c1825, 5in (12.5cm) high. This is a good example of how decoration can affect price. Without the anonymous monogram this rummer could have achieved 50 per cent more. However, without the decorative engraving its value would be reduced by half.
£165–195 / €240–280
$280–330 DN 🪓

Regency cut-glass rummer, engraved with ears of wheat, hops and initials 'WEW', on a multi-faceted knopped stem and star-cut foot, c1830, 7½in (19cm) high.
£175–210 / €260–310
$310–370 DN(BR) 🪓

To find out more about antique glass see the full range of Miller's books at
www.millers.uk.com

Wine glass, the funnel bowl above a double-series opaque-twist stem, on a conical foot, c1760, 6½in (16.5cm) high.
£200–240 / €300–360
$350–420 G(L) 🪓

Firing glass, the ogee bowl with a hammered flute lower section, on a terraced foot, c1750, 3½in (9cm) high. The moulded foot of this glass is unusual. With a plain foot it might have sold for half this price, showing that it is possible to pick up a bargain.
£200–240 / €300–360 $350–420 DN ⚒

The look without the price

These glasses are early 20th-century reproductions of an early 19th-century design. The Edwardian appetite for Regency-style domestic finery encouraged British manufacturers in all fields to recreate their former glories. The result is that today early 20th-century reproductions out-number genuine period pieces by a significant factor. 'Antique' glassware produced between 1910 and 1935, such as these rummers, was generally of a clearer crystal than the earlier models it copied. Although these reproductions are now approaching genuine antique status, they can still be purchased for less than a quarter of the price of pieces twice as old.

Set of six glass rummers, moulded and engraved with a band of acorns and oak leaves, c1900, 5¼in (13.5cm) high.
£240–280 / €360–420 $420–500 DN(Bri) ⚒

Set of 12 hock glasses, with cut-glass stems, 1900–10, 6¾in (17cm) high.
£260–310 / €390–460 $460–550 SWO ⚒

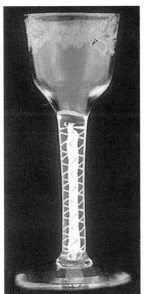

Wine glass, etched with foliage, on an opaque-twist stem and folded foot, 18thC, 6in (15cm) high. This glass was a good buy. With its attractive engraving it could have achieved a further £50 / €75 / $90.
£220–260 / €330–390 $390–460 WL ⚒

▶ **Glass rummer,** engraved with stars supported within swags above a broad-fluted lower section, c1830, 7¾in (19.5cm) high. With its Adamesque neo-classical design, this rummer offers good value for money.
£260–310 / €390–460 $460–550 DN ⚒

Glass goblet, decorated with a view of Berkley Lodge, dated 1905, 8in (20.5cm) high.
£270–300 / €400–450
$480–530 BrW ⊞

Miller's compares...

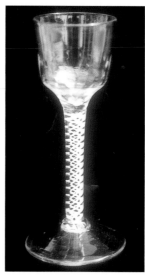

A. Wine glass, the ogee bowl on a double-series opaque-twist stem and conical foot, c1765, 6in (15cm) high.
£270–300 / €400–450
$480–530 GS ⊞

B. Glass, with mercury-twist stem, c1740, 6½in (16.5cm) high.
£540–600 / €800–890
$960–1,050 CHAC ⊞

Item A is smaller and later than Item B, but the main difference between the two is the twists in the stems. Item A has a double-series opaque twist, which is quite a common stem. Item B, however, has a much rarer mercury-twist stem, which has flat rather than round threads giving a greater reflective surface, hence the name, and the higher price.

Wine glass, the ogee bowl engraved with fruiting vine, on a double-series opaque-twist stem and conical foot, c1765, 5¾in (14.5cm) high. The engraving has probably added £75–100 / €110–150 / $135–175 to the price of this glass.
£300–340 / €450–500
$530–600 GS ⊞

◀ **Wine glass,** the ogee bowl on a multiple opaque-twist stem and raised conical foot, c1765, 6¼in (16cm) high.
£300–340
€450–500
$530–600 PSA ⊞

▶ **Wine glass,** the ogee bowl on an opaque-twist stem with swollen centre knop and a conical foot, c1760, 7in (18cm) high.
£300–360
€450–540
$530–640 G(L) 🖊

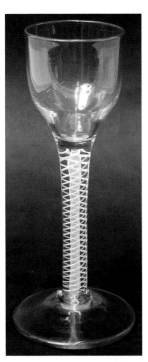

◄ **Wine glass,** the ogee bowl above a double-series spiral gauze opaque-twist stem and conical foot, c1760, 7in (18cm) high. The double-series twist in the stem has added £100 / €150 / $175 to the value of this glass.
**£300–360 / €450–540
$530–640** G(L) 🔨

Find out more in

Miller's Glass Pocket Fact File, Miller's Publications, 2001

Pair of wine glasses, the bell bowls on multiple air-twist stems with two knops, c1750, 6¾in (17cm) high. Knops can add interest and therefore value to a glass – and a double knop is more unusual and interesting than a single one. However, the price of these glasses will not have been greatly affected by being a pair, as they do not sell for much more than singles. The reason for this is possibly that most collectors only want one example of each type of glass.
**£350–420 / €520–620
$620–740** TEN 🔨

Glass, with double opaque-twist stem and single knop, c1760, 6½in (16.5cm) high. The knop has increased the value of this glass by around £100 / €150 / $175.
**£340–380 / €510–570
$600–670** CHAC ⊞

Wine glass, the bell bowl on a double-series opaque-twist stem and conical foot, c1760, 6¾in (17cm) high.
**£330–390 / €490–580
$580–690** G(L) 🔨

▶ **Glass,** with double opaque-twist stem, c1760, 6½in (16.5cm) high.
**£440–490 / €660–730
$780–870** CHAC ⊞

Wine glass, the pan-top bowl on a multiple-spiral air-twist stem with swollen knop, c1755, 5¾in (14.5cm) high. Pan tops and swollen knops are unusual features and can increase value by £200 / €300 / $350.
£450–500 / €670–750
$800–890 GS ⊞

Baluster wine glass, engraved with ships and an inscription, on a folded foot, Dutch, c1760, 7½in (19cm) high.
£460–550 / €690–820
$810–970 LAY ⚒

Wine glass, the ogee bowl with 'hammered' decoration to the lower section, the stem with air-twist gauze and two spiral threads, on a conical foot, c1760, 6¾in (17cm) high. This piece achieved its price as it originates from Harvey's Wine Museum collection. It also has a moulded bowl giving the effect known as hammered because it looks as if it has been created by countless tiny hammer blows.
£470–560 / €700–830
$830–990 B ⚒

◀ **Wine glass,** the bell bowl on a stem with two opaque spiral threads and two six-ply spiral bands, on a domed conical foot, c1765, 6in (15cm) high. The high price achieved by this glass is in part due to the unusual domed foot. The added benefit is that it originates from Harvey's Wine Museum collection. Such provenance can add another 10 to 15 per cent to the price.
£470–560 / €700–830
$830–990 B ⚒

◀ **Set of six champagne glasses,** engraved with a Greek key border, 1870–80, 5in (12.5cm) high. A set of six glasses will command a far higher price than a set of a lower quantity, and will be proportionally more than if the glasses are sold individually.
£500–550 / €750–810
$890–970 JAS ⊞

Wine glass, with air-twist stem, c1740, 6½in (16.5cm) high.
£500–550 / €750–810
$890–970   CHAC ⊞

Armorial wine glass, the funnel bowl engraved with an ecclesiastical armorial, the folded conical foot engraved with flowers, minor scratch, German, 1730–40, 7½in (19cm) high. The cutting and engraving on this glass is of superb quality and is typical of work produced in Germany during this period.
£510–610 / €760–910
$900–1,050   S(Am) ✎

Wine glass, the funnel bowl above an air-twist stem with three knops, on a conical foot, c1765, 6¾in (17cm) high.
£630–750 / €940–1,100
$1,100–1,350   G(L) ✎

The Glass Excise Duty (1745–1845)

Contrary to received wisdom, Glass Excise Duty is now thought to have had virtually no effect on the style of glassware produced in Britain over its duration. This is because when originally imposed, the duty added less than one penny to the cost of a wine glass at a time when the market for glass remained the exclusive preserve of the rich. The introduction of the duty coincided with the arrival in Britain of the rococo decorative style, which tended towards light and airy effects and motifs.

Find out more in

Miller's Glass Buyer's Guide, Miller's Publications, 2001

◀ **Excise wine glass,** the funnel bowl with hammered and fluted lower section, the hollow stem on a conical foot, c1745, 6½in (16.5cm) high. Ex-Harveys Wine Museum sale. It was once thought that a glass such as this, with a rare hollow stem, would have been made in reaction to the imposition of the weight-related Glass Excise Duty, which gave rise to the trade name of excise glass. This association is now widely discounted.
£630–750 / €940–1,100
$1,100–1,350   B ✎

Jugs

Victorian optic-moulded glass jug,
with a clear handle, 8½in (21.5cm) high.
£55–65 / €80–95
$95–110 HOLL ✗

Pair of satin-glass ewers, each with a
folded rim above a basal knop and a body
with six lobes, painted with flowers, with
applied handles, late 19thC, 9½in (24cm)
high. This style of ewer would have been
made in any one of the numerous glassworks
in Britain, America, France and Germany.
£95–110 / €140–165
$170–195 PFK ✗

▶ **Usher's Whisky glass water jug,**
1900–10, 12in (30.5cm) high. This kind
of item is popular among whisky and
breweriana collectors.
£200–230 / €300–340
$350–410 MURR ▦

Coloured glass

Chemical advances during the Victorian age led to
the discovery that certain additions to molten glass
could produce vessels that changed colour when
reheated. The chemicals used to produce these
effects included arsenic, uranium and gold, and
additional decoration such as enamelling, etching
or gilding was often added later. Manufacturers,
including Libbey Glass Co in America and Thomas
Webb & Sons, produced ranges such as Amberina,
which shaded from yellow to red, and peach and
opaque pink that shaded to yellow.

Acid-etched glass pitcher,
signed 'G. de Feuvre', French,
c1910, 7in (18cm) high.
£180–210 / €270–310
$320–370 G(L) ✗

**Pair of Victorian cranberry
glass claret jugs,** with clear
handles and stoppers, 11in
(28cm) high. Cranberry glass is
very popular. However, buyers
should be aware that there are
some very authentic-looking
reproductions available.
£130–155 / €195–230
$230–270 FHF ✗

**Bos Whisky glass water
jug,** 1890–1910, 8½in (21.5cm)
high. The letters on this glass
are in hand-painted enamels
that were fired onto the
surface of the jug in a kiln,
therefore leaving them virtually
impregnable to damage.
£270–300 / €400–450
$480–530 MURR ▦

Lustres

Pair of Victorian opaline glass lustres, each with a wavy rim, with clear drops, some damage, 9in (23cm) high.
£110–130 / € 165–195
$195–230 FHF 🔨

Miller's compares...

A. Pair of Victorian cut-crystal lustres, with prism drops, 6¾in (17cm) high.
£105–125 / € 155–185
$185–220 DD 🔨

B. Pair of Victorian opaque vaseline glass lustres, with gilded rims and enamel-painted with garlands of flowers, one prism cracked, 12¼in (31cm) high.
£260–310 / € 390–460
$460–550 DD 🔨

Pendant lustres remain popular table centrepieces two centuries after their introduction. These examples show how prices can vary. While the lustres in Item A are slightly earlier and finely cut, they are relatively small, being almost half the size of the lustres in Item B. However, the yellow opaque glass, shaped rims and hand-painted decoration of Item B, together with the fact that it is almost twice the size of Item A, account for the difference in price.

◀ **Bohemian glass mantel lustre,** with prism drops, 19thC, 22in (56cm) high, converted to a lamp. If it had not been converted, this piece could be worth 50 per cent more. It has superb cutting and floral decoration on high-quality glass.
£160–190 / € 240–280
$280–330 JAA 🔨

Pair of Bohemian lead-crystal lustres, the crenellated rims above prism drops, minor chips, two drops missing, 1860–80, 12½in (32cm) high. This is a high quality piece which accounts for the price. However, it could be very difficult to replace a single drop as they were made in so many different styles. All the drops may have to be replaced in order to match and achieve perfect symmetry.
£740–880 / € 1,100–1,300
$1,300–1,550 GAK 🔨

The term 'lustre' can be confusing as it has been applied to a number of different items over the past 300 years. They have included a chandelier (18th century), a cut-glass table centrepiece supporting a single candlestick (19th century), and a single drop suspended from a chandelier, centrepiece or candlestick, which is the current usage.

Paperweights & Dumps

Victorian glass dump,
enclosing graduated bubbles,
4½in (11.5cm) high. As well as
being decorative pieces, glass
dumps were often used as
doorstops. This means that
many suffered damage, and
these are best avoided as the
repairs can be costly.
**£90–105 / €135–155
$160–185 PFK** 🔨

Stourbridge glass dump,
enclosing silver-foil flowers,
19thC, 6¾in (17cm) high. The
flowers in this dump are made
of silver foil, but other examples
can be found with patterns of
powdered chalk or graduated
bubbles. Pieces with more
unusual decoration are usually
of higher value.
**£165–195 / €240–290
$290–340 DA** 🔨

Glass inkwell and stopper, with millefiori
canes, slight damage, 19thC, 5in (12.5cm)
high. Although this has a damaged stopper,
which has reduced its value and interest for
serious collectors, it is still an interesting
example of a paperweight inkwell.
**£140–165 / €210–240
$250–290 FHF** 🔨

Pair of glass dumps, enclosing cockerels,
late 19thC, 3in (7.5cm) diam.
**£180–200 / €270–300
$320–360 RWA** ⊞

**New England Glass Co
paperweight,** with intaglio
portraits of Queen Victoria and
Prince Albert, American, 1851,
3¼in (8.5cm) wide. Although
collectors usually prefer home-
produced pieces, this example
of an American paperweight
featuring a British motif would
appeal to collectors on both
sides of the Atlantic, a fact that
enhances its value.
**£160–190 / €240–280
$280–330 JDJ** 🔨

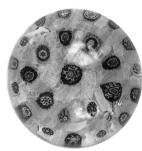

Clichy glass paperweight,
with two concentric circles of
canes and spiral cables, mid-
19thC, 3¾in (9.5cm) diam.
**£270–320 / €400–480
$480–570 RTo** 🔨

French paperweight manufacturers

The three best known French manufacturers are Baccarat, St
Louis and Clichy. Perfect examples from these factories can make
four-figure sums although, like all paperweights, the value will
be dependent on date, design and rarity. Both Baccarat and St
Louis used lead glass in their antique paperweights, but Clichy
used a clearer, lighter glass that makes their designs seem more
defined. Baccarat are best known for their mushroom weights,
St Louis for their fruit and vegetable weights and Clichy for
their distinctive Rose weights. Rare examples can go for huge
amounts of money – sometimes five- or six-figure sums.

Baccarat glass paperweight, set with a flower and a floral garland, star cut to base, mid-19thC, 1¾in (4.5cm) diam.
£270–320 / €400–480
$480–570 RTo ➹

Locate the source

The source of each illustration in Miller's can be found by checking the code letters below each caption with the Key to Illustrations, pages 286–290.

Miller's compares...

A. Clichy spaced millefiori glass paperweight, with an assortment of canes, surface damage, c1850, 3in (7.5cm) diam.
£360–430 / €540–640
$640–760 B ➹

B. Baccarat Mushroom double-overlay glass paperweight, cut with windows and printies, with star-cut base, some damage and repair, mid-19thC, 3in (7.5cm) diam.
£900–1,050 / €1,350–1,550
$1,600–1,850 B ➹

While both these paperweights have suffered damage, reducing their value to serious collectors, they are still attractive examples of the high quality of Clichy and Baccarat factories. However, it is the more complicated overlaying and star-cut base of Item B that makes it the more desirable design, and more valuable than Item A which is simpler in construction.

Clichy spaced millefiori glass paperweight, with a central pastrymould cane bordered by two concentric circles and a cane garland, surface damage, c1850, 2½in (6.5cm) diam.
£300–360 / €450–540
$530–640 B ⚒

▶ **St Louis glass paperweight,** set with a nosegay and a cane garland on a muslin ground, 1845–60, 2½in (6.5cm) diam.
£720–800 / €1,050–1,200
$1,250–1,400 SWB ⊞

St Louis glass paperweight, set with a posy of flowers, with honeycomb faceting and eight side printies, slight damage, mid-19thC, 3in (7.5cm) diam.
£500–600 / €750–890
$890–1,050 B ⚒

▶ **St Louis concentric glass paperweight,** with a muslin ground, 1845–60, 2½in (6.5cm) diam.
£850–950 / €1,250–1,400
$1,500–1,700 SWB ⊞

St Louis glass paperweight, set with a double clematis on a latticinio ground, cut with printies and honeycomb faceting, mid-19thC, 2¾in (7cm) diam.
£450–540 / €670–800
$800–960 B ⚒

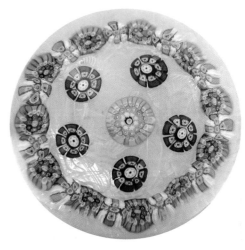

Scent Bottles

Victorian glass perfume bottle, 5½in (14cm) high. This perfume bottle was possibly made by Richardsons of Stourbridge. The small chip to the spire of the stopper will have reduced the price by about 50 per cent, but it could be easily restored by a qualified restorer.
£75–85 / €110–125
$135–150 TASV ⊞

Ruby glass perfume bottle, with gilded decoration, c1860, 5in (12.5cm) high.
£125–140 / €185–210
$220–250 TASV ⊞

Cut-glass scent bottle, with a silver top by William Comyns, 1893, 6¼in (16cm) high. It appears that the release mechanism of the opening top is broken and this may have adversely affected the price.
£180–210 / €270–310
$320–370 G(L) ⚒

Double-ended overlay glass scent bottle, with silver stoppers, c1870, 4½in (11.5cm) high. This is a good quality bottle that still has both its stoppers. Quite often the stoppers are either missing or damaged, which could reduce the value by 25 per cent.
£490–550 / €730–820
$870–970 CoS ⊞

Miniature overlay glass scent bottle, with a silver top, c1840, 1in (2.5cm) high. Miniature scent bottles are worth double the price of standard-sized examples.
£270–300 / €400–450
$480–530 VK ⊞

Thomas Webb & Sons cameo glass scent bottle, with a silver flip top, c1880, 3in (7.5cm) high.
£520–580 / €770–860
$920–1,050 LBr ⊞

Thomas Webb & Sons

Thomas Webb & Sons are renowned for their colourful cameo glass range. In the late 17th century they employed the services of George Woodall, a cameo engraver, and his signature on a piece of work would more than double its value. However, in recent years, items with fake marks have appeared on the market, and although experienced buyers will be able to identify an authentic piece, it is best to seek professional advice if there is any doubt.

Vases

Glass vase, with hand-painted overlay, c1880, 11in (28cm) high. The age of this piece and the hand-painted decoration offer very good value for money. This style of work is currently unfashionable which makes this Victorian piece, with its hand-painted decoration, very good value for money if it is the type of item you like.
£20–24 / € 30–35
$35–40 DuM ⚒

Pair of glass vases, with crenellated rims, each hand-painted with female portraits, c1860, 10in (25.5cm) high.
£160–190
€ 240–280
$280–330 DA ⚒

The Harrachor Glass Co

The Harrachor Glass Co produced a large variety of work. Founded in 1712 in Novy Svet, Bohemia, it employed 500 people and was the first Bohemian works to produce glass on coal furnaces. It was best known for its English-style cut crystal but later produced some monumental pieces of coloured glass around 1840. Its work can occasionally be identified by the presence of its trademark logo, which resembles an aeroplane propeller within a circle.

Josef Rindskopf Grenada glass vase, c1900, 9in (23cm) high. A large quantity of glass manufactured by Loetz, Rindskopf, Kralik and Harrachor was exported to the US where it is of great interest to collectors, probably more so than in the UK.
£110–130
€ 165–195
$195–230 JAA ⚒

▶ **Pair of Mary Gregory vases,** decorated by Mühlhaus, c1895, 8in (20.5cm) high.
£240–280
€ 360–420
$430–500 JAA ⚒

Harrachor glass vase, with enamel decoration, three-feather plume mark, c1900, 4½in (11.5cm) high.
£95–100 / € 140–150
$170–180 JAA ⚒

◀ **Mary Gregory glass vase,** c1910, 6in (15cm) high.
£130–145 / € 195–220
$230–260 GRI ⊞

Mary Gregory

The term Mary Gregory glass is one of the great misnomers of the antiques world. While a decorator called Mary Gregory worked for the American Boston & Sandwich glassworks during the 1880s, the company never produced pieces of the type that now bear her name. The style probably originated in Bohemia around 1870, where it is still produced today. It is distinguished by the presence of a child wearing old fashioned costume, usually depicted playing, and painted in white enamels onto the surface of a coloured glass vessel. Potential buyers should be aware that it can be difficult to distinguish old from recently made examples.

Bohemian cut-glass vase, painted with flowers, early 20thC, 15in (38cm) high. Glass of this standard of cutting and enamelling would be far too expensive to make today.
£260–310 / €390–460
$460–550   DN(BR) ✦

Loetz Marmorierte glass vase, with Carneol finish, c1880, 11½in (29cm) high. It is rare to find marked pieces of Loetz glass, and fake 'Loetz Austria' signatures are known. Much Bohemian Art Nouveau iridescent glass is falsely attributed to Loetz because it produced the best quality examples. Buyers should be aware of wishful attributions.
£260–310 / €390–460
$460–550   JAA ✦

Federzeichnung-style air-trap glass vase, painted with gilt vermicelli, drilled, marked, late 19thC, 8½in (21.5cm) high. Federzeichnung or octopus glass derives its name from the mother-of-pearl glaze 'arms' and the gold-line decorations on the body. It was produced in Bohemia and is currently very popular with American art glass collectors, who will pay up to four-figure sums for good examples. Pieces with bold background decoration and pinched-top vases are particularly popular.
£310–370 / €460–550
$550–650   DN(BR) ✦

Glass epergne, with three supports and hanging baskets, 19thC, 21in (53.5cm) high. Epergnes are prone to damage, and missing parts are difficult to replace.
£420–500 / €630–750
$740–890   E ✦

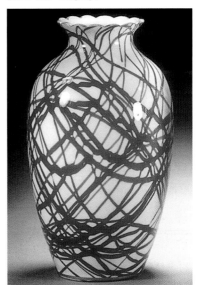

➤ **Glass epergne,** the central flute flanked by three further flutes, with crimped base, late 19thC, 20in (51cm) high.
£460–550 / €690–820
$810–970   E ✦

Pair of opaque glass vases, overlaid with stringing, scalloped rim and foot each highlighted in gold, late 19thC, 10¼in (26cm) high.
£570–680 / €850–1,000
$1,000–1,200   S(O) ✦

Miscellaneous

Glass rolling pin, c1875, 12in (30.5cm) long. This item is reasonably priced. Examples that are colour-splashed or cold-painted with slogans are more sought after, and therefore more expensive.
£100–110 / € 150–165
$175–195 GRI ⊞

Victorian glass and silver-plated table cruet set, comprising six pieces, with etched decoration, 19in (48.5cm) high. It is important that cruet stands are complete and contain matching bottles, as replacements can be very difficult to find. This American cruet set is based on a Continental, rather than British, design.
£75–90 / € 110–130
$135–160 JAA ⚶

The look without the price

James Tassie was an 18th-century modeller whose designs were adopted by Wedgwood. Originally made to imitate the cameos made of shell or hardstone, glass portraits, known as Tassies, can fetch around £200 / € 290 / $350 depending on the subject. Hardstone cameos can be worth four- and five-figure sums, depending on the quality, date and subject.

Glass paste double portrait, inscribed 'Maria F 25 April 1791', mounted in a gilt frame, medallion 2¾in (7cm) high.
£140–165 / € 210–240
$250–290 WW ⚶

C. F. Monroe Wave Crest glass ferner, decorated with flowers, with original insert, c1890, 7in (18cm) diam. Wave Crest was a particular range of white opal glassware, often fitted with metal mounts or insets, produced by C. F. Monroe. Although the company is virtually unknown in Britain, its products are a popular collecting field in America.
£110–130 / € 165–195
$195–230 JAA ⚶

Chrystoleum, after William Strutt, entitled 'Peace', mounted in an ornate frame, 19thC, 6¾ x 9½in (17 x 24cm). Chrystoleum paintings were popular in the late 19th century. They were produced by transferring photographs from the paper on which they were taken onto glass. The artist then painted a picture producing an effect which resembled a painting on ivory. The process required skill rather than artistic talent.
£140–165 / € 210–240
$250–290 SWO ⚶

Cranberry glass model of a boot, with applied crystal decoration, c1900, 4in (10cm) high. Glass novelties such as boots, bellow, hats and walking sticks are known as 'friggars' in Britain and 'whimsies' in America. They have been produced as standard novelties by glassworks across the world for several centuries.
£150–165 / €220–240
$270–290 GRI ⊞

Edwardian rich-cut-glass suite, comprising 33 pieces. This style of suite or service is currently unfashionable, hence the attractive price of this item.
£230–270 / €340–400
$410–480 SWO ⚲

Find out more in

Miller's Collecting Glass: The Facts At Your Fingertips, Miller's Publications, 2000

Pair of glass *bonbonières* and covers, cut and frosted with swags, c1800, 9½in (24cm) high. Cut in the Regency style, these *bonbonières* were not easy to make. Ensuring that the covers fitted was a time-consuming task and cutting each one was a day's work. These pieces would make ideal mantelpiece decorations and are very good value for money.
£270–320 / €400–480
$480–570 DN(Bri) ⚲

► **Glass double-ended telescope,** the gold-plated mounts set with turquoise stones, c1880, 5½in (14cm) long.
£430–480 / €640–720
$760–850 JAS ⚲

► **Bohemian glass comport,** the scalloped rim engraved with a woodland scene, on a faceted stem, c1870, 6¼in (16cm) high.
£300–360
€450–540
$530–640 SWO ⚲

Clocks, Watches & Barometers

Man's enduring fascination with the accurate measurement of time has always meant that those households that could afford one possessed either a clock, or a more humble timepiece, that would regulate their daily routine.

In the 17th and 18th centuries clock making was very much a cottage industry, with the various component parts being made independently of each other. This has given rise to interesting regional variations which can often be the focus of attention for a collector. These early clocks also have a timeless quality. Their rudimentry construction has meant that probably more pieces from this period have survived than from any other. I still find it amazing that an early 18th-century oak longcase clock can be purchased for under £1,000 / €1,500 / $1,800, and a silver pair-cased verge watch can be bought for only £200 / €300 / $350.

During the 19th century general advancements in clock making, as a result of the Industrial Revolution, led to a huge output of clocks with mass-produced movements. However, as with other areas of antiques, a change in what is regarded as fashionable design has led to many of these clocks, together with the more classically and romantically-inspired examples, being less sought after. Consequently I believe that now the opportunities are greater than ever for people to buy attractive well-made clocks at prices of less than those of a few years ago. Look out for good gilt-metal and porcelain panel clocks. These were once the darlings of the saleroom, but now only make three-figure sums.

The French, Americans and Germans made a large quantity of clocks and watches which were exported all over the world. Be aware that the name on the dial of a clock may well only be that of the retailer, not the maker.

Carriage clocks come in all shapes and sizes – the better made and the more complicated the movement, the higher the value. Having said that, standard brass-cased French-movement carriage clocks are making almost exactly what they were 10 years ago, so I can't help feeling that, at the moment, these represent great opportunities for collectors.

Wristwatches have continued to grow in popularity. Good makes and good looks nearly always go hand-in-hand. Rolex, Jaeger le Coultre, Patek Phillipe and other distinguished makes are still commanding a premium. However, there are many fakes on the market, so collectors should be very wary of entering this field before gaining some knowledge of what is genuine and what is not.

As a means of being able to forecast the weather when modes of transport were less watertight and a prevailing wind could spell disaster, barometers played a major part in households throughout the late 18th and 19th centuries. Good Georgian stick barometers are fast becoming beyond the pocket for most of us, but Victorian wheel barometers and their aneroid sucessors are still very affordable and accessible.

As with all categories of antiques, the best advice I can give is buy the best quality whenever possible. This is not an investment tip but I can guarantee that you will derive more pleasure from owning the best rather than the 'also-ran'

Jeremy Sparks

Bracket Clocks

Miller's compares...

A. Edwardian mahogany and brass-inlaid bracket clock, 11in (28cm) high.
£260–310 / €390–460
$460–550 WilP ⚘

B. Inlaid mahogany and brass bracket clock, with striking movement, French, c1900, 9½in (24cm) high.
£420–500 / €630–750
$740–890 WilP ⚘

Item A does not have a striking mechanism and has a relatively plain case, whereas, Item B has a striking movement, attractive marquetry decoration and domed top. All of these combine to make Item B the more pleasing and valuable clock.

Edwardian mahogany and inlaid bracket clock, the enamel dial painted with floral swags, the sides with fretwork grilles, French, 13in (33cm) high. The dial on this clock is in good condition and has very attractive festoon decoration. Although this style of clock is currently unfashionable, at this price it is a good buy.
£470–560 / €700–830
$830–990 SWO ⚘

Mahogany-veneered bracket clock, the enamel dial inscribed 'Scott, Charing Cross', the eight-day movement striking on a bell, with brass handle and ball feet, 19thC, 16in (40.5cm) high. This plain clock is in good, original condition.
£620–740 / €920–1,100
$1,100–1,300 WW ⚘

◀ **Edwardian walnut bracket clock,** the brass dial with cast spandrels and enclosed by a glass door, the German eight-day movement striking on two coils, with ormolu finials, side grilles and scroll feet, 16in (40.5cm) high. Although the good quality walnut case of this bracket clock is highly decorative, it contains a standard movement, making it an affordable piece.
£760–910
€1,150–1,350
$1,350–1,600 DD ⚘

To find out more about antique clocks see the full range of Miller's books at **www.millers.uk.com**

Carriage Clocks

Miller's compares...

A. Brass carriage timepiece, the enamel dial with gilt decoration, with simulated bamboo columns, late 19thC.
£140–165 / €210–240 $250–290 GAK ✗

B. Gilt-brass desk timepiece, with silvered Reamur thermometer and compass within a silvered dial, with lever escapement, movement stamped 'DH', French, c1900, 8¾in (22cm) high.
£600–720 / €890–1,050 $1,050–1,250 B(Kn) ✗

Gilt-brass striking carriage clock, with porcelain chapter ring and bevelled glass panels, French, 19thC, 7in (18cm) high, with leather-covered wood travelling case. A travelling case is an added bonus but does not always increase the value. It can however add up to 30 per cent to the price of a plain clock.
£240–280 / €360–420 $420–500 JAA ✗

Both Items A and B are of a similar date and have attractive brass cases. Item A, however, is a simple timepiece, whereas Item B has visible escapement, a stamped movement and a thermometer and compass facility. These unusual features make it the more desirable of the two clocks and therefore more valuable.

Mignonettes

Miniature carriage clocks, also known as *mignonettes*, were mainly produced in France during the late 19th century. They were not made in huge numbers, the result being that they are now sought after by collectors. Although there are three standard sizes – No. 1 at 1¾in (4.5cm) high, No. 2 at 4in (10cm) high and No. 3 at 4¼in (11cm) high – they often varied according to the maker. The dials of miniature carriage clocks are often unsigned as they are too small to accommodate a signature.

Brass carriage clock, the enamel dial marked 'Benetfink & Co Ltd, London, Made in Paris', late 19thC, 5¼in (13.5cm) high.
£260–310 / €390–460 $460–550 FHF ✗

Edwardian silver miniature carriage clock, by The Goldsmiths & Silversmiths Co, London 1904, 2in (5cm) high. Miniature carriage clocks are always popular with collectors. They often have Continental movements and this can add £150 / €220 / $270 to the price
£290–340 / €430–510 $510–600 GAK ✗

◄ **Silver-plated carriage clock,** the enamel dial with retailer's name 'J. Edmonds', the eight-day two-train movement with lever escapement striking the hours on a gong and with half-hour passing strike, French, late 19thC, 6½in (16.5cm) high, with a leather-covered wood carrying case.
£300–360
€450–540
$530–640 DN ⚚

Brass carriage clock, the porcelain dial above an alarm dial, the movement with silver lever platform escapement, strike, repeat and alarm, decorated with simulated bamboo, repolished, damaged, French, c1900, 7½in (19cm) high, with original travel case. This is a decorative clock but damage to the alarm dial has reduced its value. In good condition it could be worth almost £450 / €670 / $800.
£340–400 / €510–600
$600–710 ROSc ⚚

◄ **Brass *mignonette*,** by Margaine, silvered dial, c1890, 3½in (9cm) high. The hump-backed design of this brass clock is unusual. Margaine is a well-known and collectable carriage clock maker, one of only a few who marked their work, thus making this a desirable and more valuable piece.
£360–400
€540–600
$640–710 BELL ⊞

The look without the price

Brass and glass carriage clock, striking the half-hours and repeating on a gong, worn, c1890, 5½in (14cm) high.
£480–570 / €720–850
$850–1,000 GAK ⚚

This clock is in good condition, although the gilding is worn. If regilded it could be worth £650–700 / €970–1,050 / $1,150–1,250. When purchasing an item, the cost of repair should always be taken into account.

Gilt-brass carriage clock, the enamel dial with subsidiary alarm dial, the repeating movement with later club–tooth lever escapement, striking on a bell, French, c1850, 5¼in (13.5cm) high. This decorative piece has the extra features of alarm and repeat functions, which increases its appeal to collectors.
£500–600 / €750–890
$890–1,050 S(O) ⚚

Brass carriage clock, the enamel dial with foliate-engraved mask, the repeating movement with ratchet-tooth lever platform escapement and striking on a gong, French, c1880, 6½in (16.5cm) high, with a travelling case.
£540–640 / €800–950
$960–1,150 S(O) ⚒

Find out more in

Miller's Clocks Antiques Checklist,
Miller's Publications, 2001

Gilt-brass carriage clock, the enamel dial within a gilt surround, the movement with ratchet-tooth lever escapement, striking and repeating on a gong, French, c1895, 6¾in (17cm) high, with a leather-covered travelling case. A repeater is a very desirable feature on a carriage clock, and such examples always fetch higher prices.
£580–690 / €870–1,050
$1,050–1,200 S(O) ⚒

▶ **Lacquered-brass electric timepiece,** the brass dial with enamel chapter ring, engraved 'Eureka 1000 Day Motion', the chromium-plated English movement with oversize balance wheel to battery cavity, marked 'ACME', French, early 20thC, 14½in (37cm) high. Electric clocks have become more popular recently. They are widely available but interesting, quirky examples such as this are more attractive to collectors.
£640–760 / €950–1,150
$1,150–1,350 B(Kn) ⚒

Brass carriage timepiece, the enamel dial with subsidiary alarm dial, the movement with cylinder platform escapement, quarter-repeating on two bells, the backplate stamped 'V. R.', in a corniche case, French, c1870, 5¾in (14.5cm) high. The alarm on this clock has added to its value.
£600–720 / €890–1,050
$1,050–1,250 S(O) ⚒

◀ **Brass carriage timepiece,** with a silvered dial, the lever escapement with countersunk balance, the case engraved with flowers and leaf scrolls, with acorn finials, mid-19thC, 5in (12.5cm) high. This simple timepiece has an attractively engraved case which adds greatly to its appeal and therefore its value.
£640–760 / €950–1,150
$1,150–1,350 G(L) ⚒

Mantel Clocks

The look without the price

This clock has a simple movement in a good-quality plain case, and would not be out of place in a modern interior. Mantel clocks with more elaborately decorated cases can be worth twice this price.

Edwardian mahogany balloon clock, with an enamel dial and single-barrel movement, inlaid sycamore decoration, 8¼in (21cm) high.
£65–75 / €95–110
$115–135   AMB ✎

The look without the price

Gilt-metal French-style Trianon clock, by Ansonia, with later paper dial, American, c1900, 14½in (37cm) high.
£125–150 / €185–220
$220–270   ROSc ✎

This ornate mantel clock is an American copy of a French design and has a gilt-metal case. If it were an original French clock with an ormolu case its value would be three times this amount.

▶ **Pine mantel clock,** by E. Ingraham & Co, the eight-day movement with strike and alarm, the grained gesso door with gilt trim, American, c1880, 13in (33cm) high. At first sight this American clock appears to be of German origin. It is an example of how European and American companies copied each other in their attempts to remain competitive.
£130–155 / €195–230
$230–270   ROSc ✎

Painted cottage mantel timepiece, by Henry Sperry & Co, dial signed, American, c1855, 11in (28cm) high. This style of clock is still popular with the American market. The mass-produced movement, 'cottage' styling and later date have made this item less desirable in the UK, where prices have remained stable for the last 10 years.
£125–150 / €185–220
$220–270   ROSc ✎

Find out more in

Miller's Clocks & Barometers Buyer's Guide, Miller's Publications, 2003

Victorian slate mantel clock, with a painted ceramic dial and frieze, the French movement striking on a gong, 14in (35.5cm) high. This clock has a very attractive and unusual dial, which is possibly the reason for it achieving twice its estimated value at auction.
£190–220 / €280–330
$340–390 G(L) 🔨

Cast-brass mantel clock, with an eight-day striking movement, the case surmounted by an urn, with two handles and cast feet, Continental, early 20thC, 16in (40.5cm) high.
£175–210 / €260–310
$310–370 L&E 🔨

Mahogany mantel clock, the eight-day movement striking on a bell, with turned pilasters surmounted by acorn finials, French, c1890, 13¾in (35cm) high. This good-quality clock has a decorative case and would appeal to collectors.
£165–195 / €240–290
$290–350 AMB 🔨

Brass novelty mantel timepiece, modelled as a lifebelt with crossed oars and rudder stand, early 20thC, 12¼in (31cm) high. Novelty clocks are not uncommon, but they are a strong collecting area.
£220–260 / €330–390
$390–460 DN(EH) 🔨

The look without the price

Spelter and onyx mantel garniture, with ivorine dial and movement, with outside countwheel striking on a bell, sidepieces associated, French, c1900, clock 22in (56cm) high.
£250–300 / €370–440
$450–530 B(Kn) 🔨

Garnitures are not currently fashionable but this spelter example would be of more interest if it were made of bronze. The associated sidepieces are so similar to the clock that they will not have made a great difference to the overall price. This garniture is affordable and good value for money.

Marble mantel clock, French, c1870, 17¾in (45cm) wide. The large, plain design of this mantel clock is popular at the moment. It was probably made with side pieces that have since been lost.
£270–320 / €400–480
$480–570 SWO 🔨

Miller's compares...

A. Gilt-metal and porcelain-mounted mantel clock, the dial painted with a windmill scene with gilt highlights, the movement striking on a bell and stamped 'Japy Frères & Co', case stamped 'P. H. Mourey 79', under a glass dome, French, late 19thC, 15¼in (38.5cm) high.
£250–300 / €370–440
$450–530 B(Kn) 🔨

B. Gilt-metal and porcelain mantel clock, the dial signed 'Carter, Salisbury' and flanked by two urns, the movement with outside countwheel and striking on a bell, the pediment surmounted by two lovebirds, under a glass dome, French, late 19thC, 15in (38cm) high.
£580–690 / €860–1,000
$1,050–1,200 Bea 🔨

Both Item A and Item B are porcelain-mounted gilt-metal clocks of a similar date. However, Item B has finer decoration and the porcelain panels are of much better quality, which is why it sold for over twice the price of Item A.

Paris porcelain mantel clock and stand, with a drum dial, the rococo-style case applied with flowers and painted with floral panels, minor damage, dial glass missing, c1860, 16in (40.5cm) high. The ornate style of this clock is not to modern tastes and its condition will have detracted from the price. When purchasing clocks such as this it is very important to note the condition of the porcelain case, as damage can be costly to repair.
£300–360 / €450–540
$530–640 S(O) 🔨

Gilt-metal and porcelain-mounted mantel clock, the dial with gilt hands and a floral painted panel, the movement striking on a gong, French, late 19thC, 20½in (52cm) high. Finer examples of clocks of this type were made in ormolu, but in smaller numbers. Such examples are more desirable and therefore more valuable. However, this clock is very affordable and would still be attractive in the home.
£300–360 / €450–540
$530–640 B(Kn) 🔨

Champlevé-enamelled mantel clock, with a brass dial stamped 'Vincenti et Cie', the movement striking on a gong, on an ogee pediment with brass finials, French, 19thC, 11in (28cm) high. The ornate and decoratively enamelled case of this clock has increased its value.
£320–380 / €480–570 $570–670 G(L) 🔨

Gilt-brass mantel clock, with a painted enamel dial, the eight-day movement striking on a bell, with presentation inscription, French, late 19thC, 14in (35.5cm) high. Although this clock is attractive the style is currently unfashionable. It is a very good buy at this affordable price – if you like the look.
£340–400 / €510–600 $600–710 B(Kn) 🔨

Early Victorian burr-walnut mantel clock, the enamel dial and twin-train movement striking on a gong, 15in (38cm) high. Walnut is an attractive and desirable wood and this is a good-quality clock. However, there appears to be a small fault in the moulding and this would account for the rather low price of this item.
£350–420 / €520–630 $620–740 SWO 🔨

Miller's compares...

A. Gilt-spelter and marble figural mantel clock, with a floral painted dial, the brass twin-train drum movement striking on a bell, with pendulum, the pedestal case surmounted by Fortune and Cupid, entitled 'La Fortine Guidant L'Amour', French, late 19thC, 27½in (70cm) high.
£350–420 / €520–630 $620–740 B(Kn) 🔨

B. Ormolu mantel clock, with enamel dial, the movement with outside countwheel striking on a bell, the case surmounted by a reclining classical figure, French, late 19thC, 17½in (44.5cm) high.
£800–960 / €1,200–1,400 $1,400–1,650 B 🔨

Item A is a very large mantel clock made of spelter. Item B, however, is a finer and more elegant piece and is also made of ormolu, which makes it a better quality piece and therefore the more valuable of the two clocks.

Alabaster and gilt-metal-mounted mantel clock, the dial with incised numerals, the case with simulated lapis lazuli medallions, on a wooden stand, under a glass dome, French, late 19thC, 13½in (34.5cm) high. Alabaster is a very soft stone and therefore prone to damage. The use of a glass dome helps to keep the clock in good condition.
£370–440 / €550–660 $650–780 FHF 🔨

Marble and bronze-mounted Egyptian-style mantel clock, the marble dial signed 'Thos. Dixon, Norwich', the movement with Brocot escapement and striking on a bell, the case surmounted by a sphinx and flanked by Egyptian figures, with a presentation plaque, French, c1880, 15¼in (38.5cm) high. Clocks were often made with Egyptian-style decoration and are therefore widely available. This item appears to have a foot missing, which also will have detracted from its value. Egyptian style is currently a fashionable trend with the French market.

€400–480 / €600–720
$710–850 S(O) 🔨

Empire-style rosewood and marquetry mantel clock, the silvered dial with cast-gilt-metal surround, the movement with count-wheel, striking on a bell and with gridiron pendulum, French, 19thC, 22½in (57cm) high. This clock has attractive marquetry inlay which adds to its appeal – marquetry is always a desirable feature in clocks.

€520–620 / €770–920
$920–1,100 G(L) 🔨

Miller's compares...

A. Rosewood portico mantel clock, the silvered dial with cast-gilt surround, the movement with outside countwheel striking on a bell, gridiron pendulum and decorative bob, the case with a moulded cornice supported by turned columns, French, c1840, 20¾in (52.5cm) high.
£480–570 / €720–850
$850–1,000 S(O) 🔨

B. Marble and ormolu portico mantel clock, the annular enamel dial with milled bezel and engine-turned centre, the Vincenti et Cie movement signed 'Roblin à Paris', with early Brocot escapement, associated sunmask pendulum and striking on a bell, French, c1840, 20in (51cm) high.
£840–1,000
€1,250–1,500
$1,500–1,750 S(O) 🔨

Item A is made of rosewood, which although a good quality wood, is not as desirable as the black marble and ormolu of Item B, which is also a better quality clock than item A. It is these factors that have enabled Item B to sell for nearly twice the price of Item A.

▶ **Brass mantel clock,** retailed by Bennett & Co, with mercury pendulum and glass sides, French, c1880, 10½in (26.5cm) high. Mercury pendulums are very accurate and are a sign of a good quality clock. Always check for movement in the mercury as *faux* mercury was also used.
£530–630
€790–940
$940–1,100 GAK 🔨

Gilt-brass and *champlevé* enamel mantel clock garniture, with a gilt dial, the movement striking on a gong, the case decorated with floral panels and flanked by columns, French, c1900, clock 11¾in (30cm) high. This is a good quality clock garniture. However, garnitures have fallen from fashion and this has adversely affected prices. A year ago this item could have sold for £800–1,200 / €1,200–1,800 / $1,400–2,100, so now is a good time to buy if you like this style.
£550–660 / €820–980
$970–1,150 S(O) ♪

▶ **Gilt-brass and *champlevé* enamel mantel clock,** with enamel dial, mercury pendulum and eight-day striking movement, the case with Corinthian columns, under a glass dome, French, 19thC, 16in (40.5cm) high. The good quality craftsmanship, generous size and mercury pendulum all make this item a desirable collector's piece.
£600–720
€890–1,050
$1,050–1,250
SWO ♪

The look without the price

Empire-style gilt-brass-mounted mahogany table clock, the enamel dial signed 'Pearce & Sons', the plated movement with Brocot escapement, sun mask pendulum and striking on a gong, French, c1900, 15½in (39.5cm) high.
£720–860 / €1,050–1,250
$1,250–1,500 S(O) ♪

This good quality clock has a fine mahogany case. However, had it actually been made during the French Empire period (1799–1815) this clock could be worth twice this amount.

Louis XV-style tulipwood mantel clock, with a porcelain dial, the two-train spring-driven movement striking the half-hour on gongs, stamped 'G. Megnin', the case with marquetry floral bouquets, French, early 20thC, 16¾in (42.5cm) high. This clock is a typical French style and shape with a simple movement. Its value lies in the elegant marquetry and brass mounts of the case.
£660–790 / €980–1,150
$1,150–1,350 PFK ♪

▶ **Louis XIV-style boulle and gilt-metal-mounted table clock,** the brass dial with two blind winding holes and porcelain numerals, the replacement English single-train fusee movement with anchor escapement, damaged, French, late 19thC, 32¼in (82cm) high. This decorative French clock could be worth at least £1,500 / €2,200 / $2,650 if it still had its original movement and the case was in perfect condition.
£720–860 / €1,050–1,250
$1,250–1,500 DN ♪

Wall Clocks

Oak wall timepiece, by Seth Thomas Clock Co, with a painted dial, the eight-day No. 10 double-spring movement with lever escapement, American, c1924, 14¾in (37.5cm) high. Clocks by this well-known maker are very popular with the American market. It is generally true to say that collectors prefer to buy items that were made in their own country.
£125–150 / €185–220
$220–260 ROSc ⚒

Late Victorian mahogany drop-dial wall clock, by J. Sewell, West Bromwich, the painted dial with traces of inscription, damaged, 21¼in (54cm) high.
£240–280
€360–420
$420–500 PFK ⚒

▶ **Carved walnut wall clock,** by Thompson & Vine, London, with an enamel dial, the eight-day single-train fusee movement with anchor escapement, late 19thC, 17¾in (45cm) high. The good quality carving on this piece has added to its value.
£380–450
€570–670
$670–800 DN ⚒

William IV rosewood drop-dial timepiece, with a single fusee movement, 22in (56cm) high.
£260–310 / €390–460
$460–550 G(L) ⚒

Mahogany wall clock, the dial inscribed 'A. Miles, Stockwell', with a single fusee movement, 19thC, dial 11¾in (30cm) diam. This clock has attractive mother-of-pearl decoration and original hands which add to its desirability.
£290–340 / €430–510
$510–600 SWO ⚒

Locate the source

The source of each illustration in Miller's can be found by checking the code letters below each caption with the Key to Illustrations, pages 286–290.

◀ **Regency mahogany drop-dial wall clock,** the painted dial signed 'Sm'l Firderen, Birmingham', with a twin fusee movement, 24in (61cm) high.
£390–460
€580–690
$690–810 G(L) ⚒

Miller's compares...

A. Mahogany drop-dial wall clock, the enamel dial inscribed 'David Thomas, 6 Castle St, Swansea', with a single fusee movement, late 19thC, dial 12in (30.5cm) diam.
£400–480 / €600–720 $710–850 PF ✎

B. Mahogany wall timepiece, with an enamel dial, the single fusee movement inscribed 'Frodsham, Gracechurch Street, London', 14¾in (37.5cm) diam.
£700–840 / €1,050–1,250 $1,250–1,500 WW ✎

Item A bears the name 'David Thomas' which may be the name of the retailer, rather than the maker. Item B has the name of a well-known maker, Frodsham of London. The fact that Item B can be attributed to a manufacturer of quality clocks is the reason it sold for nearly twice as much as Item A.

Gilt-stucco and giltwood wall clock, the alabaster dial with enamel cartouche numerals and steel hands, the movement with anchor escapement, with countwheel and striking on a gong, the case with ebonized surround and boulle-inlaid panels, French, c1870, 36¼in (92cm) high. The ornate rococo style of this clock appeals more to Continental and American collectors than it does to those in the UK.
£480–570 / €720–850 $850–1,000 S(Am) ✎

◀ **Ebonized regulator wall timepiece,** the enamel dial with steel hands, the spring-driven movement with anchor escapement, Austrian, mid-19thC, 21¼in (54cm) high. Ebonized clocks are more popular on the Continent than in the UK. If this clock had been made of walnut it could have been worth a further £200 / €300 / $350 on the UK market.
£670–800 / €1,000–1,200 $1,200–1,400 S(Am) ✎

Mahogany wall timepiece, the repainted dial inscribed 'Thwaites & Reed, Clerkenwell', the fusee movement with anchor escapement, c1890, 14¾in (37.5cm) diam. This clock has a well-made and attractive frame that is popular with collectors. This has added to its value.
£570–680 / €850–1,000 $1,000–1,200 S(O) ✎

▶ **Late Victorian mahogany and brass-inlaid drop-dial wall timepiece,** the enamelled dial inscribed 'J. D. Grant, Broad St, Ilfracombe', the eight-day single-train fusee movement with anchor escapement, slight damage, 20¾in (52.5cm) high. The brass inlay on this item is an attractive feature collectors will look for.
£700–840 / €1,050–1,250 $1,250–1,500 DN ✎

Miscellaneous

Miller's compares...

Victorian brass skeleton timepiece, with a pierced silvered dial and a single fusee movement, on a marble base, under a glass dome, 15in (38cm) high. The good condition and complexity of this clock make it desirable and have increased its value. Skeleton clocks vary in quality, so do be sure to check the plates and the frame, and avoid any clocks that are thin or not well finished. Better quality clocks have five or six spokes on the wheels, and the best dials are of silvered brass with black numerals.
**£600–720 / €890–1,050
$1,050–1,250 G(L) ➚**

A. Glass and gilt-brass strut clock, with a lever movement and easel back, late 19thC, 6¼in (16cm) high.
**£260–310 / €390–460
$460–550 NSal ➚**

B. Gilt-brass strut timepiece, in the style of Thomas Cole, the silvered dial signed for Mackay Cunningham & Co, the lever fusee watch movement signed 'E. Gosheron', c1850, 6in (15cm) high.
**£720–860 / €1,050–1,300
$1,250–1,500 S ➚**

Item A has the advantage of being a striking clock whereas Item B is a timepiece. However, Item B is a desirable and good quality timepiece made in the style of Thomas Cole, who was a well-known maker. This accounts for Item B achieving almost three times more than Item A.

The look without the price

Brass lantern clock, the dial with a foliate-engraved centre and signed 'Dent No. 60486, 61 Strand, London', the signed and numbered fusee movement with anchor escapement and striking on the hour, the case with pierced foliate frets and top-mounted bell, late 19thC, 15¼in (38.5cm) high.
**£660–790 / €980–1,150
$1,150–1,350 S(O) ➚**

Dating from the late 16th century, lantern clocks are the oldest domestic English clock and have also been the most vulnerable to alteration and repair. It is therefore advisable to ascertain the age of a clock before buying by checking the movement. If this particular example were a genuine 17th-century lantern clock it could be worth £1,000–1,500 / €1,500–2,250 / $1,800–2,700.

Pocket Watches

Gunmetal pocket watch, the enamelled dial plate with gilt numerals, marked, Swiss, 19thC, 2¾in (7cm) high.
£30–35 / €45–50
$55–60 JAA ⚒

Silver cased watch, the porcelain dial decorated with a locomotive and engraved 'Remontoir', minor damage, Swiss, c1870, 3¾in (9.5cm) diam. This watch will appeal to collectors of both watches and railwayana, making it a very desirable and valuable item.
£110–130 / €165–195
$195–230 JAA ⚒

Miller's compares...

A. 18ct gold half-hunter-cased keyless lever watch, the enamel dial with pink enamel chapter ring, the bar movement with wolf's-tooth winding to a cut and compensated bimetallic balance, with associated bar brooch, Swiss, late 19thC, 1¼in (3cm) diam.
£100–120 / €150–180
$175–210 B(Kn) ⚒

B. 18ct gold half-hunter-cased pocket watch, by Patek Philippe, the enamel dial with floral centre, with a frosted gilt movement, the polished case with enamel-set monogram to the rear and enamel-set chapter ring to the front, late 19thC, 1¼in (3cm) diam, with associated chain.
£460–550 / €690–820
$810–970 B(Kn) ⚒

Item A is an attractive gold watch by an unknown maker that has an associated gold bow brooch of a later date. Item B is the more desirable and valuable because it was made by the renowned and sought-after watch-maker Patek Philippe, and although the rope-link chain is associated, it is of a contemporary date. These factors contributed to Item B achieving over four times more than Item A at auction.

◄ **Silver keyless lever chronograph,** the enamel dial with outer dial inscribed 'Miles per hour from ¼ mile distances', the movement numbered, early 20thC, 2in (5cm) diam. The simplicity of design and clarity of the dial make this watch an appealing item.
£150–180 / €220–270
$270–320 B(Kn) ⚒

► **Silver keyless pocket chronograph,** by Omega, with an enamel dial, 1909.
£160–190 / €240–280
$280–330 G(L) ⚒

18ct gold hand-wound mechanical fob watch, the enamel dial with gold 'jewelling' and enamel decoration, c1890, 2in (5cm) diam. The ornate decoration on this watch has added to its value.
£180–200 / €270–300
$320–350 Bns ⊞

Silver key-wind half-hunter-cased pocket watch, the porcelain dial with subsidiary seconds dial, movement signed 'Haas Puivat & Co, Genève' and numbered '38002', Swiss, c1890, 2in (5cm) diam.
£180–200 / €270–300
$320–350 Bns ⊞

Miller's compares...

A. Silver and tortoiseshell open-faced key-wind pocket watch, by Bevington, Stourbridge, bezel damaged, movement signed, London 1827, 2in (5cm) diam, with a fitted leather case.
£180–210 / €270–310
$320–370 L 🔨

B. Silver and tortoiseshell triple-cased verge watch, the dial signed for Markwick, Markham and Perigal, the movement signed for Marcm. Borrell, maker's mark 'RO', London 1750, 2¼in (5.5cm) diam.
£450–540 / €670–800
$800–960 B(Kn) 🔨

Item A has the more unusual Roman numerals but it has also been damaged. Tortoiseshell is brittle and can be cleaned but not easily repaired. Minor cracks to tortoiseshell cases are acceptable, but major restoration is expensive. Item B is older and has a desirable triple case, it also has an unusual dial with Arabic numerals and fancy pillars, which help to date it. Item B is rarer and more desirable than Item A, which helped it to achieve a much higher price at auction.

▶ **18ct gold cylinder pocket watch,** with an engraved gilt dial, the gilt three-quarter keywind movement with going barrel, engraved cock with polished-steel regulator and three-arm gilt balance with blue steel spiral hairspring, Swiss, late 19thC, 1½in (4cm) diam. Swiss, French and American ladies' watches are highly sought after.
£210–240 / €310–360
$370–420 PT ⊞

◀ **Silver pair-cased pocket watch,** by Thomas and Richard Carpenter, London, with an enamel dial and gilt verge movement signed 'George Philpot, Maidstone', with a silver chain and key, early 19thC, 2in (5cm) diam. Pair-cased watches are unusual and of interest to collectors. Unfortunately the dial of this watch appears to be damaged. In perfect condition this item could possibly sell for £250 / €370 / $440.
£180–210 / €270–310
$320–370 WW 🔨

Miller's compares...

Silver pair-cased verge pocket watch, by W. Roberts, Long Marton, c1825, 1in (2.5cm) diam. This watch is in good condition and was a good buy at auction.
£240–270 / €360–400
$420–480 TIC ⊞

A. Gold and enamel pocket watch, chain and key, with a silvered dial and gilt movement, late 19thC, 1in (2.5cm) diam.
£200–240 / €300–360
$350–420 B(Kn) ⚒

B. Gold and enamel cylinder watch, the silvered dial with gold hands, with a gilt movement, decorated with birds of paradise, signed 'Breguet', c1830, 1½in (4cm) diam.
£360–430 / €540–640
$640–760 S(O) ⚒

Both Item A and Item B are watches from the same period with enamel decoration. The maker of Item A is unknown, but Item B is attributed to Breguet. Most Breguet timepieces were signed in two places to avoid fakes, but this example has only been signed once, making its origins doubtful. Had Item B definitely been made by Breguet its value could have been £8,000–10,000 / €11,900–14,900 / $14,200–17,700. However, the decoration of Item B is of superior quality to that of Item A, making it more desirable and therefore the more valuable watch.

Verge watches

The verge escapement was used from the early 16th century until the first half of the 19th century, when it was gradually replaced by the lever (the verge is rarely found on watches produced after 1850). It is also known as 'crown-wheel escapement' because the escape wheel, with its 11 or 13 teeth, looks like a crown. Although it was a durable and reliable mechanism, it was not particularly accurate and needed constant power provided by a vulnerable fusee chain.

◄ **18ct gold half-hunter pocket watch,** early 20thC, 2in (5cm) diam. Half-hunter watches are currently more popular than full-hunter watches and consequently achieve higher prices. This good quality watch is in excellent condition.
£240–280
€360–420
$420–500 L&E ⚒

Nickel alarm pocket watch, the enamel dial with fluorescent numbers and skeleton hands, the three-quarter plate lever movement with compensated balance, early 20thC, 2in (5cm) high. The case has a hinged back, allowing it to be used as a bedside alarm clock. This interesting feature increases its appeal to collectors and adds value.
£250–280 / €370–420
$440–500 FOF ⊞

Silver pair-cased pocket watch, the enamelled dial with gilt hands, the gilt verge movement inscribed 'Willm Preston, Lancaster', maker 'VR', Chester 1800, 3in (7.5cm) high. When buying, be aware that watch cases should fit well and pair cases should be hallmarked with matching dates and maker's initials.
**£250–300 / €370–440
$440–530 WW** 🔨

Silver repoussé pair-cased verge watch, by J. Bannister, Wrexham, with enamel dial, gilt movement with lace-edged cock and cock-foot over baluster pillars, signed and numbered, the outer case depicting four classical figures, hallmarked 'TB', London 1755, 2in (5cm) diam. The Victorians often took early plain-cased watches and added fashionable decoration, but unfortunately this detracts from the original value. This watch possibly has later decoration which may account for the low price achieved at auction.
**£250–300 / €370–440
$440–530 B(Kn)** 🔨

14ct gold chronograph pocket watch, 1930s, 2in (5cm) diam.
**£260–290 / €390–430
$460–510 TIC** ⊞

Silver pocket watch, by Charles Frodsham, the enamelled dial with subsidiary seconds and single hand, signed, the movement numbered and inscribed 'Gold Medal of Honour. Paris 1855', Chester 1887, dial 2in (5cm) diam, ¾oz. Watches made by Charles Frodsham are very desirable. If it had been by another maker, this watch may only have been worth about £100–150 / €150–220 / $175–270 less.
**£260–310 / €390–460
$460–550 WW** 🔨

14ct gold-filled open-faced Waltham pocket watch, the porcelain dial with subsidiary seconds, with a gilt-frosted keyless movement, the case engraved with a stag and floral decoration, American, c1893. This piece is by a well-known American maker and is in good condition. It would, however, be of greater appeal and achieve a higher price if it were sold on the American market.
**£350–390 / €520–580
$620–690 Bns** ⊞

Silver pocket watch, by Thomas Carpenter, the enamel dial decorated with a hunter and his dog by a river, the fusee movement numbered and signed 'Fleming, London', London 1804, 2¼in (5.5cm) diam. Painted dials are keenly sought after and attractive scenes can increase value. If this watch had a verge movement it could be worth £100–150 / €150–220 / $175–270 more.
**£320–380 / €480–570
$570–670 WW** 🔨

Find out more in

*Miller's Watches:
A Collector's Guide,*
Miller's Publications,
1999

18ct gold keyless lever dress watch, by Paul Ditisheim, the silvered dial with Breguet numerals and subsidiary seconds, nickel lever movement, bimetallic compensation balance, five adjustments and precision regulator, with a twist-link white gold chain, signed, Swiss, Solvil, c1910, 1¾in (4.5cm) diam. The twist-link chain and Breguet numerals are attractive to buyers and have added value to this watch.
**£360–430 / €540–640
$640–760 S(O)**

18ct gold open-faced lever pocket watch, the gilt dial with applied numerals and floral and turquoise-set border, with a gilt fusee movement and engine-turned case, signed 'Clerke, Royal Exchange No. 7407', 1820, 1¾in (4.5cm) diam. The early lever movement in this item appeals to collectors and although the glass appears to be damaged, this has not affected the auction price.
**£460–550 / €690–820
$810–970 TEN**

Rolex silver and enamel travelling watch, with a two-tone silvered dial, nickel lever movement, bimetallic compensation balance, timed to six positions and all climates, Glasgow 1928, 1¼in (3cm) diam. There is always demand from collectors for items such as this unusual novelty watch by the well-known maker Rolex.
**£360–430 / €540–640
$640–760 S(O)**

Silver repoussé pair-cased watch, with an enamel dial, the gilt full plate verge movement with pierced and engraved balance bridge, square baluster pillars and fusee, with associated outer case, signed, London 1741, 2¼in (5.5cm) diam. This watch has an ill-fitting and worn outer case which will have detracted from the price.
**£480–580 / €720–860
$850–1,050 S(O)**

Gold repeating watch, by Jean Baptiste Baillon, the swing-out movement with quarter repeat, chipped, crystal missing, marked, French, mid-18thC, 2¾in (7cm) high. The damage to this watch has detracted from its value, especially as it could be costly to repair.
**£420–500 / €630–750
$740–890 JAA**

Silver repoussé pair-cased watch, by Samson, the dial painted with a scene of a maiden bidding farewell to an English ship, the full plate verge movement with a steel three-arm balance, pierced and engraved balance cock, the outer case depicting a classical scene, silver key, with later hands, marked, London 1797, 2in (5cm) diam. The quality of painting will determine the value of a dial. Minor flaws are acceptable, but only badly damaged painted decoration should be restored. The replacement of the original hands has devalued this watch by around £100 / €150 / $175.
**£500–600 / €750–890
$890–1,050 TEN**

18ct gold keyless lever watch, by Patek Philippe, with an enamel dial, wolf's-tooth winding and moustache lever, the case with engraved monogram, PPCo stamp, signed, Swiss, mid-19thC, 1¾in (4.5cm) diam. This rare watch is by a well-renowned maker and its unusual movement has added to its value.
**£520–620 / €770–920
$920–1,100 B(Kn)** 🔨

Silver keyless lever watch, by Cervine, the silvered dial with Masonic symbols and signature, the nickel lever movement with 17 jewels and monometallic compensation balance, Swiss, c1930, 2in (5cm) high. Masonic watches of this type were made from c1900 to 1940. Masonic items continue to be popular with collectors, which adds to their value.
**£720–860 / €1,050–1,300
$1,250–1,500 S(O)** 🔨

Silvered and tortoiseshell verge watch, with a polychrome enamel dial depicting a soldier and a lady, full plate gilt fusee movement, damaged, German, c1790, 2¾in (7cm) diam. This piece would appeal to collectors of both watches and tortoiseshell items, and this has added to its value.
**£750–830 / €1,100–1,250
$1,300–1,450 PT** ⊞

Gold and enamel cylinder watch, the engine-turned silver dial with subsidiary seconds and gold Breguet hands, the keywind gilt Lepine calibre movement with suspended going barrel, blue steel regulator, three-arm gilt balance with blue steel spiral hairspring, cylinder and escape wheel, with clip, Swiss, c1830, 1¼in (3cm) diam.
**£770–860 / €1,150–1,300
$1,350–1,500 PT** ⊞

Gold and enamel consular-cased verge watch, by Julien Le Roy, with a later enamel dial, the full plate gilt verge movement with steel three-arm balance, pierced and engraved balance cock, faceted baluster pillars, the case decorated with flowers, French, Paris, c1755, 1¾in (4.5cm) diam. This decorative watch by a well-known maker has the added benefit of a rare adjustable movement, which accounts for its value. This is a very desirable piece.
**£780–940 / €1,100–1,400
$1,400–1,650 S(O)** 🔨

Enamel-set cylinder pocket watch, the enamel dial with Turkish hour markers, with a gilt movement, mid-19thC, 1½in (4cm) diam. The enamel decoration on this watch appears to be damaged and this will have detracted from its value. Good condition is vital, as the original decorative techniques are often difficult and expensive to restore.
**£820–980 / €1,200–1,450
$1,450–1,700 B(Kn)** 🔨

> To find out more about antique pocket watches see the full range of Miller's books at **www.millers.uk.com**

Wristwatches

18ct gold wristwatch, with an enamelled bezel, Glasgow 1912, 1in (2.5cm) diam. The unusual Glasgow hallmark on this enamel-decorated watch makes it more collectable and therefore adds to its value.
£120–140 / €180–210
$210–250 SWO 🔨

Miller's compares...

A. Jaeger-LeCoultre chrome-plated wristwatch, with manual wind movement, case worn, Swiss, 1940s, 1¼in (3cm) diam.
£160–190 / €240–290
$290–340 FHF 🔨

B. Jaeger-LeCoultre gold-plated alarm wristwatch, the silvered dial with seconds and rotating alarm ring, the 17 jewel movement with steel dust cover, Swiss, 1940s, 1¼in (3cm) diam.
£400–480 / €600–720
$710–850 B(Kn) 🔨

Although both Items A and B are by the same maker and were manufactured during the same period, Item A is chrome plated. Item B is is a superior quality watch and is gold plated. This accounts for Item B having sold for twice as much as Item A.

Officer's watch, the enamel dial with subsidiary seconds dial, inset with a compass, the case inscribed 'Frank from Sadie August 3rd 1915', 1914–15, 1in (2.5cm) diam. Military watches are a popular collecting niche. The unusual shape of this watch makes it a sought-after and desirable item.
£220–260 / €330–390
$390–460 CHTR 🔨

Omega stainless steel wristwatch, the two-tone dial with raised gold batons and centre sweep seconds, marked and signed, 1937, 1¼in (3cm) diam, with original strap and box. The value of this quality wristwatch has been increased by the presence of the original strap and box.
£300–340 / €450–510
$530–600 FOF ⊞

Rolex

Rolex was established in Geneva in 1908 and gained a worldwide reputation that it still enjoys today. This reputation is in part due to its limited production range which is sold through selected retailers at tightly controlled prices. The company is also famous for its innovations such as the first waterproof watch, the 'Oyster', which appeared in 1926, and other now highly collectable watches such as 'GMT', 'Prince' and 'President', as well as bubble-back watches.

Rolex stainless steel Oyster Speedking Precision wristwatch, the silvered dial with subsidiary seconds, Swiss, c1950, 1¼in (3cm) diam. This wristwatch has an associated bracelet, and this has reduced its value. With its original Rolex bracelet it could be worth around £100 / €150 / $175 more.
£350–420 / €520–630 $620–740 TEN ✦

Omega stainless steel and aluminium British Air Military issue wristwatch, case inscribed '6B/159 A11902', Swiss, c1943, 1¼in (3cm) diam. Pilots' watches are particularly sought after by collectors of military watches.
£360–420 / €540–600 $640–710 Bns ⊞

◄ **Longines steel military wristwatch,** with rotation bezel and adjustable stop ratchet, Swiss, 1940s, 1¼in (3cm) diam. This item has an unusual dial and is by a good maker. These factors have increased its desirability and value.
£420–500 / €630–750 $740–890 FHF ✦

◄ **Rolex steel Oyster wristwatch,** with subsidiary seconds dial, Swiss, 1930s, 1¼in (3cm) diam. Oyster watches are one of the most collectable series of Rolex designs and early examples are particularly sought after. Rolex watches should never be bought from an unknown source. The company keeps detailed records of all watches, including stolen ones, so it is advisable to check before purchase.
£610–730 / €910–1,100 $1,100–1,300 G(L) ✦

Darly 18ct gold wristwatch and bracelet, with gilt dial, Continental, 1950s, 6¼in (16cm) long. The price of this attractive watch is attributable to its high gold content.
£530–630 / €790–950 $940–1,100 FHF ✦

▶ **Longines 18ct gold wristwatch,** the dial with subsidiary seconds, with a hinged back, signed, Swiss, 1920s, 1in (2.5cm) diam. This gold watch is by a good maker and its style is popular at the moment. These factors have helped this item to achieve its high price.
£760–910 / €1,150–1,350 $1,350–1,600 B(Kn) ✦

Barometers

Ebony and ivory desk barometer, with a silvered dial and easel back, late 19thC, 4½in (11.5cm) high. This barometer has an unusual frame which could be of Eastern origin, making it of interest to collectors.
£100–120 / €150–180
$175–210 WW ⚲

Miller's compares...

A. Edwardian marquetry-inlaid mahogany aneroid wheel barometer, the silvered dial inscribed 'J. Halden & Co, Manchester', the spirit thermometer with silvered scale, 38½in (98cm) high.
£200–240 / €300–360
$350–420 PF ⚲

B. Mahogany wheel barometer, by J. Colombar Co, Newcastle-upon-Tyne, inlaid with boxwood and harewood, with an alcohol thermometer, inscribed with maker's name, damaged, 1760–1812, 38in (96.5cm) high.
£640–760 / €950–1,150
$1,150–1,350 PFK ⚲

Item A is an early 20th-century aneroid barometer. These were produced in large numbers and as a result are readily available at reasonable prices. Item B, however, is Georgian and has attractive inlay to the case. Although it is damaged, Item B is the more sought after and therefore more valuable barometer of the two.

◄ **Rosewood wheel barometer,** with silvered dials and registers, with hygrometer, thermometer and spirit level, c1890, 37in (94cm) high. This item has sold for a reasonable price, possibly because it appears to have some damage to the case and hands. It is always advisable to check the cost of repairs as they can be expensive.
£210–250 / €310–370
$370–440 G(B) ⚲

Silver aneroid pocket barometer, the case engraved with interlacing initials surmounted by a crown, London 1912, 2¼in (5.5cm) diam. The silver case, good quality and size of this barometer account for its high value.
£380–450 / €570–670
$670–800 S(O) 🔨

Mahogany wheel barometer, by J. Fesana, Bath, with a silvered alcohol thermometer and dial with brass bezel, signed, early 19thC, 36¾in (93.5cm) high.
£400–480
€600–720
$710–850 B(Kn) 🔨

Victorian mahogany Admiral Fitzroy barometer, with single mercury column and thermometer, 35½in (90cm) high. This barometer sold for more than twice its estimate, possibly because there were two very keen bidders on the day.
£350–420
€520–630
$620–740 PF 🔨

George IV mahogany wheel barometer, by F. Bernasconi & Son, Newcastle, with four silvered dials and a convex mirror, 38in (96.5cm) high. This barometer was a good buy – examples with this number of dials are sought after and would normally command a higher price.
£260–310 / €390–460
$460–550 G(L) 🔨

▶ **Mahogany wheel barometer,** by C. Barnaschina, Newcastle-upon-Tyne, the silvered dial with thermometer, inlaid with satinwood shell and floral motifs, early 19thC, 38¼in (97cm) high.
£480–570 / €720–850
$850–1,000 DD 🔨

Mahogany wheel barometer, the silvered dial signed 'D. Luvate, Preston', the case with box stringing and inlaid with shell decoration, c1830, 37¾in (96cm) high.
£400–480 / €600–720
$710–850 TEN 🔨

Mahogany wheel barometer, with a silvered dial, hygrometer, bowfronted alcohol thermometer and spirit level, c1835, 44in (112cm) high.
£540–640
€800–950
$960–1,150 S(O) 🔨

◄ **Carved oak Admiral Fitzroy wall barometer,** the interior with a printed chart, dated 1881, 46in (117cm) high.
£580–690
€860–1,050
$1,050–1,200
NOA ⚒

► **Mahogany wheel barometer,** the silvered dial with brass bezel, the case with inlaid shell decoration and thermometer box, signed 'Pozzi & Co', 1800–25, 38½in (98cm) high. The decorative inlay adds to the appeal and therefore value of this barometer.
£600–720
€890–1,050
$1,050–1,250
TEN ⚒

Victorian mahogany Admiral Fitzroy barometer, the ivory thermometer with glass missing, 49½in (125.5cm) high. The Gothic case has added value to this barometer. In a plainer case this item would be worth only £200–300 / €300–450 / $350–530.
£580–690 / €860–1,050
$1,050–1,200 GAK ⚒

Locate the source

The source of each illustration in Miller's can be found by checking the code letters below each caption with the Key to Illustrations, pages 286–290.

◄ **Mahogany wheel barometer,** with a silvered dial, hygrometer alcohol thermometer, convex mirror and spirit level, the case with boxwood stringing, c1840, 38½in (98cm) high.
£600–720
€890–1,050
$1,050–1,250
S(O) ⚒

► **Mahogany Admiral Fitzroy barometer,** c1870, 34in (86.5cm) high.
£760–850
€1,150–1,250
$1,300–1,500
RAY ⊞

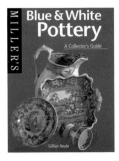 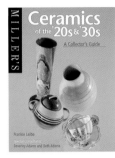 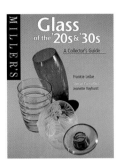
 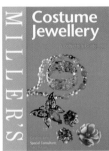 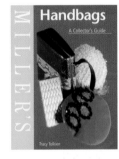
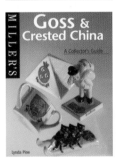 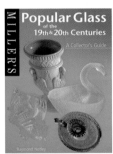 

Other Antiques

This section contains a wide range of items, some categories of which have been subject to falls in demand, which of course, offers great opportunities to the keen collector. Other categories have seen less dramatic price variations, mostly because they were not affected by the inflationary spirals of the 1980s and 1990s.

A typical example of this latter group is the field of antiquities. Although some high calibre buyers of headline-grabbing pieces have recently had quite a shock when trying to resell them, the more modestly priced pieces have not fluctuated in the same way and are consequently very affordable. For instance, you can still acquire Egyptian ushabti (tomb figures), dating from c500 BC, for less than £200 / €300 / $350 each, and amulets (good luck charms) from the same period will cost you little more. The wonderful example of Anubis (page 220), measuring over 24in (61cm) high, seems very good value even if it has been restored. After all, £200 / €300 / $350 does not seem much to pay for a piece of ceramic sculpture that is 2,500 years old.

On a slightly more prosaic level, boxes remain popular although condition is all important due to the relatively high cost of restoration. If you are a do-it-yourself enthusiast you can turn this to your advantage, but remember that nothing depreciates an item more quickly than a bad repair. Some restoration is so simple as to seem almost magical, as is the case when a little olive oil is applied to a tired piece of tortoiseshell, returning it to its pristine glory in a matter of minutes. Nevertheless, avoid trying to flatten out warped lids or replacing that little piece of brass inlay that has come adrift. It is also worth remembering that almost any type of conversion will reduce value, so why not use this to your advantage? A George III knife box that has been converted to hold stationery will always fetch substantially less than one with its original interior. However, the former is far more useful in a modern setting and, when closed, will look identical to an unconverted example.

Dolls, Teddy Bears & Toys is another area where condition is the watchword. Again, this offers huge opportunities for the buyers who can live with their dolls having replacement clothing and perhaps even a new wig. Teddy, too, will be much cheaper if his ear has been gnawed beyond recognition by an over-affectionate former owner rather than being in pristine and sadly unloved condition. You will even be able to buy mint condition examples of your favourite childhood Dinky toys if you are prepared to forego the original box.

Finally, perhaps one of the best fields for anybody with a taste for both exotic beauty and practicality is that of rugs and carpets. Most of the examples shown in this guide date from the late 19th century to around 1920. This era accounts for a lot of collectable rugs and carpets which are now sought after by private buyers and dealers alike and which, if they are in good condition, can make appreciable sums of money. Once again, however, damage or wear can bring prices down to very reasonable levels, particularly in the case of rugs. For country house chic, large carpets with quite a bit of scuffing can give a new residence that instant lived-in look.

Leslie Gillham

Antiquities

Stone axe, European, Neolithic period 3000–2000 BC, 7in (18cm) wide. Neolithic axes are fairly common and, unlike this example, are generally made of flint shaped to fit into the hand. Flint axes can cost upwards of £100–200 / €150–300 / $175–350.
£35–40 / €50–60
$60–70 HEL ⊞

Latch key, the latch lifter with four open fretwork fields, East Anglia, Viking, 9th–11thC, 2in (5cm) long. This interesting item would also appeal to collectors of keys.
£65–75 / €95–110
$115–135 ANG ⊞

Pottery bowl, modelled as a pine cone, Roman, 1st–2ndC AD, 5in (12.5cm) diam. This item was possibly a drinking vessel. The decoration has increased its value, plainer examples are more frequently found at around £50–80 / €75–120 / $90–140. Those modelled as gods' or animals' heads are more valuable and could fetch £500 / €750 / $890 or more.
£160–180 / €240–270
$280–320 HEL ⊞

Miller's compares...

A. Faïence bead necklace, Egypt, 4th–2ndC BC, 22in (56cm) long.
£40–45 / €60–65
$70–80 HEL ⊞

B. Faïence bead necklace, Phoenician, 3rdC BC, 24in (61cm) long.
£80–90 / €120–135
$140–160 HEL ⊞

Item A and Item B have been restrung to make them wearable, which does not affect the value. The price difference is due to the appeal of the design. The beads of Item B are large and decorative. The Egyptian beads of Item A are plainer and less attractive, which is why Item A cost less than Item B.

▶ **Bronze phalera/ roundel,** from a horse harness, Gloucestershire, 3rdC AD, 3½in (9cm) diam. This rare and interesting item is in good condition and will appeal to collectors.
£175–195
€260–290
$310–350 ANG ⊞

◀ **Painted pottery barrel flask,** Cypriot, 1050–650 BC, 4in (10cm) high. This item has a typical geometric design. Plain, undecorated examples can be purchased for £40–60 / €60–90 / $70–105.
£180–200 / €270–300
$320–350 HEL ⊞

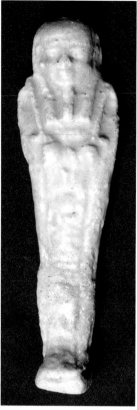

The look without the price

Alabaster head of a male,
Egyptian, Roman period,
2nd–3rdC AD, 2½in (6.5cm) high.
**£200–220 / €300–330
$350–390** HEL ⊞

This item is probably a fragment from a larger piece. Alabaster was plentiful and popular but soft and prone to damage, and this example has been eroded. If it had been made of marble, which is preferred by collectors as it denotes quality, it could be worth seven times this amount.

Faïence ushabti figure,
Egyptian, 730–332 BC,
5½in (14cm) high. Ushabti of this colouring were only made during the New Kingdom period and less detailed examples were of a later date. They were placed in tombs to help the deceased in the afterlife. Condition does affect the price – an example in good condition could fetch £300 / €450 / $530.
**£180–200 / €270–300
$320–350** HEL ⊞

Locate the source

The source of each illustration in Miller's can be found by checking the code letters below each caption with the Key to Illustrations, pages 286–290.

◄ **Faïence amulet of Anubis,** the jackal-headed god of embalming, ears missing, nose restored, c600 BC, 25½in (65cm) high. Although terracotta tends to be easily damaged, a small amount of damage is acceptable. This is a well-detailed and unusually large mummy amulet. Its size and decorative quality will appeal to collectors, hence its high value.
**£200–220 / €300–330
$350–390** MIL ⊞

► **Redware terracotta cup,** with handle, Romano-Egyptian, Akhmim Cemetery, 220–250 AD, 4¾in (12cm) high. This item dates from the end of the Egyptian period. It has an unusually bright glaze colour and is in very good condition. These attributes contributed to the good price of this cup.
**£220–250 / €330–370
$390–440** MIL ⊞

Pottery demon bowl, inscribed with an Aramaic exorcist incantation, Mesopotamian, 5th–6thC AD, 5in (12.5cm) diam. This item would appeal to collectors of historical mystical objects. It is an interesting and desirable piece, and could possibly sell for nearly double this amount.
**£240–270 / €360–400
$420–480** A&O ⊞

Find out more in

Miller's Antiques Price Guide, Miller's Publications, 2004

Demon bowls

Thought to be for trapping or exorcizing demons, demon bowls are only found in Babylon (now Iran and Iraq) and are believed to be a local tradition. They are inscribed mainly in Syriac, Aramaic or Mandaic, but examples have been found with Persian inscriptions. Some bowls have mock writing, suggesting the inscription may not have been essential to their purpose. When found in situ, they have either been buried in the floor of a house or placed in corners of rooms where the floor meets the walls – places where it was thought that demons could enter a property.

Miller's compares...

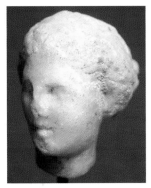

A. Marble head of a female, Egyptian, Ptolemaic, 3rd–1stC BC, 2in (5cm) high.
**£250–280 / €370–420
$440–500** HEL ⊞

B. Marble head of Aphrodite, Hellenistic, 2nd–1stC BC, 1¾in (4.5cm) high.
**£630–700 / €940–1,050
$1,100–1,250** HEL ⊞

Item A and Item B are fragments from larger statues. Item A is badly worn and almost unidentifiable as a head. Item B has crisp, clear features and is recognizably Aphrodite, thus making it more desirable and valuable than Item A.

Stone cat amulet, with attachment loop, Egyptian, Third Intermediate period, c1069–525 BC, 1¼in (3cm) high. Amulets were worn as protective charms. Cat amulets in particular are very popular with collectors, which is why they tend to sell for higher prices than other animals, which can be acquired for £150–200 / €220–300 / $270–350.
**£260–310 / €390–460
$460–550** B(Kn) ⚒

◄ **Painted pottery 'eye' jug,** Cypriot, 1050–650 BC, 6in (15cm) high. This jug is popular and would appeal to collectors because of its large size and decoration. Although the paint is worn, it is still intact and undamaged. An undecorated example might only be worth £100–150 / €150–220 / $175–270.
**£270–300 / €400–450
$480–530** HEL ⊞

Bronze incense burner, with hinged cover, suspension loop and chain, eastern European or Byzantine, possibly 14thC, 6in (15cm) high. The value and appeal of this item are due to its patina. Bronze items should never be cleaned, as this would destroy the patina, rather they should be handled frequently to build the patina up.
£330–400 / €490–600
$580–710 B(Kn) ⚒

Pottery relief fragment, moulded with a crocodile and a snake, some red pigment, Romano-Egyptian, 1stC BC/AD, 3¼ x 4in (8.5 x 10cm). Pottery fragments are very popular but are becoming more difficult to find since Egypt imposed restrictions on the export of such pieces. Remember to ask for provenance when buying antiquities, and be aware of export and import regulations, as some items will require a special passport.
£350–420 / €520–630
$620–740 B(Kn) ⚒

> To find out more about antiquities
> see the full range of
> Miller's books at
> **www.millers.uk.com**

► **Metal patera (skillet) handle,** East Anglia, 1stC AD, 3¼in (8.5cm) wide. This item could possibly be a mirror handle.
£350–390
€500–550
$600–660 ANG ⊞

◄ **Bronze dish,** damaged, 1stC AD, 7¼in (18.5cm) diam. Items that were used for domestic purposes are more sought after than burial items. This dish has good crisp decoration and without the damage could be worth £1,000 / €1,500 / $1,800.
£350–390
€510–560
$600–660 ANG ⊞

Wooden cartonnage mask, traces of original stucco, four pegs for attachment to the mummy case, Egyptian, Ptolemaic period, 300 BC, 9½in (24cm) high. This mask is from the front of a sarcophogus and would originally have been covered in plaster with painted decoration. A more finely carved mask in good condition could be worth £1,000–1,500 / €1,500–2,200 / $1,750–2,650.
£400–450 / €600–670
$710–800 MIL ⊞

Bronze figure of Nike/ Victory, Hellenistic, 1stC BC/AD, 2¾in (7cm) high.
£400–450 / €600–670
$710–800 HEL ⊞

◄ **Roman bronze flagon,** with applied base, handle and rim, west European, c3rd–4thC AD, 10½in (26.5cm) high. This item is possibly French or German. Household items are very popular with collectors and this is an unusually large example, hence the high value.
£440–490 / €660–730 $780–870 A&O ⊞

► **Bronze Herm,** modelled with the head of Ptolemy, Greek/Egyptian, 3rd–2ndC BC, 3¼in (8.5cm) high. Greek bronzes from this later period can be found relatively easily, and therefore tend to attract lower prices than the earlier rarer examples.
£440–490 / €660–730 $780–870 ANG ⊞

Red-figure kantharos, painted with the head of a lady of fashion, slight damage, 4thC BC, 8in (20.5cm) high. This vase is in good, bright, unrestored condition and is of an excellent shape. It will appeal to both collectors and interior decorators, a fact which has boosted its value. If the painting could be attributed to a specific artist, it might be worth £2,000–3,000 / €3,000–4,500 / $3,550–5,300.
£680–750 / €1,000–1,100 $1,200–1,350 A&O ⊞

► **Composition amulet of a lion-headed goddess,** wearing a *uraeus*, with a suspension loop, incised with impressed hieroglyphics, Egyptian, Third Intermediate period, 1069–702 BC, 3in (7.5cm) high, mounted. This is an unusual figure to find as an amulet. Although there appears to be some damage, this will not have affected the value significantly as the hieroglyphics increase the interest and collectability of this piece.
£760–910 / €1,150–1,350 $1,350–1,600 B(Kn) ⚒

► **Pottery vessel,** with burnished red decoration, Egyptian, c4000–3,000 BC, 10¼in (26cm) high. This very early vessel is an interesting collector's piece. These items were not glazed but polished instead, and are usually found with a black rim. Prices have remained stable over the last five years.
£700–840 / €1,050–1,250 $1,250–1,500 B(Kn) ⚒

Architectural

Brass door knob, c1900, 2½in (6.5cm) diam.
£18–22 / €30–35
$35–40 Penn ⊞

Architectural salvage

Many people now visit architectural salvage yards in search of period pieces with which to restore their homes. When buying architectural items it is worth remembering that they were not mass-produced to conform with modern sizing and may well not be the correct size for your property, so it is always best to take a tape measure with you just to make sure. Also, period bathroom suites may not meet modern building regulations and making them fit may be a costly operation, so do bear in mind the costs that might be involved before making a purchase. Ideally, salvaged items should be contemporary to the property.

Brass fittings

There are many reproduction brass architectural items on the market and they can be worth a fraction of their period counterparts. Older, original brass fittings tend to be darker, and more orange in colour than modern brass which tends to be of a more yellow tone. If in doubt, always consult a specialist, although eventually experience will help you tell the difference between an original and a reproduction piece. Items in pairs or sets are more valuable than single examples.

Brass door handle, cast with a rose, c1900, 2½in (6.5cm) diam. This door handle is a good example of crisp casting, and could be worth up to £40 / €60 / $70. Reproductions are often pitted with sand marks from the casting process.
£30–35 / €45–50
$55–60 Penn ⊞

Brass letter plate, c1880, 7in (18cm) wide. There are many reproduction brass letter plates on the market and it is advisable to check the quality of casting and look for bolts and spring mechanisms that are aged but intact. Buyers should also be aware that today's larger envelopes may not fit through smaller antique letter boxes.
£35–40 / €50–60
$60–70 WRe ⊞

Copper finger plate, c1900, 12in (30.5cm) high. Copper is an unusual material for finger plates and this example could be worth up to £50 / €75 / $90.
£30–35 / €45–50
$55–60 Penn ⊞

The look without the price

Brass door pull, c1900, 9½in (24cm) long.
£40–45 / €60–65
$70–80 Penn ⊞

This door pull would have been manufactured as part of a pair. With its matching pair it could be worth up to £90 / €135 / $160.

Iron hook and eye, c1870, 10½in (26.5cm) long. Hook and eye latches from the 17thC can be worth three times the value of later examples such as this.
£45–50 / €65–75
$80–90 Penn ⊞

Cast-iron door knocker, c1900, 6in (15cm) high. Brass door knockers are more popular than cast-iron ones and can achieve higher prices, especially examples with rococo and floral decoration, or those cast with bats.
£40–45 / €60–65
$70–80 Penn ⊞

▶ **Cast-iron vent,** early 20thC, 39in (99cm) high. These vents are often sought after by buyers wishing to use them as bollards within their gardens or driveways.
£45–50 / €65–75
$80–90 WRe ⊞

Early Victorian brass fender, with pierced friezes, on three butter-curl feet, 39in (99cm) wide. This style of fender is currently very popular and can fetch up to four times this amount depending on condition and size. This was a good buy.
£55–65 / €80–95
$95–115 PFK 🔨

◀ **Pair of brass Suffolk latches,** c1900, 9in (23cm) high.
£50–55 / €75–85
$90–100 Penn ⊞

Locate the source

The source of each illustration in Miller's can be found by checking the code letters below each caption with the Key to Illustrations, pages 286–290.

Set of four brass finger plates, French, 1880s, 10½in (26.5cm) high.
£55–65 / €80–95
$95–115 each Penn ⊞

Iron door pull, c1870, 6in (15cm) long. It is worth noting that authentic Victorian door fittings have British Standard Whitworth thread, whereas later reproductions will have a metric or unified thread.
£55–65 / €80–95
$95–115 Penn ⊞

Pair of brass Suffolk latches, c1900, 9in (23cm) high.
£55–65 / €80–95
$95–115 Penn ⊞

◄ Brass finger plate, c1880, 10½in (26.5cm) high. Victorian brass finger plates are often very ornately decorated and they should be crisply cast with clear details.
£60–70 / €90–105
$105–120 Penn ⊞

Wooden boot jack, early 19thC, 11in (28cm) long.
£65–75 / €95–110
$115–135 SDA ⊞

Cast-iron wall-mounted water pump, 20thC, 28in (71cm) high. Water pumps with decoration or with a maker's mark can command up to £120 / €185 / $220.
£70–80 / €105–120
$125–140 WRe ⊞

Pair of Victorian pressed-brass finger plates, 11in (28cm) high. These finger plates are high quality and offer good value for money.
£85–95 / €125–140
$150–170 SAT ⊞

▶ **Brass bell,** 19thC, 13in (33cm) high. Brass bells are currently unfashionable, although examples with their fittings intact are able to attract higher prices. If you like brass bells, now is a good time to buy them.
£105–120 / €155–180
$185–210 DRU ⊞

Toleware coal scuttle, painted with flowers, fruit and birds, with a tin liner and two handles, some paint flaking, 19thC, 20in (51cm) wide. Toleware is collectable in its own right, and fireplace accessories are currently very sought after. This attractive coal scuttle will appeal to collectors in both these areas and could be worth as much as £200 / €300 / $350.
£120–140 / €180–210
$210–250 G(L) ⋏

◀ **Brass letter plate and bell push,** c1910, 17in (43cm) wide. Although this letter plate has lost its bell-push button, it is an unusual piece and would appeal to buyers of door furniture. If the bell-push button were not missing, this piece could be worth £125 / €185 / $220.
£85–95 / €125–140
$150–170 Penn ⊞

Brass and steel servants' bell, c1900, 10½in (26.5cm) high.
£105–120 / €155–180
$185–210 Penn ⊞

Victorian walnut coal box, the retractable front decorated with flowering plants and enclosing a liner, with a brass carrying handle, on four bun feet, 13½in (34.5cm) wide. Coal boxes are still useful items and are very sought after. Examples with their original tin liners and shovels could be worth up to £200 / €300 / $350.
£150–180 / €220–270
$270–320 PFK ⋏

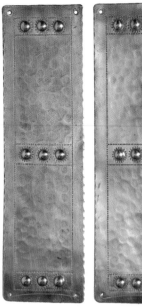

Three pairs of Victorian steel door handles, 2½in (6.5cm) diam. These door handles are a very good buy, not only because they are matching pairs, but their connecting bars are still intact.
£155–175 / €240–260
$280–310 SAT ⊞

▶ **Victorian brass and iron two-tier trivet,** 13in (33cm) high. The low price of this piece reflects the fact that trivets are currently out of fashion. If you like trivets, now is a good time to buy them.
£165–195
€240–290
$290–350 SWO ⊞

Set of four Arts and Crafts copper finger plates, c1900, 11¼in (28.5cm) high. Arts and Crafts finger plates are extremely popular with collectors.
£155–175 / €240–260
$280–310 Penn ⊞

Miller's compares...

A. Pair of cast-iron urns, with egg-and-dart rims and lion-mask handles, early 20thC, 18¾in (47.5cm) diam.
£175–210 / €260–310
$310–370 WL ⚒

B. Pair of cast-iron urns, with fluted and reeded decoration, 19thC, 25in (63.5cm) diam.
£780–930 / €1,200–1,400
$1,400–1,650 E ⚒

There are many good reproduction garden urns on the market and it can be difficult for the beginner to tell the difference between a modern reproduction and an original. Of the two items shown, the urns in Item A are the most ornate and their later date and clean appearance make them an attractive and affordable option. Item B have rusted paintwork which is a sign of age that is difficult to fake, are the more desirable campana shape, have classical decoration and are the larger of the two pairs. It is these factors that make Item B more desirable and valuable than Item A.

Brass bell pull, c1890, 5in (12.5cm) wide. This bell pull is an example of the fine craftmanship that can be found in Victorian brass fittings.
£175–195 / €260–290
$310–350 SAT ⊞

Set of eight brass pulls, c1890, 5in (12.5cm) wide. These brass pulls would originally have been fitted to a chest of drawers. They are a perfect buy for a restoration project.
£175–195 / €260–290
$310–350 SAT ⊞

William IV brass and polished-steel curb fender, 54in (137cm) wide. This fender was an extremely good buy, since it still has its original poker stands it might have achieved a further 40 per cent on this price.
£200–240 / €300–360
$350–420 L ⚒

Brass and mesh bowfronted fender, 19thC, 28in (71cm) wide. High fenders such as this offer a stylish alternative to modern child guards.
£190–220 / €280–330
$340–390 WW ⚒

Victorian steel fender, applied with fruiting vines, the front with pierced roundels, 59in (150cm) wide. This fender has an attractive serpentine shape which would appeal to buyers.
£220–260 / €330–390
$390–460 L ⚒

Find out more in

Miller's Antiques Price Guide, Miller's Publications, 2004

◀ **Brass servants' bell,** with original fittings, 19thC, 12in (30.5cm) high. The fact that this bell has all its original fittings makes it an attractive purchase.
£230–260
€340–390
$410–460 DRU ⊞

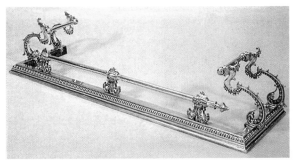

Late Victorian brass fender, with scroll supports, 52½in (133.5cm) wide. This ornate brass fender does not fit with today's trend for minimalism. However, it is in good condition and could possibly be worth £330 / €490 / $580.
£250–300 / €370–530
$440–530 WW ⚒

Cast-iron 12-gallon wash boiler, by Jack Horner, 1904, 30in (76cm) high.
£360–400 / €540–600
$640–710 OLA ⊞

▶ **Alabaster and gilt-metal pedestal,** with associated top, French, c1880, 48½in (123cm) high. Alabaster is a soft stone and is easily damaged. However, this pedestal is in excellent condition and its classical design would appeal to American and Continental buyers.
£360–430 / €540–640
$640–760 S(O) ✗

Set of nine embossed finger plates, c1890, 9in (23cm) high. It is unusual to find such a large set of finger plates. Sets of this size are very desirable and are consequently more expensive than sets of a lower quantity.
£360–400 / €540–600
$640–710 SAT ⊞

The look without the price

Louis XIV-style gilt-bronze bowfronted fender, decorated with scrolls and foliage, French, late 19thC, 53in (134.5cm) wide.
£380–450 / €570–670
$670–800 WW ✗

Although rather ornate, this fender is still a very attractive piece and would not look out of place in a modern interior. However, had it been made of brass, rather than gilt-bronze, it would have sold for a higher price – possibly twice as much.

◀ **Pair of Gothic-style painted and parcel-gilt doors,** 1850–1900, 88in (223.5cm) high. The Gothic style is very fashionable at the moment, particularly in America.
£420–500 / €620–740
$740–890 NOA ✗

Leaded and stained-glass window, decorated with birds and foliage, early 20thC, 19 x 38in (48.5 x 96.5cm). Stained-glass windows are popular decorative items and although this particular example appears to have some damage, this has not affected the value. It may be because the damage is on the outer edge of the glass. Damage to the central panel or the main pattern could significantly affect the value as it can be complex and expensive to restore.
£430–510 / €640–760
$760–900 S(S) 🔨

Victorian pine fire surround, with applied paterae and husk decoration, 66in (167.5cm) wide. This fire surround is an excellent buy as it is a good size and has attractive decoration.
£490–590 / €730–880
$870–1,050 SWO 🔨

Steel lock, with chased decoration, possibly 17thC, 13in (33cm) long. Locks are a popular collecting area and larger, more ornate examples are particularly valuable.
£500–550 / €750–820
$890–970 KEY ▦

Set of three stained-glass armorial panels, each depicting a family coat-of-arms and Latin mottos, 19thC, 16¼ x 11½in (41.5 x 29cm). These panels would be of particular interest to historians and collectors of heraldic items.
£540–640 / €800–950
$960–1,150 G(L) 🔨

▶ **Set of five Victorian painted cast-iron urns,** campana shape, with everted rims above fluted and semi-reeded bodies, 19¾in (50cm) high.
£560–670 / €830–1,000
$1,000–1,200 B(WM) 🔨

Set of panelled oak doors, with linenfold moulding, 19thC, 28in (71cm) wide.
£570–680 / €850–1,000
$1,000–1,200 S(O) 🔨

◀ **Pair of terracotta urns,** with leaf-moulded rims, the fluted columns with lion masks, damaged, 19thC, 43¼in (110cm) high. Terracotta garden ornaments are very popular but are prone to damage and weathering. Such faults will reduce the value and it is always worth checking an item before purchase.
£590–700 / €880–1,050
$1,050–1,250 DN 🔨

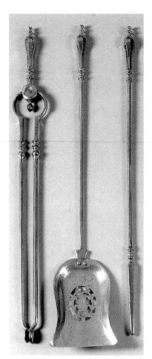

Locate the source

The source of each illustration in Miller's can be found by checking the code letters below each caption with the Key to Illustrations, pages 286–290.

Set of three polished steel fire irons, c1820, 28¾in (73cm) long. Polished steel fire accessories are currently more popular than brass examples. This may be because polished steel is better suited to current decorating trends and modern homes.
£640–760 / €950–1,150
$1,150–1,350 S(O) 🔧

◀ **Painted wall panel,** oil on canvas, with a crowned monogram, probably Spanish, 18thC, 106½ x 62¼in (270 x 158cm). The exceptional size and unusual decoration of this panel have added significantly to its value.
£660–790 / €980–1,200
$1,150–1,400 S(O) 🔧

Set of four gilt-bronze fire irons, comprising a pair of tongs, a poker, a shovel and a brush, with stand, c1880, 33¾in (85.5cm) high. Fire irons with original stands are rare. This example is very decorative and would appeal to buyers looking to recreate a traditional interior.
£720–860 / €1,050–1,300
$1,250–1,500 S(O) 🔧

Wrought-iron seat, 1850–1900, 60in (152.5cm) wide. When looking to purchase a wrought-iron seat such as this, it is important to check the rivets for signs of rust or damage, which can detract from the value and be expensive to restore.
£720–860 / €1,050–1,300
$1,250–1,500 S(S) 🔧

The look without the price

Victorian Coalbrookdale-style painted cast-iron garden seat, in Fern pattern, with a slatted wood seat, 25½in (65cm) wide.
£800–960 / € 1,200–1,400
$1,400–1,650 Bea ✗

The Coalbrookdale Company was best known for its Fern and Nasturtium pattern benches and had this example been manufactured by Coalbrookdale it would have been worth double or triple this amount. Originally these benches would not have been white but, as with this example, many have been repainted.

◀ **Pair of carved wood panels,** inscribed 'De Drie Fontenne' and 'Rosius', Flemish, 18thC, 19¾in (50cm) high.
£810–970 / € 1,200–1,400
$1,450–1,700 BERN ✗

Empire-style bronze and gilt-bronze fender, stamped 'Bouhon Frères', French, c1890, 40½in (103cm) wide. The French Empire style is currently very popular and this fender could possibly have fetched a further 20 per cent.
£960–1,150 / € 1,450–1,700
$1,700–2,000 S(O) ✗

Arms & Armour

Flintlock boxlock pocket pistol,
by Johnson & Collins, with a slab-sided walnut butt and turn-off barrel, early 19thC, 6in (15cm) long. These pistols were originally sold in pairs. If they were still a pair they could be worth £400 / €600 / $710.
£160–190 / €240–280
$280–340 PFK ✂

Travelling pistol, with a walnut stock and iron flintlock mechanism, ramrod and cock missing, signed 'I. H. Bolton', the barrel with proof marks, early 19thC, 8½in (21.5cm) long. The ramrod and cock are missing from this travelling pistol. If this item had been complete it could have fetched £350 / €520 / $620.
£180–210 / €270–310
$320–370 G(L) ✂

Miller's compares...

A. Artillery hanger, with a brass hilt and ribbed grip, slight wear, the blade marked 'Art Fab De Toledo', Spanish, 1902, blade 27½in (70cm) long.
£175–195 / €260–290
$310–350 FAC ⊞

B. Infantry hanger, with a brass hilt and ribbed grip, marked with a crowned 'GR' cipher, slight wear, 1812, blade 23in (58.5cm) long, with original leather scabbard.
£400–450 / €600–670
$710–800 FAC ⊞

Item A is Spanish and was made in the early part of the 20th century. Item B is an English sword dating from the Napoleonic period, which adds significant value to this piece. English and French swords are more desirable to collectors than Spanish examples, thus increasing the price of Item B.

The look without the price

East India Company-style brass-mounted flintlock holster pistol, the barrel engraved with armoury inventory number 'S.L.3.79', Indian, 19thC, 17½in (44.5cm) long.
£180–210 / €270–310
$320–370 PFK ✂

If this pistol had actually been made by the East India Company it might have been worth £400–600 / €600–890 / $710–1,050. However, this piece still makes a good decorative item for a fraction of the cost.

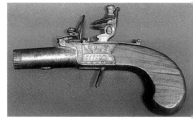

Flintlock pistol, engraved 'Mabson and Labron', early 19thC, 6in (15cm) long. This pistol has the unusual and interesting feature of a hidden trigger. It also carries Birmingham proof marks which are less sought after than the well-known London marks.
£200–240 / €300–360
$350–420 HOLL ✂

To find out more about antique arms and armour see the full range of Miller's books at
www.millers.uk.com

.45–70 calibre Springfield Model 1873 trapdoor rifle, with a low arch breech block and ski jump rear sight, dated 1873, 32½in (82.5cm) long. The Springfield trapdoor rifle is a single-shot, black powder weapon. The name refers to the method of loading the cartridge by opening the rifle at the top of the breech, which is more accurate than muzzle loaders. The 1873 is a modified version of the first model, which was made in 1868.
£220–260 / €330–390
$390–460 JDJ 🔨

Victorian truncheon, inscribed with crowned 'VR' and 'Constable', 18in (45.5cm) long. This truncheon would have been for ceremonial use; the plainer ones that were used daily are more affordable, costing £100 / €150 / $175.
£250–280 / €370–420
$440–500 TLA ⊞

Steel-mounted flintlock pocket pistol, with a steel barrel and walnut stock, impressed proof marks, 18thC, 7½in (19cm) long. This pistol was a bargain. It could have achieved £600–700 / €890–1,050 / $1,050–1,250 on a different day.
£280–330 / €420–490
$500–580 G(L) 🔨

Percussion transition revolver, by Hollis & Sheath, London, with foliate scroll-engraved decoration, mid-19thC, 9in (23cm) long. The firm of Hollis & Sheath was based in London and Birmingham between 1849 and 1861, thereafter becoming Hollis & Sons of London. This is a popular transition revolver and could easily have fetched a further £300 / €450 / $530.
£250–300 / €370–450
$440–530 RTo 🔨

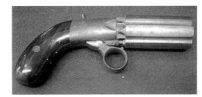

Early Victorian six-shot pepperbox percussion pistol, with a laburnum butt and under-mounted hammer, ring trigger, the lock engraved with scrollwork, 8in (20.5cm) long. Like many pepperbox percussion pistols, this example is not named. Those with a named maker are more sought after by collectors, and therefore command higher prices.
£300–360 / €450–540
$530–640 PFK 🔨

Reuthes cast-iron patent percussion animal trap pistol, with two pronged arrows, maker's mark, 19thC, 13in (33cm) long. These particular pistols are not usually marked, making this an interesting example.
£300–360 / €450–540
$530–640 G(L) 🔨

▶ **.32 calibre Derringer-style rimfire pistol,** with four barrels and chequered wood grips, stamped '9 H.S.', Continental, c1860, 6in (15cm) long.
£310–350 / €460–520
$550–620 MDL ⊞

.36 calibre six-shot pinfire revolver, inscribed 'London No 77669', c1880, 10in (25.5cm) long. This revolver is good value at this price.
£320–380 / €480–570
$570–670 TMA 🏹

Enfield sea service percussion pistol, with a walnut grip, swivel ramrod and brass buff cap with lanyard loop, the lock marked 'Enfield 1858' and with a crowned 'VR', 14in (35.5cm) long. As this is a military type pistol with a lanyard, it could be worth £400 / €600 / $710.
£320–380 / €480–570
$570–670 HOLL 🏹

Percussion transitional revolver, c1850, 12in (30.5cm) long.
£360–400 / €540–600
$640–710 WSA ⊞

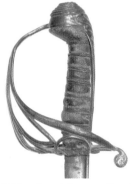

Imperial hussar's sabre, German, c1914, 36in (91.5cm) long.
£390–440 / €580–660
$690–780 TLA ⊞

1822 pattern infantry officer's sword, with a folding side guard, wire-wrapped sharkskin grip and pipe back blade, minor damage, the gilt hilt with cipher of William IV, 1830s, 30¾in (78cm) long, with original brass scabbard.
£350–390 / €520–580
$620–690 FAC ⊞

Sword/bayonet, for a Baker rifle, the hilt locking mechanism with field repair, c1815, 27in (68.5cm) long. Although the repair is contemporary, if it had been in original condition one could expect to pay £600–700 / €890–1,050 / $1,050–1,250 for this rare sword.
£400–450 / €600–670 / $710–800 TLA ⊞

◄ **NCO sword,** the wooden grip with a brass hilt and langet moulded as a shell, with expanded cross guard, American, 1840–50, blade 26in (66cm) long. Civil War weapons are of particular interest to American collectors.
£430–480
€640–720
$760–850 FAC ⊞

Smith & Wesson Model No. 1½ six-shot revolver, with sheath trigger and ebony grips, c1890, barrel 6in (15cm) long. Guns manufactured by Colt, Smith & Wesson and Starr are of interest to British and American collectors, and therefore command similar values in both countries.
£400–480 / €600–720
$710–850 WD 🏹

The look without the price

Replica of a close helmet, German, 19thC, 15¾in (40cm) high.
**£480–570 / €720–850
$850–1,000** SWO ⚲

An original helmet would be much more expensive, possibly costing 10 to 15 times as much. However, this is a good reproduction and would make a fine display piece.

Bowie knives

Bowie knives are usually classified as any large knife with a chipped point. They were particularly popular in America between 1840 and 1865 and are believed to have been designed by Rezin Bowie, brother of James Bowie who played a leading role in the Texas revolution of 1835. Bowie knives were designed to be used when fishing and hunting but there are stories of more sinister uses as well. Some of the most desirable knives were made in Sheffield and exported to America and the Hudson Bay Company, Canada. Bowie knives are very popular with American collectors.

◀ **Bowie knife,** with a cutlery handle, c1860, 13in (33cm) long.
**£580–650 / €860–970
$1,050–1,150** MDL ⊞

.65 calibre officer's flintlock holster pistol, by Gill, with a walnut fullstock and brass mounts, the trigger guard with acorn finial and the horn-tipped ramrod with steel worm, minor damage, engraved mark, c1790, 15in (38cm) long. This pistol has a decorative shell plate to the handle, which indicates that rather than it being standard issue, it would have been purchased by the officer himself.
**£610–730 / €910–1,100
$1,100–1,300** WAL ⚲

▶ **Cavalry trooper's sword,** the steel hilt with two sidebars and pierced guard, with a wirebound leather-covered grip, later wire, c1788, blade 35½in (90cm) long. This sword could have achieved an extra £200 / €300 / $350 if it had retained its original grip.
**£670–800 / €1,000–1,200
$1,200–1,400** WAL ⚲

Boxes

◀ **Oak box,** with mother-of-pearl inlay, c1860, 9½in (24cm) wide. The slightly poor condition of this box has reduced its value. Restoring it could prove expensive, and it may not be worth the invesment.
£50–60 / €75–90
$90–105 AL ⊞

Tortoiseshell

If you intend to purchase tortoiseshell items when travelling abroad, do remember to obtain the correct documentation needed for importing them into the UK. The relevant information can be obtained from your local customs office. If you buy from an auction house they should be able to supply the necessary paperwork.

Tortoiseshell-veneered pillbox, early 19thC, 2¼in (5.5cm) wide. Items made with dark tortoiseshell that has a defined pattern are more sought after than examples made with paler, less well defined veneers. If the tortoiseshell appears dull it is possible to restore it by rubbing gently with a soft cloth and a little olive oil.
£65–75 / €95–110
$115–135 CHTR ⚒

Miller's compares...

A. Edwardian oak humidor, with brass 'Cigars' motif, 11in (28cm) wide.
£55–65 / €80–95
$95–115 AMB ⚒

B. Edwardian walnut-veneered humidor, with figured veneer and ebony borders, the interior with a box of cigars and a cigar cutter, 13¼in (33.5cm) wide.
£280–330 / €420–490
$500–580 NSal ⚒

Item A is slightly smaller than Item B, and is made of oak, which is the less desirable of the two woods. Item B, which is veneered in figured walnut and has ebony bands, is the more pleasing of the two items, and this, together with its larger size, accounts for the higher value of Item B.

The look without the price

George III mahogany and inlaid jewellery casket, 13¼in (33.5cm) wide.
£95–110 / €140–165
$170–195 FHF ✥

This casket has developed a 'smile', where the cover no longer sits flush when closed, and this can be costly to repair. Without the 'smile' this box might be worth £200–300 / €300–450 / $350–530. However, it is still an attractive and useful piece.

◄ **William IV rosewood workbox,** inlaid with mother-of-pearl, 11¾in (30cm) wide. This workbox is excellent value at this price. It was obviously a lucky purchase as it could have sold for twice this amount.
£100–120 / €150–180
$175–210 DN(EH) ✥

Mahogany and rosewood-crossbanded needle-work box, with a fitted interior, ivory escutcheon and ebonized base, c1820, 9½in (24cm) wide. This workbox has had a busy life, as it is showing signs of wear. It has, however, retained its fitted interior, and this has enhanced its value.
£130–155 / €195–230
$230–270 WL ✥

The look without the price

Velvet-covered vanity/jewellery box, with silk lining, 1890, 11in (28cm) wide.
£135–150 / €200–220
$240–270 LBe ⊞

This affordable late Victorian jewellery box would grace any dressing table. The best quality examples of this style of vanity/jewellery case were made on the Continent and would have had silver mounts. Depending on size and condition, they would sell for four times as much as this example.

Mahogany box, with brass banding, c1830, 11in (28cm) wide.
£140–155 / €200–230
$240–270 WAA ⊞

Rosewood tea caddy, inlaid with cut brass, with ring-pull handles, early 19thC, 8in (20.5cm) wide. This caddy is showing signs of wear and this has reduced its value. However, the inlaid brasswork, which would be expensive to repair, is still in good condition.
£150–180 / €220–270
$270–320 TMA

Gilt-metal box, the cover with a porcelain plaque, the sides with embossed decoration, late 19thC, 4¼in (11cm) diam. This Empire-style box has a porcelain plaque – which adds value as well as appeal to collectors. Top-quality examples would have been made from gold, and therefore much more expensive to buy.
£170–200 / €250–300
$300–350 SWO

Mother-of-pearl *nécessaire,* c1875, 2½in (6.5cm) high.
£175–195 / €260–290
$310–350 JTS ⊞

Miller's compares...

A. Regency rosewood and inlaid tea caddy, on gilt-metal feet, 7in (18cm) wide.
£160–190 / €240–280
$280–340 WilP

B. Regency satinwood tea caddy, with boxwood stringing, the cover enclosing two lidded compartments, on brass paw feet, 8in (20.5cm) wide.
£240–290 / €360–430
$430–510 PFK

Item A is made of rosewood which, although a good-quality wood, is not as desirable as the satinwood of Item B. Also, the wood of Item B has a pleasing 'fiddle-back' grain, the shape is a more elegant design and it has finer lion-paw feet. All these features make Item B the more attractive, and more valuable purchase than Item A.

Tortoiseshell box, early 19thC, 3in (7.5cm) wide. This unusual box has been made with good quality tortoiseshell which exhibits good colour and strong design.
£180–200 / €270–300
$320–360 HTE ⊞

◀ **Late Georgian rosewood-and maple-veneered needle-work box,** 11½in (29cm) wide. Rosewood and maple is an unusual combination of woods which adds to the appeal of this box. However, the patina appears to be faded.
£180–210 / €270–310
$320–370 TMA

Mahogany candle box, with a dummy drawer, early 19thC, 9¾in (25cm) wide. Although this candle box has a 'smile', where the cover no longer sits flush when closed, the leather hinge is still intact and the dummy drawer adds character.
£210–250 / €310–370
$370–440 SWO

Miller's compares...

A. Burr-amboyna-veneered jewellery casket, with brass fittings, mid-19thC, 9in (23cm) wide.
£260–290 / €390–430
$460–510 GGD ⊞

B. Walnut jewellery box, with mother-of-pearl escutcheon and decoration, brass handle and velvet lining, French, c1875, 11in (28cm) wide.
£540–600 / €800–890
$960–1,050 JTS ⊞

While Item A is made of amboyna, which is an exotic wood, Item B has the advantage of marquetry inlay, mother-of-pearl decoration and its original velvet lining. The workmanship of Item B is of a very high standard and, despite being slightly later in date, is the more valuable of the two pieces.

▶ **Satinwood trinket box,** with burr-yew banding, the interior with silk lining, on chased brass ball feet, French, early 19thC, 7in (18cm) wide.
£260–290
€390–430
$460–510 GGD ⊞

William IV cedarwood memorial box, the hinged cover inset with a pencil and watercolour picture of a Blenheim spaniel, the cover interior with a printed card, 11in (28cm) wide. This box is made from the wood of a tree that was planted by Dr Samuel Johnson in the garden of his London home. This interesting provenance would make it more desirable to collectors and add to the price.
£260–310 / €390–460
$460–550 DN(BR) ⚹

For more examples of
Boxes see Silver & Plate (pages 135–139)

Ebonized and rosewood-crossbanded cylinder music box, playing six airs on four combs, accompanied by six bells, drum and castanets, Swiss, c1880, 22¾in (58cm) wide. When buying musical instruments, it is important to ensure that there are no teeth missing from combs and the cylinder needles are not broken, as this can require expensive specialist restoration.
£300–360 / €450–540
$530–640 S(O) ⚹

▶ **Mahogany-veneered tea chest,** with chequer stringing, on restored brass feet, 19thC, 11in (28cm) wide. This attractive *bombé* tea chest is very good quality and an excellent buy, even though its brass feet have been restored.
£320–380
€480–570
$570–670 WW ⚹

Late Victorian figured walnut jewellery casket, with a hinged cover and bevelled glass front enclosing three drawers, 7in (18cm) high.
£350–420 / €520–630
$620–740 DN(EH) 🏹

The look without the price

This box is a very good quality piece and could easily have sold for £1,000–1,500 / €1,500–2,200 / $1,800–2,650, which proves that it is possible to make a lucky purchase on the day when buying at auction.

Marquetry, ivory and ebony-inlaid box, with scrolling Renaissance-style decoration and an ivory portrait, Italian, 19thC, 15in (38cm) wide.
£400–480 / €600–720
$710–850 HYD 🏹

Tortoiseshell and ivory-strung card box, modelled as a knife box, with divided silk interior, mid-19thC, 2½in (6.5cm) wide. This box would appeal to collectors as it is made from high-quality tortoiseshell with a good contrast to the markings. It is also a very interesting shape.
£420–500 / €630–750
$740–890 DN(EH) 🏹

◀ **Walnut and inlaid writing and jewellery box,** c1870, 12¼in (31cm) wide. One would expect to pay a higher price for a dual-purpose box such as this.
£420–500
€630–750
$740–890 S(O) 🏹

◀ **Mahogany and inlaid cutlery box,** the base with a dummy drawer, c1820, 22¾in (58cm) high. The decorative inlay and fan-shaped carving on this cutlery box are an interesting feature. Similar boxes can also be found in oak which are used for storing candles, but would be much lower in price.
£450–540 / €670–800
$800–960 S(O) 🏹

Mother-of-pearl tea caddy, c1850, 7in (18cm) wide. Victorian mother-of-pearl decoration is always popular with buyers but be aware that any damage can be expensive to repair and restore, and will affect the value.
£500–600 / €750–890
$890–1,050 S(O) 🏹

▶ **Walnut tea caddy,** with three divisions and a concealed drawer, c1750, 9in (23cm) wide. Walnut is a very desirable wood. If this tea caddy had been made from mahogany it would have achieved a lower price.
£480–570 / €720–850
$850–1,000 S(O) 🏹

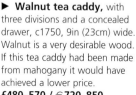

Edwardian silver-mounted ivory tea caddy, carved with ivy leaves, silver mount Sheffield 1900, 4¾in (12cm) high.
£520–620 / €770–920
$920–1,100 AH ⚒

Tortoiseshell and ivory card box, with silver chinoiserie decoration, c1865, 4in (10cm) high. Card boxes are very popular with collectors, and this is a good-quality example.
£540–600 / €800–890
$960–1,050 JTS ⊞

Tea caddy, in the form of a coal wagon, c1890, 5in (12.5cm) high. Novelty-shaped tea caddies are unusual. Attractive designs such as this can command high prices.
£800–900 / €1,200–1,350
$1,400–1,600 HAA ⊞

> **For more examples of**
> Tea Caddies see Silver & Plate (page 137)

Regency figured flame mahogany-veneered tea caddy, with two removable lidded caddies and a bowl, 13in (33cm) wide.
£540–600 / €800–890
$960–1,050 GGD ⊞

▶ **Oyster kingwood table box,** 18thC, 18¾in (47.5cm) wide. Kingwood is sometimes referred to as violet wood due to its dark purple hue. It is often used in Continental furniture, or as inlays and veneers, such as the unusual oyster pattern on this box.
£840–1,000 / €1,250–1,450
$1,500–1,750 L ⚒

Dolls, Teddy Bears & Toys

Miller's compares...

A. Bisque figure of a girl, German, c1920, 4in (10cm) high.
£35–40 / €50–60
$60–70 YC ⊞

B. Bisque figure of a boy, c1910, 3in (7.5cm) long.
£90–100 / €135–150
$155–175 YC ⊞

Item B has the higher quality of moulding and decoration that collectors look for, therefore making it more valuable.

Chad Valley felt doll, with a moulded and painted face, with glass eyes, wearing a felt and Draylon dress, 1920s–30s, 12in (30.5cm) high. This felt doll is susceptible to marks and damage. Collectors look for good quality, clean items.
£35–40 / €50–60
$60–70 FHF ↗

The look without the price

This is a later version of the desirable and higher-priced bisque doll. The composition body of this example is less easily damaged than bisque.

Armand Marseille bent-limbed composition baby doll, German, 1920s–30s, 15in (38cm) high.
£75–85 / €110–125
$135–150 POLL ⊞

Wax fairy doll, wearing original clothes, 1920s, 10½in (26.5cm) high, with box. Wax dolls are particularly collectable, poured-wax dolls being more desirable than composition with wax overlay. It is important to maintain the condition of the doll by keeping it away from heat sources and direct light, as these can discolour or melt the wax.
£55–65 / €80–95
$95–110 BaN ⊞

◄ **Limoges Min doll,** c1900, 8in (20.5cm) high.
£75–85 / €110–125
$135–150 DOL ⊞

Hornby gauge 0 electric 4–4–2 tank locomotive, No. 492 Southern Electric, minor damage.
£100–120 / €150–180
$175–210 CGC 🔨

Bisque-headed doll, with original kid body, wearing later clothes, German, early 20thC, 20in (51cm) high.
£85–100 / €125–150
$150–175 JAA 🔨

► **Bisque-headed doll,** the leather body marked '250.5, MOA Wand C' for Max Oscar Arnold, wearing later clothing and wig, German, c1920, 24in (61cm) high. A replacemnt wig can reduce the price of a doll by 10–15 per cent. The condition of the wig is an important factor, especially if it is original.
£115–135 / €170–200
$200–240 JAA 🔨

Double pack of playing cards, 1898, 4½ x 3in (11.5 x 7.5cm). Bright colours and attractive designs are important factors to collectors of playing cards.
£150–175 / €220–260
$260–310 MURR ⊞

Steiff bear on wheels, with hump back and pull-cord growler, on cast wheels, growler broken, early 20thC, 26¼in (66.5cm) high. The damage to this bear has reduced its price significantly. An example in good condition could fetch £800–1,000 / €1,200–1,500 / $1,400–1,650.
£180–210 / €270–310
$320–370 CHTR 🔨

Doll's silk outfit, comprising coat and dress, c1860, 30in (76cm) long. Dolls' clothes in good condition are popular with collectors.
£180–200 / €270–300
$320–360 DOL ⊞

Cast-iron money box, c1910, 4in (10cm) high. Large numbers of money boxes were produced in America from the late 19th to the early 20thC. Cast iron was the favoured material, and they were manufactured in a wide variety of designs, both still and mechanical. This item will therefore appeal to American collectors.
£200–220 / €300–330
$350–390 MFB ⊞

Poured-wax doll, with glass eyes and inserted hair, the cloth body with wax lower arms, legs, shoulders and head, wearing a cotton nightgown, underclothes, slippers and bonnet, left leg missing some wax, c1860, 14in (35.5cm) high. Damage to the head and shoulders can reduce value, but damage to the body is of less importance.
£210–250 / €310–370
$370–440 B(Kn) ✺

Find out more in

Miller's Toys & Games Buyer's Guide, Miller's Publications, 2004

Märklin gauge 1 0–4–0 clockwork tank locomotive, 326, one piston rod and con-rods missing, slight wear, 9¾in (25cm) long.
£220–260 / €330–390
$390–460 CGC ✺

Ernst Heubach bisque-headed baby doll, German, Kopperlsdorf, c1915, 10in (25.5cm) high. This is a good quality doll, similar to a Dream Baby, and is therefore desirable to collectors.
£250–280 / €370–420
$440–500 BaN ⊞

Armand Marseille

Armand Marseille was established in 1885, earlier than other companies such as Heubach, which was established in 1887. Early examples of Armand Marseille Dream Babies, including model 341 and other similar closed-mouth dolls, are extremely popular with collectors and are therefore the most valuable. Later examples such as the Armand Marseille model No. 351 open-mouthed Dream Baby doll were produced in much larger quantities. These dolls are not of the high quality seen in earlier bisque dolls and are therefore less desirable.

Armand Marseille Dream Baby doll, AM 341, composition, bent-limbed baby body, c1915, 11in (28cm) high. Dolls with composition bodies command higher prices than those with later cloth bodies.
£250–280 / €370–420
$440–500 BaN ⊞

► **Victorian doll's mahogany half-tester bed,** 17¼in (44cm) long, with a mattress, blankets and a patchwork quilt. This bed offers good value for money, particularly as there is a growing interest in doll's furniture in both America and the UK.
£350–420
€520–630
$620–740 PFK ⚒

Ernst Heubach character doll, mould No. 414, German, c1915, 19in (48.5cm) high. The moulded racial features on this doll are unusual, thus making it more desirable to collectors than the more common Caucasian features that have been sprayed/painted black.
£360–400 / €540–600
$640–710 BaN ⊞

◄ **Chiltern bear,** with glass eyes and a velvet muzzle, 1920s–30s, 21in (53.5cm) high. Chiltern bears are not as desirable to collectors as Farnell or Steiff.
£420–470 / €630–700
$740–830 BBe ⊞

Ivory and ebony folding chessboard, c1870, 18in (45.5cm) square. Chess is a popular game and, as a result, good quality antique chess boards and related items can fetch four- or five-figure sums.
£500–600 / €740–890
$880–1,050 BBe ⊞

Find out more in

Miller's Teddy Bears: A Complete Collector's Guide, Miller's Publications, 2001

◄ **Peg doll,** with painted features and hair and jointed limbs, wearing a period outfit, early 19thC, 9in (23cm) high. Early peg dolls, especially those with original clothing, are a popular collecting field. There are few examples found in good condition as originally these dolls were cheap to buy and were played with often.
£880–1,050 / €1,300–1,550
$1,550–1,850 G(L) ⚒

Schuco felt and mohair bear, wearing a bell hop's uniform, German, 1920s, 14in (35.5cm) high. This bear is very collectable as he is in good condition and still has his hat, which is often lost. As well as bears, Schuco has made a Yes/No bell hop monkey and Yes/No undressed bears, monkeys and cats. They patented the Yes/No mechanism in 1921.
£540–600 / €800–890
$960–1,050 MSh ⊞

Kitchenware

Wood and metal herb chopper, c1900, 6in (15cm) wide. The decorative join between the handle and the blade is a typical design of the early 20th century. Triangular joins are also a common feature. The tarnish that is evident on this blade can be buffed out, but it shows that it is an original surface.
£12–16 / €16–20
$20–24 AL ⊞

▶ **Butter dish,** with wooden surround, ceramic dish replaced, c1900, 6¾in (17cm) diam. Willow pattern dishes such as this would originally have been sold separately. In the 1940s and '50s glass dishes were used with similar wooden surrounds.
£25–30 / €40–45
$45–50 CHAC ⊞

▶ **Wood and metal grain measure,** c1910, 7½in (19cm) high. The crown markings on this item indicate that it was used to measure an official 'standard' gallon. These measures are highly sought after.
£30–35 / €45–50
$55–65 AL ⊞

Miller's compares...

A. Wooden butter stamp, with a carved design, late 19thC, 2in (5cm) diam.
£30–35 / €45–50
$55–65 WeA ⊞

B. Wooden butter stamp, with a carved design, c1870, 3¾in (9.5cm) diam.
£75–85 / €110–125
$135–150 WeA ⊞

While both these stamps are of good quality, Item A is smaller than Item B. Item A has been carved with an acorn motif whereas Item B has been carved with the emblem of HRH Prince of Wales, which makes it more unusual and more desirable to collectors, hence the higher price.

Meat cleavers

Large meat cleavers, or choppers, consist of a blade on a wooden handle, usually of beech, ash, sycamore or fruitwood. They were used both for chopping meat and disjointing bones. By the 19th century, cleavers were mostly made in Sheffield, home of the British steel industry, and therefore many are stamped 'Sheffield Steel' on the blade.

◀ **Wood and metal butcher's cleaver,** c1890, 20in (51cm) long. This cleaver appears to have substantial pitting. This should not affect the value as it is to be expected with pieces of this age that are in original condition.
£35–40 / €50–60
$60–70 YT ⊞

Wooden butter stamp, carved with a thistle and a rose, c1900, 3½in (9cm) diam. Stamps carved with a thistle and a rose are popular with collectors. The combination refers to the marriage in 1503 of King James IV of Scotland to Margaret Tudor, and has since represented Scotland and England's cordial relationship.
£45–50 / €65–75
$80–90 CHAC ⊞

Copper side-handled brandy saucepan, with fruitwood handle and brass seals, handle scorched, c1780, 4½in (11.5cm) high. Although some wear is acceptable on pieces such as this, the fruitwood handle on this pan has been severely damaged and this has reduced its value by around 30 per cent.
£50–60 / €75–85
$90–100 F&F ⊞

The look without the price

Wooden grain shovel, c1890, 42in (106.5cm) high.
£50–55 / €75–85
$90–100 AL ⊞

This wooden shovel has an attractive patina and its large size makes it an appealing display item. However, it appears to have been damaged and this has reduced its value. In perfect condition this shovel could possibly command double this price.

Sycamore butter stamp, carved with an acorn design, c1870, 3in (7.5cm) diam.
£60–70 / €95–105
$110–125 AL ⊞

Wooden grain shovel, French, c1900, 45in (114.5cm) long.
£60–70 / €95–105
$110–125 YT ⊞

Moulds

Ice-cream and jelly moulds made of copper and pewter are popular with collectors due to the wide range of shapes, patterns and sizes available. While often collected for their decorative appeal, buyers should be aware that not all these moulds are suitable for use with food. Copper examples may need to be retinned, lacquered moulds are unsuitable, and both copper and pewter items may have been cleaned with chemical agents. It is therefore best to check if a mould has been treated before making a purchase.

Copper jelly mould, c1890, 2½in (6.5cm) high. Small jelly moulds would have been used to make individual servings and are popular with Japanese and American collectors. Larger copper moulds can often achieve double or triple this price and interesting shapes also command higher prices, depending on their rarity, size and condition.
£60–70 / €95–105
$110–125 F&F ⊞

Ceramic meat tenderizer, with a wooden handle, c1910, 15in (38cm) long. This ceramic tenderizer is of particular interest as they are usually made entirely of wood. Ceramic tenderizers can be expected to achieve around 30 per cent more than their all-wood counterparts
£60–70 / €95–105
$110–125 SMI ⊞

▶ **Stoneware egg crock,** c1920, 11in (28cm) high. Egg crocks were used for pickling eggs in the days before refridgerators. Labelled kitchenware is more desirable to collectors, and this example has an interesting typeface which adds to its appeal.
£65–75 / €100–110
$120–135 SMI ⊞

Miller's compares...

A. Painted wood cider casket, with an iron handle, c1820, 9in (23cm) diam.
£60–70 / €95–105
$110–125 TOP ⊞

B. Elm cider casket, West Country, 19thC, 11in (28cm) wide.
£270–300 / €400–450
$480–530 SEA ⊞

Item A is smaller than Item B and of poorer quality. Item B is made of elm, a desirable wood, and still has its original stopper. These factors make Item B the more attractive piece and therefore worth substantially more than Item A.

Victorian cast-iron lace iron, with a wooden handle, 4in (10cm) wide. Small unusual irons are always popular with collectors.
£70–80 / €105–120
$125–140 HL ⊞

Maling ceramic flour shaker, decorated with Cobblestone pattern, c1920, 5in (12.5cm) high. Maling items with the Cobblestone pattern are available in blue, brown and green. Examples with unusual wording such as 'Soap Flakes' or with out-of-the-ordinary titles are rarer and more desirable.
£70–80 / €105–120
$125–140 SMI ⊞

▶ **Wrought-iron griddle,** Irish, late 19thC, 12in (30.5cm) high. This griddle appears to have rust damage, but as this is just a sign of age it should not affect the value. Iron items such as this are not always easy to find and they appeal to a specific group of collectors.
£75–85 / €110–125
$135–150 STA ⊞

Ceramic mould, by Grimwade, inscribed 'The British Lion Blanc-Mange & Jelly Mould', c1910, 11in (28cm) wide. This mould is an appealing shape and the writing around the rim is an attractive feature. It could be worth 20 per cent more than plainer examples.
£90–100 / €135–150
$155–175 SMI ⊞

Enamel coffee pot and stove, 1930s, 15in (38cm) high. This coffee pot and stove is complete, in excellent condition and could be used. Perfect examples are always desirable as damage can decrease the value considerably and restoration is expensive.
£75–85 / €110–125
$135–150 AL ⊞

Three sycamore butter stamps, carved with leaves and flowers, c1880, largest 4in (10cm) diam. Butter stamps are very collectable and the more detailed the pattern, the more sought-after the item. Animal and bird stamps are popular and examples with a heart pattern are keenly collected in America.
£110–125 / €165–185
$195–220 each MFB ⊞

Locate the source

The source of each illustration in Miller's can be found by checking the code letters below each caption with the Key to Illustrations, pages 286–290.

Brass and oak barrel jug, c1890, 16in (40.5cm) high. The very good condition of this jug has added to its value.
£110–125 / €165–185
$195–220 AL ⊞

▶ **Sycamore wash board,** Continental, 18thC, 18in (45.5cm) long. Laundry items are very collectable, especially examples such as this which are in good condition.
£155–175 / €230–260
$280–310 SEA ⊞

Find out more in

Miller's Complete A–Z of Collectables, Miller's Publications, 2004

Cast-iron and japanned coffee grinder, by Kenrick, cast in the style of York Minster font, 1870, 7in (18cm) high. Kenrick manufactured a range of kitchen equipment including juicers and mincers. Items made by Kenrick are very collectable.
£180–200 / €270–300
$310–350 WeA ⊞

▶ **Ceramic jug,** by T. G. Green, decorated with Delft pattern, 1900–10, 7½in (19cm) high. The Delft pattern is much less common than T. G. Green's ever-popular Cornishware range, but this jug would still appeal to collectors as it is good quality and has an attractive pattern.
£135–150
€200–220
$240–270 CAL ⊞

Brass cream skimmer, with an iron handle, c1760, 23in (58.5cm) long.
£170–190 / €250–280
$300–330 F&F ⊞

▶ **Metal coffee grinder,** by Peugeot Frères, French, 1880–90, 14in (35.5cm) high. Coffee grinders made of wood and brass from the 1920s are worth around a quarter of the value of this Victorian example. Metal coffee grinders are found in different sizes and can still be used today.
£190–220
€280–320
$330–380 PaA ⊞

Copper and wrought-iron kettle, with two handles, French, probably early 19thC, 10in (25.5cm) high. This kettle's unusual design would appeal to collectors of Aesthetic Movement and Arts and Crafts pieces, even though it is of a much earlier date.
£270–320 / €400–470
$470–560 JAA ⚒

Boxwood three-tier spice tower, c1810, 6in (15cm) high. Wooden spice towers, some of which had four sections, are very collectable. The original paper labels on this example add to its value.
£270–300 / €400–440
$480–530 F&F ⊞

Auction or dealer?

All the pictures in our price guides originate from auction houses ⚒ and dealers ⊞. When buying at auction, prices can be lower than those of a dealer, but a buyer's premium and VAT will be added to the hammer price. Equally, when selling at auction, commission, tax and photography charges must be taken into account. Dealers will often restore pieces before putting them back on the market. Both dealers and auctioneers can provide professional advice, so it is worth researching both sources before buying or selling your antiques.

Wrought-iron flesh fork, 1740, 28in (71cm) long. This fork would make a decorative feature in the inglenook of a traditional country house.
£430–480 / €640–720
$760–850 SEA ⊞

Cast-iron coffee grinder, with a brass hopper, c1900, 32½in (82.5cm) high.
£290–340 / €420–500
$510–600 GK ⚒

◄ **Beech butcher's block,** on a painted base, c1900, 24in (61cm) wide. With current concerns about food hygiene and the discovery that wooden blocks are a more hygienic option than plastic chopping boards, there has been a revival of butcher's blocks such as this.
£590–650 / €880–970
$1,000–1,100 MIN ⊞

Lighting

Victorian cranberry glass shade, 6¾in (17cm) high.
£50–60 / €75–90
$90–105 BrL ⊞

While some British dealers use the term 'vaseline glass' to refer to opalescent glass of a yellow hue, most specialists use the term 'uranium glass'.

Miller's compares...

A. Cranberry glass shade, with etched decoration, c1910, 6in (15cm) high.
£60–70 / €90–105
$105–125 JeH ⊞

B. Pink uranium glass shade, etched with a floral pattern, 1890–1900, 12in (30.5cm) high.
£670–750 / €1,000–1,100
$1,200–1,350 JeH ⊞

Item A is a cranberry glass shade and although it has some decorative etching, Item B is larger, with two-tone uranium glass and crisper etching, which is why it is worth 10 times as much as Item A.

◄ **Edwardian table lamp,** with an oxidized finish, original glass shade and lion-paw feet, 16in (40.5cm) high. The lion-paw feet on this lamp are an attractive feature which adds to its desirability.
£105–120 / €155–180
$185–210 EAL ⊞

Pair of brass-mounted candle lanterns, with glass storm shades, 19thC, 18in (45.5cm) high. These lanterns were a good buy. Straight-sided lanterns usually fetch £120 / €180 / $210 and these curved examples could have sold for £200 / €300 / $350.
£120–140 / €180–210
$210–250 PFK ➶

Victorian brass-framed kerosene parlour lamp, the milk glass shade decorated with flowers and leaves, the brass font decorated with cut-out flowers, leaves and vines, shade 13¾in (35cm) diam. Victorian lamps are very popular with American buyers – they have become less fashionable in the UK.
£130–155 / €195–230
$230–270 JDJ ➶

The look without the price

Pair of Sitzendorf oil lamps, converted for electricity, with floral-encrusted bodies supported by cherubs, painted marks, 19thC, 9in (23cm) high.
£150–180 / €230–270
$270–320 G(L) 🔨

These lamps are by a good maker and are decorated with cherubs, a feature popular with collectors. They also have the advantage of still being a pair, rather than being sold as singles. However, the fact that they have been modified has reduced their value – they could have been worth up to £500 / €750 / $890.

Slag glass lamp, early 20thC, 27in (68.5cm) diam. Tiffany-style slag glass is popular with American buyers and this is a very reasonable price for such an item.
190–220 / €280–330
340–400 JAA 🔨

Bronze table lamp, converted from a vase, on a lion monopodia base, foundry mark, 19thC, 17¼in (44cm) high.
190–220 / €280–330
340–400 SWO 🔨

Pair of Victorian satin glass shades, with moulded decoration, 11½in (29cm) high. Pairs of shades are more sought after than single examples, and if they have attractive decoration they can command even higher prices.
210–250 / €310–370
370–440 SWO 🔨

Set of three ormolu wall lights, with three branches, converted for electricity, 19thC, 20in (51cm) high.
£210–250 / €310–370
$370–440 NSal 🔨

▶ **Silver-plated brass rise-and-fall lamp,** with glass shades, c1910, 28in (71cm) wide. The design of these lamps requires them to be hung from a high ceiling, which limits the number of buyers able to use them, and therefore decreases the value.
£230–260
€340–390
$410–460 EAL ⊞

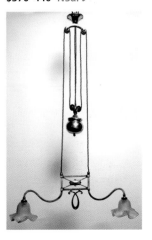

◄ **Ceiling *plafonnier*,** with pierced brass gallery, the satin glass bowl with etched decoration, c1910, 12in (30.5cm) diam. The pierced gallery of this *plafonnier* creates an appealing shadow pattern when it is lit.
£250–280 / €370–420
$440–500 JeH ⊞

Silver-plated pendant lamp the etched glass bowl moulded with swags, c1900, 16in (40.5cm high. This lamp has simple decoration that is Art Deco in style. It could be used to complement an Art Deco scheme
£270–300 / €400–450
$480–530 EAL ⊞

▶ **Pair of Victorian gas lamps,** with original cut-glass shades, 14in (35.5cm) wide. These ornate gas lamps would appeal more to Continental buyers than to those in the UK, where the current fashion is for rather plainer styles. This is a very reasonable price for a pair of lamps with original shades.
£320–360
€480–540
$570–640 EAL ⊞

Pair of bronze Grecian-revival candelabra, on tripod bases with paw feet, late 19thC, 25¼in (64cm) high. This is a good price for such large bronze candalabra and they could have fetched a further 50 per cent. This shows that it is possible to pick up a bargain on a good day.
£350–420 / €520–630
$620–740 WW ⚒

Pair of cut-glass lamps, French, 1825–50, 10in (25.5cm) high. These French lamps were sold in America but could possibly sell for £600–800 / €890–1,200 / $1,050–1,400 in the UK, where they are more to collectors' tastes.
£440–530 / €670–800
$800–960 NOA ⚒

Victorian brass oil lamp, with a cut-glass oil well and original etched-glass shade, on tripod base, 25in (63.5cm) high. This lamp, with its unusual stand and original glass shade, is a desirable piece and offers good value for money .
£340–380 / €510–570
$600–670 EAL ⊞

Miller's compares...

A. Porcelain table oil lamp, by Moore Bros, decorated with a model of an owl and encrusted with flowers, on a gilt base with four scroll feet, some losses, c1885, 18in (45.5cm) high.
£540–650 / €800–960
$960–1,150 B(W) ✎

B. Porcelain table oil lamp, by Moore Bros, modelled as a tree trunk encrusted with pine cones and branches, surrounded by dancing cherubs, on four Oriental pierced gilt feet, some losses, c1885, 18½in (47cm) high.
£760–910 / €1,150–1,350
$1,350–1,600 B(W) ✎

Both Items A and B are of a similar date, by the same manufacturer and have suffered losses. The difference in price is due to the design and decoration of each piece. Although Item A is attractive and has pale cream glazes, Item B has more complicated moulding and the applied cherubs are a more sought-after feature, which is why it achieved a higher price than Item A.

Silver-plated table oil lamp, the cut-glass reservoir on a Corinthian column, with a Hinks burner, the original glass shade etched with cherubs and urns, late 19thC, column 25in (63.5cm) high. This is a good price for such a piece, which may be due to oil lamps being relatively unfashionable at the moment. This could have sold for £600–800 / €890–1,200 / $1,050–1,400.
£570–680 / €850–1,000
$1,000–1,200 DMC ✎

Silver-plated six-branch chandelier, with a cut-glass stem, c1890, 23in (58.5cm) wide.
£630–700 / €940–1,050
$1,100–1,250 EAL ⊞

▶ **Twelve-branch chandelier,** with engraved rose glass shades and hung with back-cut spear-point prisms, the canopy with suspended glass bellflowers, converted for electricity, early 20thC, 34in (86.5cm) diam. This style of chandelier is more popular with the American and Continental markets. It would probably have sold for less in the UK where it is not to current tastes. Chandeliers should always be checked for missing drops as this can adversely affect value.
£740–890 / €1,100–1,300
$1,350–1,600 NOA ✎

Metalware

Victorian brass padlock, 2in (5cm) diam. This padlock would probably be sought after by key collectors. It would be an ideal item to start off a first collection as it is small, well made and a relatively common item.
£12–16 / €15–20
$20–25 WiB ⊞

Two late Victorian compasses, 1¾in (4.5cm) diam These compasses have a low price as they are not a popular collecting area.
£18–20 / €20–30
$25–35 each VB ⊞

Metal jotter, by Barringer, Wallis & Manners, 1905, 4 x 2½in (10 x 6.5cm).
£35–40 / €50–60
$60–70 HUX ⊞

◄ **Victorian brass safe plaque and keyhole,** 7in (18cm) high. The crest on this plaque adds interest and without it the plaque would be worth around £10–15 / €15–20 / $20–25.
£25–30 / €35–45
$45–55 WiB ⊞

Brass paper clip, embossed with the Eiffel Tower, c1880, 4in (10cm) long.
£50–60 / €75–90
$90–105 CB ⊞

Pair of brass chimney ornaments, early 19thC, 5in (12.5cm) high. These brass chimney ornaments would look good with brass fireplace furniture. To be sure that items such as these are genuine, it is advisable to consult a specialist.
£40–45 / €60–65
$70–80 TOP ⊞

Miner's brass tobacco tin, inscribed 'Frank Hinge 1892', 3in (7.5cm) diam. This item would be sought after by collectors of smoking-related items.
£60–70 / €90–105
$105–120 MB ⊞

Miller's compares...

A. Brass chamberstick, c1830, 7½in (19cm) wide.
£70–80 / €105–120
$125–140 F&F ⊞

B. Brass chamberstick, initialled 'M. S.', French, c1710, 8in (20.5cm) long.
£430–480 / €640–720
$760–850 SEA ⊞

Item A and Item B are made of brass. However, Item B is of an earlier date, has a more elegant shape and a better colour, which is why it is worth six times as much as Item A.

Pair of mother-of-pearl and brass opera glasses, by S. Avallon, French, late 18thC, 4in (10cm) wide, with case. The mother-of-pearl on these glasses adds appeal to collectors and the addition of the original case has added a further 70 per cent to the price.
£75–85 / €110–125
$135–150 SAT ⊞

Brass pestle and mortar, c1760, 3½in (9cm) high. This item would appeal to collectors of brass items or kitchenware.
€70–80 / €105–120
$125–140 F&F ⊞

◀ **Pair of gilt-brass and opaline glass tie-backs,** small repair needed, French, 19thC, 10½in (26.5cm) high. These tie-backs sold in America where they are currently popular. If sold in the UK they could have made £50–60 / €75–90 / $90–105.
£80–95 / €120–140
$140–165 JAA ⚒

The look without the price

This mortar, with its appealing relief pattern, is a desirable collectors' item. It would have been made with a matching pestle, which is now missing. If complete, it would be worth a further £35 / €50 / $60.

Bronze mortar, Spanish, 18thC, 3in (7.5cm) high.
£80–90 / €110–130
$135–160 AH ⚒

Bronze pen wipe, modelled as a greyhound, 19thC, 4¾in (12cm) long. Writing ephemera is a popular collecting area and this pen wipe is a desirable item. However, if it had been made of silver it could be worth £145 / €220 / $260.
£85–100 / €125–150
$150–175 DN(BR) 🔨

Gilt-bronze paper clip, modelled as a duck's head, with glass eyes, early 20thC, 8¾in (22cm) long. Novelty items such as this appeal to collectors.
£95–110 / €140–165
$170–195 G(L) 🔨

Pair of mother-of-pearl and brass opera glasses, with extending handle, late 19thC, 4in (10cm) wide, with case. Although already an attractive item due to the mother-of-pearl decoration, the extending handle and case have added value to these glasses.
£120–135 / €180–200
$210–240 SAT ⊞

Cut-steel-mounted velvet sewing étui, with five fittings, 19thC, 5in (12.5cm) long. Etuis are collectable items, but remember that an incomplete set will have a lower value. Examples made from hallmarked silver can be worth an additional 20 per cent.
£130–155 / €195–230
$230–270 WW 🔨

Painted tobacco tin, with decoration entitled 'The Classroom Dunce', 1800–10, 4¾ x 2¾in (12 x 7cm). Tins with unusual painted scenes such as this one are popular with buyers.
£135–160 / €200–240
$240–280 MB ⊞

Copper one-gallon 'haystack' measure, c1840, 12in (30.5cm) high. It is important to remember that dents and other forms of damage can reduce the value of an item by up to 15 per cent.
£140–160 / €210–240
$250–280 F&F ⊞

▶ **Brass table lighter,** modelled as Mr Punch smoking a cigar, 19thC, 8in (20.5cm) high. Buyers should be aware that there are many reproduction novelty items on the market. If in doubt about authenticity when buying a specific item it is advisable to seek advice from a specialist.
£140–165 / €210–250
$250–290 G(L) 🔨

The look without the price

Matched pair of cloisonné vases, decorated with birds and flowering trees, damaged, Japanese, c1880, larger 7in (18cm) high.
£200–240 / €300–360
$350–420 SWO 🔨

Cloisonné vases were often made in pairs and although these examples are a close match they are not identical. Without the damage and as a perfect pair, these vases could have achieved a further 20 per cent.

Pair of brass candlesticks, with petal bases, c1750, 8in (20.5cm) high. Although these candlesticks have unusual petal bases, brass is not very fashionable and, as a result, prices for brass items are lower than in previous years.
£250–280 / €370–420
$440–500 KEY ⊞

Cross Reference
Lighting (pages 254–257)

◀ **Bronze inkwell,** modelled as a ram, the hinged back enclosing two apertures, French, 19thC, 5½in (14cm) high. This inkwell would be popular with collectors of novelty writing ephemera. The presence of a signature would add value.
£260–310
€390–460
$460–550 LAY 🔨

◀ **Wrought-iron branding iron,** 18thC, 16in (40.5cm) long. This branding iron is unusual and would attract particular interest in the USA.
£350–390 / €520–580
$620–690 KEY ⊞

Brass and copper brazier, on a later bronze stand with claw-and-ball feet, Spanish, 16thC, 21¼in (54cm) wide. Claw-and-ball feet are an attractive feature on any antique and can increase its value.
£440–520 / €660–770
$780–920 S(Am) 🔨

Brass alms dish, with embossed decoration and inscription, 16thC, 15¾in (40cm) diam. The design of this dish would appeal to collectors of Arts and Crafts pieces and the inscription provides additional interest.
£500–600 / €750–890
$890–1,050 S(O) 🔨

Rugs & Carpets

The look without the price

This rug appears to have stretched out of shape and this may be because the weavers did not spin the warp threads tightly enough. This is a common feature of northwest Persian rugs, where wool was used as the foundation. Rugs of this age and in perfect condition are rare due to the nature of their use. If this rug were in perfect shape and condition it could be worth £800–1,200 / € 1,200–1,800 / $1,400–2,100.

Kurdish rug, northwest Persian, late 19thC, 99 x 53in (251.5 x 134.5cm). **£100–120 / € 150–180 $175–210** WW 🔨

Feraghan rug, worn, west Persian, late 19thC, 77 x 53in (195.5 x 134.5cm). This rug has paler colouring and an overall pattern, rather than one incorporating a central medallion, and this tends to be more popular with buyers. It is also rather worn and this is the reason for the low value of this rug.
£100–120 / € 150–180 $175–210 WW 🔨

Find out more in

Miller's Antiques Encyclopedia, Miller's Publications, 2003

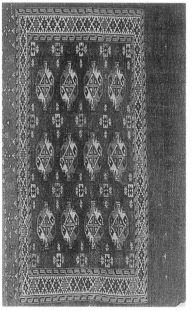

Yomud Turkoman bagface, minor losses, c1910, 47 x 32in (119.5 x 81.5cm). Turkoman pieces tend to appeal to collectors wishing to add to their collection, rather than buyers wanting an item for everyday use.
£160–190 / € 240–280 $280–330 JAA 🔨

Hamadan runner, worn, west Persian, c1920, 149 x 45in (378.5 x 114.5cm). This rug has even wear which is preferable to patchy wear and it could have fetched £400 / € 600 / $710. If it had been a more desirable width – between 34in (86.5cm) and 40in (101.5cm) – it could have achieved between £800–1,200 / € 1,200–1,800 / $1,400–2,100.
£200–240 / € 300–360 $350–420 WW 🔨

Ersari *ensis*, slight wear, north Afghani, early 20thC, 68 x 61in (172.5 x 155cm). *Ensis* were used as entrance or wall hangings. They are not very popular at the moment and this is reflected in the price.
£230–270 / € 340–400 $410–480 WW 🔨

Miller's compares...

A. Hamadan runner,
west Persian, 1900–20,
165 x 41in (419 x 104cm).
£100–120 / €150–180
$175–210 WW ✗

B. Kurdish rug, west
Persian, Hamadan region,
c1900, 114 x 47in
(289.5 x 119.5cm).
£400–480 / €600–720
$710–850 WW ✗

Item A appears to be 'abrashed' which is when
different batches of dye have faded at different
rates. It is possible that the weavers ran out of
one batch of dye and started another. Item B is a
Kurdish rug and these are often coarser. It is rare
to find examples with such detail, which is why
Item B sold for a much higher price than Item A.

Karadja rug, worn, northwest Persian,
1900–20, 74 x 56in (188 x 142cm).
Geometric patterns and contrasting colours
are popular features. Had it been in good
condition, this rug could have been worth
between £700–900 / €1,050–1,350 /
$1,250–1,600.
£240–280 / €360–420
$420–500 WW ✗

Persian rugs & carpets

When identifying the source of
Persian rugs and carpets, it is
useful to examine the foundation
and the style of design. Although
there are exceptions to the rule,
examples with formal designs
and cotton foundations tend to
be from villages or towns, while
rugs and carpets with wool
foundations and naive designs
are often tribal.

◀ **Kurd Bijar rug,** worn,
slight losses, northwest Persian,
1850–1900, 102 x 78in
(259 x 198cm). Bijar rugs are
very stiff to handle as they
are made with a very heavy
foundation which is almost
impossible to repair. Bijar rugs
in good condition are highly
sought after and command top
prices. This example has uneven
wear and has suffered slight
losses at the corners and ends,
which would account for its
lower price.
£260–310 / €390–460
$460–550 WW ✗

▶ **Herati carpet,** worn, some losses, northwest Persian, c1910,
190 x 134in (473 x 340.5cm). Larger rugs sell better in America
than in the UK, but highly detailed patterns on dark backgrounds
are unpopular with most buyers.
£300–360 / €450–540
$530–640 JAA ✗

◀ **Afshar rug,** southwest Persian, c1890, 53 x 40in (134.5 x 101.5cm).
£360–400 / €540–600 $640–710 WADS ⊞

Bakhtiari carpet, west Persian, c1900, 162 x 128in (413 x 325cm). Bakhtiari carpets are often made using dark, deep colours, which are currently unfashionable. However, this rug is a good buy at the moment as it is a large size. It could be worth £1,000–1,500 / €1,500–2,250 / $1,750–2,650 and might be more appealing to American buyers.
£310–370 / €460–550 $550–650 S(O) ⚹

Bakhtiari carpet, west Persian, early 20thC, 122¾ x 86¾in (312 x 220.5cm). Although the colours of this rug are currently out of favour with buyers, its overall pattern is preferable to a design incorporating a central medallion.
£480–570 / €720–850 $850–1,000 S(O) ⚹

Lori rug, slight damage, west Persian, late 19thC, 97 x 46in (246.5 x 117cm). This tribal rug has been coarsely woven and has appealing colours. However, there is slight damage to the edges and this would be worth repairing to prevent further deterioration and reduction in value.
£500–600 / €750–890 $890–1,050 S(O) ⚹

▶ **Feraghan rug,** overall even wear, slight damage, west Persian, 1850–1900, 124 x 61in (315 x 155cm). This piece is neither a runner nor a carpet, however it is an attractive design and if it was a larger size it could be worth £2,000–3,000 / €3,000–4,450 / $3,550–5,300.
£620–740 / €920–1,100 $1,100–1,300 WW ⚹

Sarab rug, slight dye corrosion, northwest Persian, 1900–20, 95 x 44in (241.5 x 112cm). Damage such as the natural corrosion of this iron-based dye is acceptable and does not need to be restored. Collectors will not be concerned as it should not affect the value of the rug or carpet.
£480–570 / €720–850 $850–1,000 WW ⚹

Afshar rug, decorated with stylized floral bouquets, southwest Persian, c1900, 56 x 43¼in (142 x 110cm). This tribal rug appears to be worn in the centre. The pattern is an unusual size and has an appealing white ground. Without the wear it could be worth £1,200–1,400 / €1,800–2,100 / $2,100–2,500.
£630–750 / €940–1,100 $1,100–1,300 RTo ⚒

Khamseh rug, southwest Persian, c1890, 66 x 51in (167.5 x 129.5cm). The thick pile of this rug enables it to withstand wear and tear and therefore be used on the floor. When using rugs on the floor remember to vacuum them regularly and have them cleaned professionally by a specialist every five years.
£770–850 / €1,150–1,250 $1,350–1,500 WADS ⊞

Pair of Hamadan runners, west Persian, early 20thC, 117 x 41in (297 x 104cm). Individual rugs sell better than those in pairs. This could be due to the limited space available in modern homes. Individually, these rugs could have sold for 20 per cent more.
£780–930 / €1,150–1,350 $1,400–1,650 WW ⚒

◄ **Khamseh rug,** southwest Persian, c1900, 79 x 58in (200.5 x 147.5cm). The soft wool of this rug enhances its value.
£810–900 €1,200–1,350 $1,450–1,600 WADS ⊞

▶ **Heriz carpet,** northwest Persian, c1900, 117¼ x 94¾in (298 x 240.5cm). Heriz carpets vary greatly in design and quality. Examples with good overall patterns are more desirable and this particular carpet could have fetched up to £1,500 / €2,250 / $2,650.
£840–1,000 €1,250–1,500 $1,500–1,800 S(O) ⚒

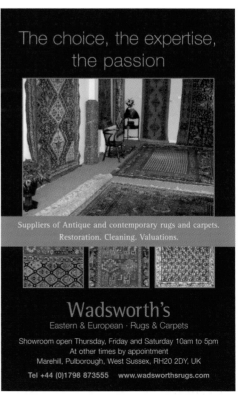

Scientific Instruments

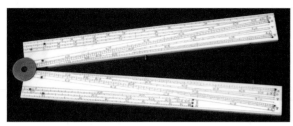

Brass and ivory rule, c1830, 6in (15cm) long. This rule belongs to the very specific and affordable collecting area of scientific instruments and, because of low demand, prices are often under £1,000 / €1,500 / $1,750. Examples with marks or signatures are more valuable.
£70–80 / €105–120
$125–140 ETO ⊞

Victorian walnut electro-medical machine, with winding handle and various electrodes, 9in (23cm) wide. Although scientific instruments do not need to be in working order, they do need to be in good condition as this can affect their value.
£100–120 / €150–180
$175–210 DA ⊞

Brass microscopic lamp, c1870, 11in (28cm) high, in original pine case. It is unusual to find an individual lamp such as this. This would make an interesting collectors item.
£135–150 / €200–220
$240–270 TOM ⊞

Lacquered-brass monocular microscope, retailed by K. J. B. Dancer, Manchester, French, c1880, 12in (30.5cm) high, in original mahogany case. Retailers' labels are crucial to value. Items with labels dating pre-1880 are the most valuable probably because they are rarer than later examples.
£135–150 / €200–220
$240–270 TOM ⊞

Set of four stainless-steel medical instruments, by Arnold & Sons, comprising a sphincterscope, two proctoscopes and a sigmoidoscope, in a mahogany case, 1925, 8¾ x 17¾in (22 x 45cm). The presence of an original case can add about 60 per cent to the value of a set of instruments. A case will always make a set such as this more appealing to collectors.
£145–165 / €220–250
$260–290 FOF ⊞

◄ **Brass monocular microscope,** with additional lenses, side-adjustable magnifying glass and slides in an internal drawer, late 19thC, 15in (38cm) high, in a mahogany case. Instruments that are complete with accessories are very desirable to collectors.
£150–180
€220–270
$270–320 G(L) ⚒

Find out more in

Miller's Collecting Science & Technology, Miller's Publications, 2001

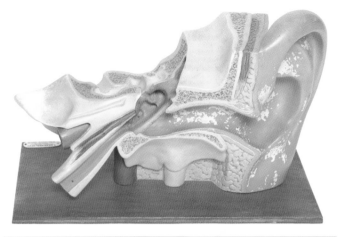

◄ **Anatomical model of the ear,** by T. Gerrard, London, paint damage, marked, c1900, 7¾in (19.5cm) high, on a mahogany base. Despite the paint damage to this model of the ear, it is a rare and unusual collector's item. This is a good buy as these items are quite rare and the damage is relatively easy to restore.
£165–185 / €240–280 $290–330 FOF ⊞

Miller's compares...

A. Lacquered- and oxidized-brass compound monocular microscope, by Watson & Sons, London, c1890, 13in (33cm) high, in a mahogany case.
£180–200 / €270–300 $320–360 TOM ⊞

B. Lacquered-brass compound monocular microscope, by Anderson & Sons, London, with accessories, c1870, 16in (40.5cm) high, in a mahogany case.
£540–600 / €800–890 $960–1,050 TOM ⊞

Although Item A is in good condition, Item B is a more complicated microscope and has a greater number of accessories. Item B is also of an earlier date and a larger size, which is why it is valued at three times the price of Item A.

Late Victorian silver-plated otoscope, by Arnold & Sons, London, in a fitted leather-covered box, marked, 3¾ x 4in (9.5 x 10cm). This silver-plated otoscope is in excellent condition. It is complete with all its parts and has retained its fitted case, making it a very desirable collectors item.
£175–195 / €260–290 $310–350 FOF ⊞

◄ **Victorian walnut-veneered apothecary box,** fitted with glass phials, stamped 'James Epps & Co', 10in (25.5cm) wide.
£200–240 / €300–360 $350–420 WW ⚒

► **Tortoiseshell double-bladed hernia bistoury,** by Wood, c1850, 9½in (24cm) long. This is an unusual blade that was used for the removal of hernias.
£220–250 / €330–370 $390–440 FOF ⊞

Set of brass postal scales, by S. Mordan & Co, 19thC, on a walnut base, 15in (38cm) wide. Scales are very collectable and this is a respectable price for an example with a walnut base and by a well-known maker.
£220–260 / €330–390
$390–460 SWO ✗

Early Victorian fruitwood monaural stethoscope, 6¾in (17cm) long, with a papier-mâché case. Instruments with cases can command higher prices and in this instance the case accounts for one third of the total value.
£250–280 / €370–420
$440–500 FOF ⊞

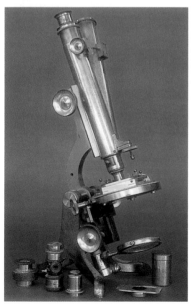

Pair of steel forceps, French, 1860, 18in (45.5cm) long.
£220–250 / €330–370
$390–440 CuS ⊞

Spring fleam, early 18thC, in a case, 1½ x 2¾in (4 x 7cm). The case for this fleam appears to be in bad condition, but it has still added about 20 per cent to the price of this piece.
£260–290 / €390–430
$460–520 FOF ⊞

The look without the price

Moritz Pillischer, a maker of instruments, was based in London where he worked from c1851 to 1887. This is one of the later models he produced and is an affordable price, whereas his earlier and rarer microscopes, such as model No. 29, can sell for four-figure sums if in good condition.

Victorian brass monocular microscope, No. 306, by M. Pillischer, London, with rack-and-pinion focusing and platform, with eight lenses, in a mahogany box, 16¼in (41.5cm) high.
£260–310 / €390–460
$460–550 DN(BR) ✗

◄ **Brass microscope,** No. 1581, by Henry Crouch, London, with spare lenses, 18in (45.5cm) high. This microscope is by a well-known maker. If it had retained its original case it could be worth upwards of £400 / €600 / $710.
£260–310 / €390–460
$460–550 BWL ✗

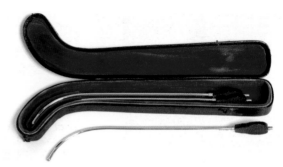

Set of Victorian walnut and brass postal scales, with brass decoration and engraved balance and weights, 8in (20.5cm) wide. The engraved and cut-brass decoration makes these scales very attractive and will appeal to collectors.
£300–340 / €450–510
$530–600 PEZ ⊞

Set of three early Victorian silver and ebony catheters, Chester 1843, 11¾in (30cm) long, in a leather-covered case. These catheters would appeal to collectors of both medical instruments and silver items.
£390–440 / €580–660
$690–780 FOF ⊞

◄ **Pine microscope slide box,** with 18 drawers containing a large assortment of slides, with ivory handles, c1880, 11in (28cm) high. Half of the value of this box lies in the slides it contains – thus illustrating the importance of the original contents.
£400–450 / €600–670
$710–800 TOM ⊞

Travelling brass microscope, with fitted shagreen case, 19thC, case 4in (10cm) wide. It is unusual to find a travelling microscope. This example is complete with all its accessories and case, which is reflected in the price.
£450–540 / €670–800
$800–960 WW ⚒

Silver thermometer, by Soloman Maw, London, with a hand-painted silvered dial, c1881, 1in (2.5cm) high. This thermometer would appeal to collectors of small, high-quality silver items as well as those seeking to collect medical instruments.
£720–800
€1,050–1,200
$1,250–1,400
FOF ⊞

Brass monocular microscope, by H. Levo, London, 19thC, on a mahogany plinth, 17in (43cm) high, with a mahogany case containing lenses and slides. The unusual shape of this box adds interest and is the reason why this microscope achieved a high price.
£610–730 / €910–1,100
$1,100–1,300 TRM ⚒

Sculpture

◄ **Parcel-gilt-bronze figure of Flora**, late 19thC, 3¼in (8.5cm) high. This figure was possibly a mount for a piece of furniture. It is made from a poor-quality moulding with little detail, and this accounts for its low value.
£120–140
€180–220
$210–260 WW ➷

The look without the price

Items made from alabaster are not as sought after as items made from marble. This is because alabaster is a softer material, which not only makes it easier to carve, but also more prone to damage. If this well-carved piece were made of marble it could be worth 15 to 20 times this amount.

Alabaster figure of a woman, plinth chipped, 1920s, 11in (28cm) high.
£50–60 / €75–90
$90–105 SWO ➷

Ivory figure of a saint, staff damaged, Spanish, 18thC, 11in (28cm) high. This ivory figure has suffered splits and other damage, but this is to be expected of an item of this age. If it were in good condition this figure could achieve £200–250 / €300–370 / $350–440.
£120–145 / €180–210
$210–250 G(L) ➷

Limewood bust of a bearded man, German, 18thC, 13¾in (35cm) high. This bust appears to be a fragment from a larger carving. Limewood is very soft, hence the cracks in this piece. This item could be worth £300–400 / €450–600 / $530–710 if it were in better condition.
£220–260 / €330–390
$390–460 DN ➷

Boxwood, oak and tortoise-shell crucifix, German, 19thC, 28¼in (72cm) high. This is a narrow collecting field. The use of tortoiseshell in this piece denotes quality. A lesser-quality crucifix could be obtained for as little as £50 / €75 / $90.
£260–310 / €390–460
$460–550 S(O) ➷

Miller's compares...

Marble bust of Dante, Italian, c1870, 12in (30.5cm) high. This good-quality bust of the Italian poet Dante was sold in the USA. However, it would be of greater interest to Continental or UK buyers, where it could have fetched £400–600 / €600–890 / $710–1,050.
£280–330 / €420–490
$500–580 DuM ✤

A. Alabaster bust of a girl, in three sections, weathered, Italian, late 19thC, 20in (51cm) high.
£200–240 / €300–360
$350–420 G(L) ✤

B. Marble bust of a young woman, repaired, some weathering, mid-19thC, 25¼in (64cm) high.
£850–1,000 / €1,250–1,450
$1,500–1,750 B(B) ✤

Item A is a Victorian alabaster bust that has weathered badly. Item B is made from white marble and is carved in the Roman style, making it the more desirable and valuable piece of the two.

▶ **Bronze statue of Salomé,** by H. Klett, German School, signed, c1900, 15in (38cm) high. This item is of poor quality and lacks detail to the face. If it had been a better quality casting it could have achieved £800–1,200 / €1,200–1,800 / $1,450–2,100.
£320–380 / €480–570
$570–670 S(Am) ✤

Cold-painted bronze model of a cat, Austrian, Vienna, c1900, 3in (7.5cm) high. Vienna bronze animals tend to be rare. Earlier examples can have wear with the bronze patination showing through the paint. Modern bronzes usually have bright, bronze bases. The cat subject in this item is a very popular one with collectors, hence the value of this piece.
£290–320 / €430–480
$510–570 RdeR ⊞

◀ **Pair of bronze figures,** after Clodion, modelled as cherubs with goat's legs, on marble plinths, 19thC, 8in (20.5cm) high. Cherub subjects appeal to collectors and interior decorators, and these are good value rococo-style examples.
£400–480 / €600–720
$710–850 RTo ✤

The look without the price

This item was cast from an original bronze and was a second casting. A second casting loses some of the definition of the original and is therefore less valuable. The harvester was a popular subject with artists such as Pieter Brugel the Elder, Jean François Millet and Vincent Van Gogh. Had this item been an original Larroux bronze, it could have been worth £600–700 / €890–1,050 / $1,050–1,250.

Patinated-bronze figure of a harvester, after Antonin Larroux, signed, 19thC, 8in (20.5cm) high.
£330–390 / €490–580 $580–690 TMA ✐

Cast-bronze group of a whippet and spaniel, by Pierre Jules Mêne, inscribed 'Coalbrookdale', signed, late 19thC, 9½in (24cm) wide. This piece is by one of the best-known and most popular bronze animal sculptors. The value has been affected by the vast quantities of well-cast patinated-bronze reproductions and forgeries that are on the market for under £50 / €75 / $90, making purchasers cautious. Without provenance even a genuine item such as this can be bought cheaply. Those with provenance are usually difficult to find under £1,500 / €2,250 / $2,650. Genuine bronzes will have varied patina, while modern examples are of one colour only.
£400–480 / €600–720 $710–850 G(L) ✐

Alabaster bust of a woman, by Professor Garella, on a marble base, Italian, late 19thC, 10½in (26.5cm) high.
£400–480 / €600–720 $710–850 G(L) ✐

Bronze model of a tuna fish, original paint, Austrian, Vienna, c1900, 5in (12.5cm) high. This is an unusual subject for a Vienna bronze, hence the low price. For some purchasers, however, rarity adds value.
£450–500 / €670–750 $800–890 RdeR ⊞

▶ **Bronze figure of a seated boy,** by F. Barbedienne Fondeur, incised mark, late 19thC, 9in (23cm) high. This bronze is of a well-known, often reproduced, subject. Its dull patina and verdigris suggest that it has been kept outside, and this accounts for its low price. In better condition this item could have achieved £600–800 / €890–1,200 / $1,050–1,400.
£480–570 / €720–850 $850–1,000 WL ✐

Find out more in

Miller's Garden Antiques: How to Source & Identify, Miller's Publications, 2003

The look without the price

Spelter figure of Diana the Huntress, 19thC, 23in (58.5cm) high.
£500–600 / €750–890 $890–1,050 SWO ⚒

Spelter was a commonly-used Victorian material which is very brittle and prone to damage. It usually has an applied patina to give it the appearance of bronze. This subject could have achieved £2,000–2,500 / €3,000–3,700 / $3,550–4,400, if it were made in bronze.

Patinated-bronze figure of Mars, after the antique, sword missing, on a later base, Italian, probably Naples, 19thC, 11¾in (30cm) high. This item is a reproduction of an antique Roman bronze and was produced as a Grand Tour tourist souvenir. The missing sword has reduced the value of this piece. Had it been complete, it could have achieved £600–800 / €890–1,200 / $1,050–1,400.
£500–600 / €750–890 $890–1,050 B(Kn) ⚒

Cold-painted bronze model of a pheasant, inscribed 'Namgreb' (Bergman), Austrian, Vienna, c1910, 14in (35.5cm) high. Pheasants are a very popular subject. This item is unusual because it is large and this accounts for its high price.
£680–750 / €1,000–1,100 $1,200–1,350 RdeR ⊞

Painted wood figure of the Christ Child, holding a silver lily staff, Spanish, 1725–75, 14½in (37cm) high. The Christ Child is a popular religious figure in South America, but it is less so in the UK where it would probably only have achieved £300–500 / €450–750 / $530–890 at auction.
£620–740 / €920–1,100 $1,100–1,300 LHA ⚒

▶ **Marble bust of a smiling child,** Italian School, late 19thC, 15½in (39.5cm) high. This is a popular and appealing subject with high-quality carving. These factors account for this piece having sold at three times its estimate.
£750–900 / €1,100–1,300 $1,350–1,600 TEN ⚒

Part-cold-painted bronze model of a capercaillie, by Bergman, on a rootwood stand, cast factory mark No. 4639, the stand impressed '1008', late 19thC, 12¼in (31cm) high. This interesting composition is well patinated and of a good colour. It is an excellent collector's piece, hence its high value.
£850–1,000 / €1,250–1,500 $1,500–1,800 SWO ⚒

Textiles

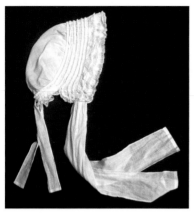

Baby's bonnet, c1900, 7in (18cm) wide. Baby clothes are very collectable. This bonnet is a good buy at this price and could be worth up to £35 / €50 / $60.
£22–25 / €30–35
$35–45 HTE ⊞

▶ **Ribbonwork sample,** worked on silk, early 19thC, 28 x 15in (71 x 38cm). Ribbonwork is a collectable area, and this sample would be particularly appealing to collectors because of its floral subject matter. It could be worth £65 / €95 / $115.
£40–45 / €60–70
$70–80 JPr ⊞

Silk and lace table runner, with silver embroidery and appliqué, c1890, 37 x 10in (94 x 25.5cm). The style of this table runner is currently very unfashionable, which accounts for its low price.
£40–45 / €60–70
$70–80 JPr ⊞

Period cushions

Good examples of period cushions abound. However, buyers should be aware not only of clever reproductions, but also of the paramount need for original cushions to have trimmings that are contemporary with the cushion material.

The very nature of their use means that cushions are subject to excessive amounts of wear, although good restoration and repair are acceptable. Lesser quality examples may be found in old material that is worked with modern trimmings and stitching. While not unacceptable, these would only be worth one-third of the original example.

Miller's compares...

A. Tapestry and beadwork cushion, c1860, 17in (43cm) square.
£60–70 / €90–105
$105–120 JPr ⊞

B. Lyon silk cut-velvet cushion, c1860, 18 x 23in (45.5 x 58.5cm).
£590–650 / €880–970
$1,050–1,150 LGU ⊞

Item A is a beaded tapestry cushion, and although these are usually sought after, this example is misshapen and the colours have run. Item B is of the same age as Item A, but the silk cut-velvet and attractive coordinating trim are in excellent condition, which is why its value is nine times that of Item A.

Miller's compares...

A. Beaded bag, 19thC,
8in (20.5cm) long.
£70–80 / €105–120
$125–140 HTE ⊞

B. Steel-beaded bag, with ormolu
frame, 1930s, 9in (23cm) long.
£170–190 / €250–280
$300–340 JPr ⊞

Item A is an attractive beaded bag with a draw-string
closure and many such examples survive today. Item B is
a collectable Art Deco bag made from unusual materials,
making it a desirable item and therefore more valuable
than Item A.

Sampler, by Jane Rumney,
dated 1824, 11in (28cm)
square. The faded colours, poor
condition and plain composition
of this sampler have detracted
from its value.
£80–90 / €120–135
$140–160 PFK ➹

Samplers

Samplers that are
worked with birds and
animals tend to be
more popular than
examples that are
worked only with text.
The more unusual the
animal, the more
valuable the sampler.
For instance, samplers
worked with zebras
are extremely rare and
are only known to
have been produced
during the 1830s.

◀ **Length of bobbin lace,**
restored, Flemish, late 17thC,
7 x 44in (18 x 112cm). Although
this lace has been restored, it is
of a good length and therefore
still holds its value.
£115–125 / €170–185
$200–220 HL ⊞

Embroidered and quilted satin purse,
late 19thC, 7 x 4in (18 x 10cm). The
embroidered phrase on this item would
appeal to collectors. If it had also been
embroidered with a date it could have been
worth an extra £50 / €75 / $90.
£115–125 / €170–185
$200–220 JPr ⊞

▶ **Velvet draw-**
string bag, c1840,
7in (18cm) long. Bags
such as this are very
desirable, especially
when decorated with
flowers. The fact that
they can easily be
displayed on a wall
adds to their value.
£140–155
€220–230
$260–270 JPr ⊞

Miller's compares...

A. Sampler, by Rosaline Augusta Tutton, dated 1884, 13in (33cm) square, framed and glazed.
£120–145 / €180–220
$210–260 G(L) 🔨

B. Tablet sampler, by Susan Snelgrove, worked with biblical verse, dated 1834, 13½ x 16in (34.5 x 40.5cm), framed and glazed.
£240–290 / €360–430
$420–510 G(L) 🔨

Woven, net and embroidered drawstring purse, late 18thC, 10in (25.5cm) long. This attractive item may well have formed part of a 'sewing book', which would have been taken to show prospective employers examples of various different sewing projects.
£220–260 / €330–390
$390–460 JPr ⊞

Item A has attractive colours and is worked with animals as well as the alphabet, but is of a later date than Item B, which has a more desirable rosewood frame. Earlier samplers tend to be more valuable and this explains why Item B sold for twice the price of Item A.

Wool curtain ties, late 19thC, 32in (81.5cm) long. Curtain ties are generally purchased for use rather than as collectors' items. The colours of this item remain vibrant and this will have had a positive affect on the price.
£200–220 / €300–330
$350–390 JPr ⊞

Part of a sampler, worked in silk on linen, late 18th/early 19thC, 6¾ x 6½in (17 x 16.5cm). As it stands, this section of a sampler would sell well as it is an attractive subject. However, had it been complete, it could have been worth three or four times this sum.
£260–310 / €390–460
$460–550 L&E 🔨

◄ **Pair of fretwork face screens,** with felt and beadwork decoration, 19thC, 18in (45.5cm) high. Fans with felt and beadwork decoration are unusual and this has accounted for the value of this pair.
£320–350 / €480–520
$570–620 JPr ⊞

Sampler, by Rebecca Slater, worked with trees and scrolling foliage, dated 1815, 9 x 7½in (23 x 19cm), together with a needlework picture. Pine trees are an unusual subject that would be desirable to collectors. This example was a good buy at auction and could be worth £500–600 / €750–890 / $890–1,050.
£340–410 / €510–610
$600–730 HYD ➤

▶ **Sampler,** by Maria Pressland, early 19thC, 18½ x 21¾in (47 x 55.5cm). This example is only part of a larger work and it is therefore of less value than the complete item. However, self-portraits and family history are highly sought after by collectors, thus improving its value.
£480–580 / €720–860
$850–1,050 DN ➤

Satin dress, with later alterations, c1730.
£600–720 / €890–1,050
$1,050–1,250 S(O) ➤

Sampler, inscribed 'Gouda' and initialled 'CA' and 'BL', dated 1824, 19½ x 18½in (49.5 x 47cm). If this sampler were English rather than Dutch it could be worth £2,000 / €3,000 / $3,550. However, it was still a good buy and could have fetched a further £200 / €300 / $350.
£380–460 / €570–690
$670–810 GAK ➤

Beaded tray, with a mahogany frame, c1880, 10 x 19in (25.5 x 48.5cm). The value of this tray has been enhanced by the beadwork, which is very collectable.
£560–620 / €830–920
$990–1,100 LGU ⊞

▶ **Tapestry fragment,** Flemish, late 17thC, 56 x 70in (142 x 178cm). Tapestries are a popular collecting area. Generally speaking, prices are size-related, so the larger the item, the higher the price.
£650–780 / €970–1,150
$1,150–1,400 G(L) ➤

Sampler, by Rebecca Bulger-Brandon, c1803, 16 x 12½in (40.5 x 32cm), in a gilt frame. This sampler depicts a hill, which is unusual, and it also has attractive 'spot motifs', which make it more appealing to collectors. This item was a good buy at auction and could have achieved £600–650 / €890–970 / $1,050–1,150.
£460–550 / €690–820
$810–970 S(O) ➤

Embroidered Cantonese silk bridal gown, decorated with beads and tassels, 1911.
£540–650 / €800–960
$960–1,150 S(O) ➤

Wooden Antiques

Wooden thatching tool, c1750, 16in (40.5cm) wide. This type of tool belongs to a very specific collecting area and because of relatively low demand for these items, pieces are usually affordable.
£80–90 / €120–135
$140–160 F&F ⊞

Tunbridge ware puzzle box, puzzle missing, c1880, 2in (5cm) square. This box would originally have contained a puzzle. In good condition and complete with the puzzle, this box could be worth around £80–140 / €120–210 / $140–250.
£50–60 / €75–90
$90–105 HTE ⊞

Tunbridge ware cribbage board, decorated with an ivory plaque engraved with a Masonic symbol, 19thC, 12¼in (31cm) long, together with a brass cribbage board on a mahogany base. This cribbage board would appeal to collectors of both cribbage and Masonic items. This is not a typical Tunbridge ware piece as it is inlaid with ivory and a mixture of native and exotic woods. Multiple lots such as this are a good way to pick up a bargain. In this instance, the brass cribbage board probably accounts for only a very small percentage of the total price.
£90–105 / €135–155
$160–185 SWO ✦

Wooden desk stand, carved as a butterfly, with two covered inkwells, 19thC, 8¾in (22cm) wide. Items modelled as, or depicting, butterflies are very collectable.
£130–155 / €195–230
$230–270 SWO ✦

Tunbridge ware

Tunbridge ware originated in the 17th century and was primarily made in Tonbridge and Tunbridge Wells, Kent, although it is defined by its method of manufacture rather than the location in which it was made. Tunbridge ware sewing items are especially popular, and items decorated with animals are more desirable than those decorated with flowers. When buying, try to avoid a damaged item or boxes that are bowed as they are difficult to restore. Makers to look out for are Edmund Nye, Thomas Barton and Henry Hollamby. They all produced exceptionally fine work and items made by them are now highly sought after.

Wooden dairy bowl, with pierced lug, 19thC, 16¼in (41.5cm) diam. A pierced lug is a loop or handle with a hole through it, which enables the item to be hung from the ceiling or on a wall. Wooden bowls such as this are popular with the American market.
£130–155 / €195–230
$230–270 PFK ✦

Tunbridge ware tape measure, by Edmund Nye, c1850, 1in (2.5cm) long. Edmund Nye produced high-quality wares. A named maker can add 10 to 20 per cent to the value of an item.
£135–150 / €200–220
$240–270 VB ⊞

Victorian coromandel Betjemann's Patent book slide, applied with Gothic-style gilt-brass motifs, 13in (33cm) closed.
£170–200 / €250–300
$300–350 TMA 🔨

Book slides

Book slides were fashionable from 1850 to 1910 and are widely available. Although they are not particularly collectable, good-quality examples with their 'stops' still intact and those with a retailer's plaque are desirable.

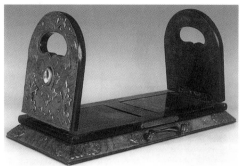

Burr-walnut and brass-mounted book slide, each end applied with a porcelain plaque painted with a portrait of a girl, inset with a brass plaque inscribed 'Toulmin & Gale, 7 New Bond St', c1870. Items marked with a retailer's details are desirable as they give added interest to a piece.
£140–165 / €210–240
$250–290 RTo 🔨

The look without the price

Tunbridge ware rosewood matchbox, modelled as a book, inlaid with tesserae mosaic, three drawers missing, 3¾in (9.5cm) wide.
£160–190 / €240–280
$280–340 DN(BR) 🔨

Complete with drawers, this matchbox could have achieved £275 / €410 / $490. However, at this price it is an affordable and attractive display piece.

◀ **Mahogany lazy Susan,** 19thC, 16in (40.5cm) diam. Antique lazy Susans are often bought by collectors to display small items such as thimbles. They are very popular in America.
£190–220 / €280–330
$340–390 SWO 🔨

George III wooden police constable's rattle, 10in (25.5cm) wide. Rattles are a popular collecting area and the early date and police connection has given this item added value.
£200–220 / €300–330
$350–390 TLA ⊞

Georgian oak book press, 13½in (34.5cm) high. Smaller examples of book presses are more desirable.
£320–360 / €480–540
$570–640 KEY ⊞

Regency Tunbridge ware rosewood work box, the hinged cover enclosing a lift-out tray, with lion-mask handles, 11in (28cm) wide. Work boxes of this period can be valuable, especially examples with Van Dyke and penwork decoration. This example is an attractive shape, but the lack of decoration to the frieze has kept the price low.
£350–420 / €520–630
$620–740 SWO ⊅

Miller's compares...

A. Mahogany tray, with inlaid decoration and brass handles, c1900, 21in (53.5cm) wide.
£300–330 / €450–500
$530–590 TOP ⊞

B. Edwardian satinwood tray, with inlaid decoration, 27in (68.5cm) wide.
£450–500 / €670–750
$800–890 HiA ⊞

While both trays are of a similar date and shape, Item A is made of mahogany and has a simple scroll decoration. Item B is made of satinwood, the more desirable of the two woods, and has a complex and attractive inlay, providing an appealing colour contrast. Hence Item B is more desirable and valuable than Item A.

► **Mahogany cigar dispenser,** with working musical mechanism and gilt-metal decoration, Continental, c1900, 11in (28cm) high. This novelty cigar case is in excellent condition and the working musical mechanism adds appeal. It would be a highly sought-after item for collectors of both wooden antiques and smoking accessories.
£360–400 / €540–600
$640–710 GGD ⊞

◀ **Tunbridge ware ebony ring box,** inlaid with a mosaic dog within tesserae bands, 19thC, 3½in (9cm) wide.
£380–450 / €570–670
$670–800 DN(BR) ✎

The look without the price

William IV mahogany boot jack, in the style of Gillows, with adjustable tongue, 30¼in (77cm) high.
£380–450 / €570–670
$670–800 B(Kn) ✎

This boot jack is in working condition and was made in the style of the well-known furniture makers, Gillows. Had it actually been made by Gillows and been in good condition, it could be worth at least 10 times this price.

Tunbridge ware clamp, with tape covers and needlecase in the form of cottages, c1820, 8in (20.5cm) high. It is rare to find a clamp with more than one tape cover in such good condition. A certain amount of wear is to be expected on such items and it is wise to be suspicious of perfect pieces, especially as painted Tunbridge ware can be repainted.
£450–500 / €670–750
$800–890 RdeR ⊞

◀ **Birch peg tankard,** with a hinged cover, Norwegian, dated 1761, 8¾in (22cm) high. This is an unusual tankard and would probably appeal to Scandinavian collectors.
£550–660
€820–980
$970–1,150 CGC ✎

Tunbridge ware travelling draughts set, c1880, 5in (12.5cm) square. Draughts sets are very popular with Tunbridge ware collectors and it is difficult to find them complete with all the original pieces.
£590–650 / €880–970
$1,050–1,200 AMH ⊞

Glossary

We have defined here some of the terms that you will come across in this book. If there are any terms or technicalities you would like explained or you feel should be included in future, please let us know.

abrashed: A slight shift in colour tone caused by the weaver running out of one batch of yarn and continuing with another: each batch of a natural dye will differ slightly from others.

armorial: A full coat-of-arms. Also a term used for any object decorated with the owner's coat-of-arms, especially silver or silver plate.

astragal: Moulding into which are set the glass panes of a cabinet or bookcase.

bergère: Originally any armchair with upholstered sides, now more often used to describe a chair with a square or round caned back and sides.

bevelled glass: Where a slope is cut at the edge of a flat surface. Usually associated with the plate glass used in mirrors.

boteh: The Paisley motif which may also be found in stylized form. It probably represents a leaf.

bright-cut engraving: Whereby the metal surface is cut creating facets that reflect the light.

cabriole leg: Tall curving leg subject to many designs and produced with club, pad, paw, claw-and-ball, and scroll feet.

canapé: A large settee with upholstered back and arms.

cartouche: A decorative frame, surrounded by scrollwork and foliage, often bearing an inscription, monogram or coat-of-arms.

chasing: Method of decorating using hammers and punches to push metal into a relief pattern – the metal is displaced, not removed.

corbel: Projecting moulding at the top of tall cabinet furniture.

coromandel: Yellow- and black-striped wood from South America which is used mainly for crossbanding.

credenza: Elaborately decorated Victorian side cabinet, sometimes with rounded ends, and often with glazed or solid doors.

doucai: Decoration on Chinese porcelain using five colours.

enamel: Coloured glass, applied to metal, ceramic or glass in paste form and then fired for decorative effect.

field: The large area of a rug or carpet usually enclosed by borders.

finial: An ornament, often carved in many forms from animal figures to obelisks, and used to finish off any vertical projection.

fleam: A type of lancet, popular from the beginning of the 18thC, for making an incision into the vein of an animal for blood letting.

gesso: Composition of plaster of Paris and size which was used as a base for applying gilding and usually moulded in bas relief.

incuse: A mark or design stamped or hammered onto an object (usually a coin).

intaglio: Incised gemstone, often set in a ring, used in antiquity and during the Renaissance as a seal. Any incised decoration; the opposite of carving in relief.

kilim: A simple, pileless rug or carpet.

KPM: Königliche Porzellan Manufactur. Mark used on Berlin porcelain 1832–1957.

lithography: Method of polychrome printing in which a design is drawn in ink on a stone surface and transferred to paper. Lithographic prints were also used to decorate ceramics.

marotte: Doll on a stick which plays a tune when spun round.

marquetry: Design formed from different coloured woods veneered onto a carcase to give a decorative effect. Many early examples are Dutch.

meiping: Chinese for cherry blossom. A term referring to a tall vase, with high shoulders, small neck and narrow mouth, used to display flowering branches.

mon: A Japanese crest, or coat-of-arms.

monopodia: Furniture leg carved as an animal's limb with a paw, usually found on console or pier tables.

nacreous: Made from mother-of-pearl, or having the lustre of, mother-of-pearl.

naos or cella: The inner room of a temple housing the statue of a deity.

ogee: Double curved shape which is convex at the top and becomes concave at the bottom. It is often found on the feet of Georgian furniture. Also known as *cyma reversa*.

papier-mâché: Paper pulp usually combined with a glue and moulded into boxes, trays and ornaments, painted or japanned. Also used to make furniture building up layers of paper with pitch and oil over an iron frame.

parquetry: Decorative veneers laid in a geometric pattern.

patera: Small flat circular ornament, often in the form of an open flower or rosette, used as a ceiling or furniture ornament.

patina: Surface colour of genuinely old wood resulting from the layers of grease, dirt and polish built up over the years, and through handling. Differs from wood to wood and difficult to fake.

pilaster: Decorative flat-faced column projecting from a wall.

porter: A dark sweet ale brewed from black malt.

pricket: A sharp metal spike on which to stick a candle.

prie-dieu: Chair with a low seat and a tall back. They were made during the 19th century and were designed for prayer.

purdonium: Form of coal box patented by a Mr A. Purdon, with slots for matching shovels, often highly ornate.

putti: Cupids or cherubs used as decoration.

retipping: Replacing the tips of chair legs.

salt glaze: Hard translucent glaze used on stoneware and achieved by throwing common salt into the kiln at high temperatures. Produces a silky, pitted appearance like orange peel.

scratchweight: A note made of the weight of a silver article at assay, usually inscribed on the base. It may show how many items were in a set and, by a change in weight, if a piece has been altered. The weights are expressed as troy ounces (oz), pennyweights (dwt) and grains (gr).

skiver: Thin skin of leather used as a writing surface on desks etc.

socle: Another name for a plinth.

spelter: Zinc treated to look like bronze. An inexpensive substitute used in Art Nouveau appliqué ornament and Art Deco figures.

spigot: A stopper or tap, usually wood, and fitted to a cask.

splat: Central upright in a chair back.

strapwork: Repeated carved decoration suggesting plaited straps. Originally used in the 16th and 17th centuries and revived in the 19th century.

tamper: An instrument for packing down tobacco in a pipe.

tine: The prong of a fork; early ones have two, later ones three.

tôle peinte: French 18th-century method of varnishing sheet iron vessels so that the surface could be painted upon. And by derivation, painted metal panels applied to furniture.

troy ounce: A measurement used to express the weight of a piece of silver. One troy ounce comprises 20 pennyweights.

Tunbridge ware: Objects decorated with wooden inlay made of bundles of coloured wood cut into sections; usually simple geometric designs, but sometimes whole scenes; mid-17th to late 19th century.

verdigris: Greenish or blueish patina formed on copper, bronze or brass.

wrought-iron: A pure form of iron often used for decorative purposes.

wucai: Type of five-colour Chinese porcelain decoration.

Directory of Specialists

f you wish to be included in next year's directory, or if you have a change of address or telephone number, please contact Miller's Advertising Department on +44 (0)1580 766411 by July 2005. We advise readers to make contact by telephone before visiting a dealer, therefore avoiding a wasted journey.

ANTIQUITIES

Dorset
Ancient & Gothic, PO Box 5390, Bournemouth, BH7 6XR
Tel: 01202 431721

Lancashire
Millennia Antiquities
Tel: 01204 690175 or 07930 273998
millenniaant@aol.com
www.AncientAntiquities.co.uk

Leicestershire
Ancient & Oriental Ltd
Tel: 01664 812044
alex@antiquities.co.uk

London
Helios Gallery, 292 Westbourne Grove, W11 2PS
Tel: 07711 955997
info@heliosgallery.com
www.heliosgallery.com

ARCHITECTURAL ANTIQUES

Gloucestershire
Olliff's Architectural Antiques, 19–21 Lower Redland Road, Redland, Bristol, BS6 6TB
Tel: 0117 923 9232
marcus@olliffs.com
www.olliffs.com

Somerset
Walcot Reclamations, 108 Walcot Street, Bath, BA1 5BG Tel: 01225 444404
rick@walcot.com
www.walcot.com

Surrey
Drummonds Architectural Antiques Ltd, The Kirkpatrick Buildings, 25 London Road (A3), Hindhead, GU26 6AB
Tel: 01428 609444
www.drummonds-arch.co.uk

ARMS & MILITARIA

Nottinghamshire
Michael D. Long Ltd, 96–98 Derby Road, Nottingham, NG1 5FB Tel: 0115 941 3307
sales@michaeldlong.com
www.michaeldlong.com

Surrey
West Street Antiques, 63 West Street, Dorking, RH4 1BS Tel: 01306 883487
weststant@aol.com
www.antiquearmsandarmour.com

East Sussex
The Lanes Armoury, 26 Meeting House Lane, The Lanes, Brighton, BN1 1HB Tel: 01273 321357
enquiries@thelanesarmoury.co.uk
www.thelanesarmoury.co.uk

USA
Faganarms, Box 425, Fraser, MI 48026 Tel: 586 465 4637
info@faganarms.com
www.faganarms.com

BAROMETERS

Cheshire
Derek & Tina Rayment Antiques, Orchard House, Barton Road,

Barton, Nr Farndon, SY14 7HT
Tel: 01829 270429 or 07860 666629 and 07702 922410
raymentantiques@aol.com
www.antique-barometers.com

BOXES & TREEN

Berkshire
Mostly Boxes, 93 High Street, Eton, Windsor, SL4 6AF
Tel: 01753 858470

London
Hampton Antiques, The Crown Arcade, 119 Portobello Road, W11 2DY Tel: 01604 863979
info@hamptonantiques.co.uk
www.hamptonantiques.co.uk

East Sussex
June & Tony Stone Fine Antique Boxes, PO Box 106, Peacehaven, BN10 8AU
Tel: 01273 579333
rachel@boxes.co.uk
www.boxes.co.uk

CLOCKS

Essex
Bellhouse Antiques
Tel: 01268 710415
Bellhouse.Antiques@virgin.net

DOLLS

Buckinghamshire
Yesterday Child Tel: 020 7354 1601 or 01908 583403

Cheshire
Dollectable, 53 Lower Bridge Street, Chester, CH1 1RS
Tel: 01244 344888/679195

Kent
Barbara Ann Newman
Tel: 07850 016729

West Sussex
Pollyanna, 34 High Street, Arundel, BN18 9AB
Tel: 01903 885198

FURNITURE

Bedfordshire
S. & S. Timms, 2–4 High Street, Shefford, SG17 5DG
Tel: 01462 851051
info@timmsantiques.com
www.timmsantiques.com

Derbyshire
Stephanie Davison Antiques, Bakewell Antiques Centre, King Street, Bakewell, DE45 1DZ Tel: 01629 812496
ask@chappellsantiquescentre.com
www.stephaniedavisonantiques.com/

Hampshire
Cedar Antiques Ltd, High Street, Hartley Wintney, RG27 8NY Tel: 01252 843222 or 01189 326628

Kent
Pantiles Spa Antiques, 4, 5 & 6 Union House, The Pantiles, Tunbridge Wells, TN4 8HE Tel: 01892 541377
psa.wells@btinternet.com
www.antiques-tun-wells-kent.co.uk

Sutton Valence Antiques, North Street, Sutton Valence, Nr Maidstone, ME17 3AP
Tel: 01622 843333/01622 675332 svantiques@aol.com
www.svantiques.co.uk

Oxfordshire
Rupert Hitchcox Antiques, Warpsgrove, Nr Chalgrove, Oxford, OX44 7RW
Tel: 01865 890241
www.ruperthitchcoxantiques.co.uk

East Sussex
Pastorale Antiques, 15 Malling Street, Lewes, BN7 2RA Tel: 01273 473259 or 01435 863044
pastorale@btinternet.com

Wish Barn Antiques, Wish Street, Rye, TN31 7DA
Tel: 01797 226797

West Midlands
Martin Taylor Antiques, 323 Tettenhall Road, Wolverhampton, WV6 0JZ
Tel: 01902 751166
enquiries@mtaylor-antiques.co.uk
www.mtaylor-antiques.co.uk

GLASS

Gloucestershire
Grimes House Antiques, High Street, Moreton-in-Marsh, GL56 0AT
Tel: 01608 651029
grimes_house@cix.co.uk
www.grimeshouse.co.uk
www.cranberryglass.co.uk

London
Christine Bridge Antiques, 78 Castelnau, SW13 9EX
Tel: 07000 445277
christine@bridge-antiques.com
www.bridge-antiques.com
www.antiqueglass.co.uk

Jasmin Cameron, Antiquarius, 131–141 King's Road, SW3 4PW Tel: 020 7351 4154 or 07774 871257
jasmin.cameron@mail.com

Norfolk
Brian Watson Antique Glass, Foxwarren Cottage, High Street, Marsham, Norwich, NR10 5QA
Tel: 01263 732519
brian.h.watson@talk21.com
By appointment only

Somerset
Lynda Brine
lyndabrine@yahoo.co.uk
www.scentbottlesandsmalls.co.uk

Somervale Antiques, 6 Radstock Road, Midsomer Norton, Bath, BA3 2AJ
Tel: 01761 412686
ronthomas@somervaleantiques glass.co.uk
www.somervaleantiquesglass.co.uk

Yorkshire
Ged Selby Antique Glass
Tel: 01756 799673
By appointment only

KITCHENWARE

Kent
Wenderton Antiques
Tel: 01227 720295
By appointment only

Lincolnshire
Skip & Janie Smithson Antiques Tel: 01754 810265 or 07831 399180
smithsonantiques@hotmail.com

East Sussex
Ann Lingard, Ropewalk Antiques, Rye, TN31 7NA
Tel: 01797 223486
ann-lingard@ropewalkantiques.freeserve.co.uk

LIGHTING

Devon
The Exeter Antique Lighting Co, Cellar 15, The Quay, Exeter, EX2 4AP
Tel: 01392 490848
www.antiquelightingcompany.com

Gloucestershire
Jennie Horrocks
Tel: 07836 264896
info@artnouveaulighting.co.uk
artnouveaulighting.co.uk

MARKETS & CENTRES

Bedfordshire
Woburn Abbey Antiques Centre, Woburn, MK17 9WA
Tel: 01525 290350
antiques@woburnabbey.co.uk

Gloucestershire
The Old Ironmongers Antiques Centre, 5 Burford Street, Lechlade, GL7 3AP
Tel: 01367 252397

The Top Banana Antiques Mall, 1 New Church Street, Tetbury, GL8 8DS
Tel: 0871 288 1102
info@topbananaantiques.com
www.topbananaantiques.com

Norfolk
Tombland Antiques Centre, Augustine Steward House, 14 Tombland, Norwich, NR3 1HF Tel: 01603 619129 or 761906
www.tomblandantiques.co.uk

Northamptonshire
The Brackley Antique Cellar, Drayman's Walk, Brackley, NN13 6BE
Tel: 01280 841841
antiquecellar@tesco.net

Oxfordshire
Heritage, 6 Market Place, Woodstock, OX20 1TA
Tel: 01993 811332/0870 4440678
dealers@atheritage.co.uk
www.atheritage.co.uk

The Swan at Tetsworth, High Street, Tetsworth, Nr Thame, OX9 7AB Tel: 01844 281777 antiques@theswan.co.uk www.theswan.co.uk

Surrey
Great Grooms of Dorking, 50/52 West Street, Dorking, RH4 1BU Tel: 01306 887076 laurence@greatgrooms.co.uk www.great-grooms.co.uk

East Sussex
The Brighton Lanes Antique Centre, 12 Meeting House Lane, Brighton, BN1 1HB Tel: 01273 823121 peter@brightonlanes-antiquecentre.co.uk www.brightonlanes-antiquecentre.co.uk

Church Hill Antiques Centre, 6 Station Street, Lewes, BN7 2DA Tel: 01273 474 842 churchhilllewes@aol.com www.church-hill-antiques.co.uk

Worcestershire
Worcester Antiques Centre, Reindeer Court, Mealcheapen Street, Worcester, WR1 4DF Tel: 01905 610680 WorcsAntiques@aol.com

OAK & COUNTRY
Buckinghamshire
Manor Farm Barn Antiques Tel: 01296 658941 or 07720 286607 mfbn@btinternet.com btwebworld.com/mfbantiques

Cambridgeshire
Mark Seabrook Antiques, PO Box 396, Huntingdon, PE28 0ZA Tel: 01480 861935 enquiries@markseabrook.com www.markseabrook.com

PAPERWEIGHTS
CHESHIRE
Sweetbriar Gallery Paperweights Ltd, 3 Collinson Court, off Church Street, Frodsham, WA6 6PN Tel: 01928 730064 sales@sweetbriar.co.uk www.sweetbriar.co.uk

Northern Ireland
Marion Langham Limited, Claranagh, Tempo, Co Fermanagh, BT94 3FJ Tel: 028 895 41247 marion@ladymarion.co.uk www.ladymarion.co.uk

PINE
Gloucestershire
Cottage Farm Antiques, Stratford Road, Aston Subedge, Chipping Campden, GL55 6PZ Tel: 01386 438263 info@cottagefarmantiques.co.uk www.cottagefarmantiques.co.uk

Hampshire
Pine Cellars, 39 Jewry Street, Winchester, SO23 8RY Tel: 01962 777546/867014

REPUBLIC OF IRELAND
Bygones of Ireland Ltd, Lodge Road, Westport, Co Mayo Tel: 00 353 98 26132/25701 bygones@anu.ie www.bygones-of-ireland.com

Delvin Farm Antiques, Gormonston, Co Meath Tel: 353 1 841 2285 info@delvinfarmpine.com john@delvinfarmpine.com www.delvinfarmpine.com

Somerset
Ministry of Pine, Timsbury Village Workshop, Unit 2, Timsbury Industrial Estate, Hayeswood Road, Timsbury, Bath, BA2 0HQ Tel: 01761 472297 ministryofpine.uk@virgin.net www.ministryofpine.com

East Sussex
Ann Lingard, Ropewalk Antiques, Rye, TN31 7NA Tel: 01797 223486 ann-lingard@ropewalkantiques.freeserve.co.uk

Warwickshire
Pine & Things, Portobello Farm, Campden Road, Nr Shipston-on-Stour, CV36 4PY Tel: 01608 663849 www.pinethings.co.uk

POTTERY & PORCELAIN
Cambridgeshire
Houghton Antiques Tel: 01480 461887 or 07803 716842

Derbyshire
Roger de Ville Antiques Tel: 01629 812496 or 07798 793857 www.rogerdeville.co.uk

Dorset
Greystoke Antiques, 4 Swan Yard, (off Cheap Street), Sherborne, DT9 3AX Tel: 01935 812833

Gloucestershire
Coco's Corner, Unit 4, Cirencester Antique Centre, Cirencester Tel: 01452 556 308 cocos-corner@blueyonder.co.uk

Fox Cottage Antiques, Digbeth Street, Stow-on-the-Wold, GL54 1BN Tel: 01451 870307

Peter Scott Tel: 0117 986 8468 or 07850 639770

Hampshire
Millers Antiques Ltd, Netherbrook House, 86 Christchurch Road, Ringwood, BH24 1DR Tel: 01425 472062 mail@millers-antiques.co.uk www.millers-antiques.co.uk

London
Aurea Carter, PO Box 44134, SW6 3YX Tel: 020 7731 3486 aureacarter@englishceramics.com www.englishceramics.com

Guest & Gray, 1–7 Davies Mews, W1K5 AB Tel: 020 7408 1252 info@chinese-porcelain-art.com www.chinese-porcelain-art.com

Hope & Glory, 131A Kensington Church Street, W8 7LP Tel: 020 7727 8424

R & G McPherson Antiques, 40 Kensington Church Street, W8 4BX Tel: 020 7937 0812 rmcpherson@orientalceramics.com www.orientalceramics.com

Rogers de Rin, 76 Royal Hospital Road, SW3 4HN Tel: 020 7352 9007

Ray Walker Antiques, Burton Arcade, 296 Westbourne Grove, W11 2PS Tel: 020 8464 7981 rw.antiques@btinternet.com

Middlesex
Royal Commemorative China Tel: 020 8863 0625 royalcommemorative@hotmail.com

Norfolk
Roger Bradbury Antiques, Church Street, Coltishall, NR12 7DJ Tel: 01603 737444

Northern Ireland
Marion Langham Limited, Claranagh, Tempo, Co Fermanagh, BT94 3FJ Tel: 028 895 41247 marion@ladymarion.co.uk www.ladymarion.co.uk

Oxfordshire
Key Antiques of Chipping Norton, 11 Horsefair, Chipping Norton, OX7 5AL Tel: 01608 644992/643777 info@keyantiques.com www.keyantiques.com

REPUBLIC OF IRELAND
George Stacpoole, Main Street, Adare, Co Limerick Tel: 6139 6409 stacpoole@iol.ie www.georgestacpooleantiques.com

East Sussex
Jupiter Antiques, PO Box 609, Rottingdean, BN2 7FW Tel: 01273 302865

Wiltshire
Andrew Dando, 34 Market Street, Bradford on Avon, BA15 1LL Tel: 01225 865444 andrew@andrewdando.co.uk www.andrewdando.co.uk

Yorkshire
Country Collector, 11–12 Birdgate, Pickering, YO18 7AL Tel: 01751 477481 www.country-collector.co.uk

RUGS & CARPETS
West Sussex
Wadsworth's, Marehill, Pulborough, RH20 2DY Tel: 01798 873555 info@wadsworthsrugs.com www.wadsworthsrugs.com

SCIENTIFIC INSTRUMENTS
Cambridgeshire
Fossack & Furkle, PO Box 733, Abington, CB1 6BF Tel: 01223 894296 fossack@btopenworld.com www.fossackandfurkle.freeservers.com

Cheshire
Charles Tomlinson, Chester Tel: 01244 318395 charlestomlinson@tiscali.co.uk

London
Curious Science, 319 Lillie Road, Fulham, SW6 7LL Tel: 020 7610 1175 curiousscience@medical-antiques.com

Surrey
Eric Tombs, 62a West Street, Dorking, RH4 1BS Tel: 01306 743661 ertombs@aol.com www.dorkingantiques.com

SILVER
Gloucestershire
Corner House Antiques and Ffoxe Antiques, Gardners Cottage, Broughton Poggs, Filkins, Lechlade-on-Thames, GL7 3JH Tel: 01367 860078 jdhis007@btopenworld.com www.corner-house-antiques.co.uk

Kent
Tenterden Antiques & Silver Vaults, 66 High Street, Tenterden, TN30 6AU Tel: 01580 765885

London
Daniel Bexfield, 26 Burlington Arcade, W1J 0PU Tel: 020 7491 1720 antiques@bexfield.co.uk www.bexfield.co.uk

Lyn Bloom & Jeffrey Neal, Vault 27, The London Silver Vaults, Chancery Lane, WC2A 1QS Tel: 020 7242 6189 bloomvault@aol.com www.bloomvault.com

TEDDY BEARS
Gloucestershire
Bourton Bears Tel: 01993 824756 help@bourtonbears.co.uk www.bourtonbears.com

TEXTILES
Devon
Honiton Lace Shop, 44 High Street, Honiton, EX14 1PJ Tel: 01404 42416 shop@honitonlace.com www.honitonlace.com

Gloucestershire
Collectable Costume, Showroom South, Gloucester Antiques Centre, 1 Severn Road, Gloucester, GL1 2LE Tel: 01989 562188 or 07980 623926

London
Linda Bee, Art Deco Stand L18–21, Grays Antique Market, 1–7 Davies Mews, W1Y 1AR Tel: 020 7629 5921

Linda Gumb, Stand 123, Grays Antique Market, 58 Davies Street, W1K 5LP Tel: 020 7629 2544 linda@lindagumb.com

Somerset
La Femme Tel: 07971 844279 jewels@joancorder.freeserve.co.uk

Joanna Proops Antique Textiles & Lighting, 34 Belvedere, Lansdown Hill, Bath, BA1 5HR Tel: 01225 310795 antiquetextiles@aol.co.uk www.antiquetextiles.co.uk

TOYS
Yorkshire
John & Simon Haley, 89 Northgate, Halifax, HX1 1XF Tel: 01422 822148/360434 toysandbanks@aol.com

TUNBRIDGE WARE
Kent
Variety Box Tel: 01892 531868

London
Amherst Antiques, Monomark House, 27 Old Gloucester Street, WC1N 3XX Tel: 01892 725552 info@amherstantiques.co.uk www.amherstantiques.co.uk

WATCHES
Hampshire
Tickers, 37 Northam Road, Southampton, SO14 0PD Tel: 02380 234431 kmonckton@btopenworld.com

London
Pieces of Time, (1–7 Davies Mews), 26 South Molton Lane, W1Y 2LP Tel: 020 7629 2422 info@antique-watch.com www.antique-watch.com

Directory of Auctioneers

Auctioneers who hold frequent sales should contact us on +44 (0)1580 766411 by July 2005 for inclusion in the next edition.

UNITED KINGDOM

Bedfordshire
W. & H. Peacock, 26 Newnham Street, Bedford MK40 3JR
Tel: 01234 266366

Berkshire
Dreweatt Neate, Donnington Priory, Donnington, Newbury RG14 2JE
Tel: 01635 553553
donnington@dnfa.com
www.dnfa.com/donnington

Law Fine Art Tel: 01635 860033
info@lawfineart.co.uk
www.lawfineart.co.uk

Special Auction Services, Kennetholme, Midgham, Reading RG7 5UX Tel: 0118 971 2949
www.invaluable.com/sas/

Cambridgeshire
Cheffins, Clifton House, 1 & 2 Clifton Road, Cambridge CB1 7EA Tel: 01223 271966
www.cheffins.co.uk

Channel Islands
Bonhams and Langlois, Westaway Chambers, 39 Don Street, St Helier, Jersey JE2 4TR Tel: 01534 722441
www.bonhams.com

Cumbria
Mitchells, Fairfield House, Station Road, Cockermouth CA13 9PY Tel: 01900 827800

Penrith Farmers' & Kidd's plc, Skirsgill Salerooms, Penrith CA11 0DN Tel: 01768 890781
info@pfkauctions.co.uk
www.pfkauctions.co.uk

Devon
Bearnes, St Edmund's Court, Okehampton Street, Exeter EX4 1DU Tel: 01392 207000
enquiries@bearnes.co.uk
www.bearnes.co.uk

Bonhams, Dowell Street, Honiton EX14 1LX Tel: 01404 41872
www.bonhams.com

Dorset
Hy Duke & Son, The Dorchester Fine Art Salerooms, Weymouth Avenue, Dorchester DT1 1QS
Tel: 01305 265080
www.dukes-auctions.com

Essex
Ambrose, Ambrose House, Old Station Road, Loughton IG10 4PE Tel: 020 8502 3951

Sworders, 14 Cambridge Road, Stansted Mountfitchet CM24 8BZ
Tel: 01279 817778
auctions@sworder.co.uk
www.sworder.co.uk

Herefordshire
Brightwells Fine Art, The Fine Art Saleroom, Easters Court, Leominster HR6 0DE Tel: 01568 611122
fineart@brightwells.com
www.brightwells.com

Hertfordshire
Tring Market Auctions, The Market Premises, Brook Street, Tring HP23 5EF Tel: 01442 826446
sales@tringmarketauctions.co.uk
www.tringmarketauctions.co.uk

Kent
Mervyn Carey, Twysden Cottage, Scullsgate, Benenden, Cranbrook TN17 4LD Tel: 01580 240283

Dreweatt Neate formerly Bracketts Fine Art Auctioneers, The Auction Hall, The Pantiles, Tunbridge Wells TN2 5QL Tel: 01892 544500
tunbridgewells@dnfa.com
www.dnfa.com/tunbridgewells

Ibbett Mosely, 125 High Street, Sevenoaks TN13 1UT
Tel: 01732 456731
auctions@ibbettmosely.co.uk
www.ibbettmosely.co.uk

Lambert & Foster, 102 High Street, Tenterden, Kent TN30 6HT
Tel: 01580 762083
saleroom@lambertandfoster.co.uk
www.lambertandfoster.co.uk

London
Bonhams, Montpelier Street, Knightsbridge SW7 1HH
Tel: 020 7393 3900
www.bonhams.com

Bonhams, 101 New Bond Street, W1S 1SR Tel: 020 7629 6602

Sotheby's, 34–35 New Bond Street, W1A 2AA Tel: 020 7293 5000
www.sothebys.com

Sotheby's Olympia, Hammersmith Road, W14 8UX Tel: 020 7293 5555 www.sothebys.com

Oxfordshire
Holloway's, 49 Parsons Street, Banbury OX16 5PF
Tel: 01295 817777
enquiries@hollowaysauctioneers.co.uk
www.hollowaysauctioneers.co.uk

Scotland
Bonhams, 65 George Street, Edinburgh EH2 2JL
Tel: 0131 225 2266

Thomson, Roddick & Medcalf Ltd, 60 Whitesands, Dumfries DG1 2RS
Tel: 01387 255366
trmdumfries@btconnect.com
www.thomsonroddick.com

Somerset
Lawrences Fine Art Auctioneers, South Street, Crewkerne TA18 8AB
Tel: 01460 73041
www.lawrences.co.uk

Staffordshire
Wintertons Ltd, Lichfield Auction Centre, Fradley Park, Lichfield WS13 8NF Tel: 01543 263256
enquiries@wintertons.co.uk
www.wintertons.co.uk
Photos: Courtesy of Crown Photos
Tel: 01283 762813

Surrey
Ewbank, Burnt Common Auction Rooms, London Road, Send, Woking GU23 7LN Tel: 01483 223101
antiques@ewbankauctions.co.uk
www.ewbankauctions.co.uk

East Sussex
Dreweatt Neate, formerly Edgar Horns, 46–50 South Street, Eastbourne BN21 4XB Tel: 01323 410419 eastbourne@dnfa.com
www.dnfa.com/eastbourne

Gorringes Auction Galleries, Terminus Road, Bexhill-on-Sea TN39 3LR Tel: 01424 212994
bexhill@gorringes.co.uk
www.gorringes.co.uk

Gorringes, inc Julian Dawson, 15 North Street, Lewes BN7 2PD
Tel: 01273 478221

auctions@gorringes.co.uk
www.gorringes.co.uk

Wallis & Wallis, West Street Auction Galleries, Lewes BN7 2NJ
Tel: 01273 480208
auctions@wallisandwallis.co.uk
grb@wallisandwallis.co.uk
www.wallisandwallis.co.uk

West Sussex
Rupert Toovey & Co Ltd, Spring Gardens, Washington RH20 3BS
Tel: 01903 891955
auctions@rupert-toovey.com
www.rupert-toovey.com

Sotheby's Sussex, Summers Place, Billingshurst RH14 9AD
Tel: 01403 833500
www.sothebys

Wales
Peter Francis, Curiosity Sale Room, 19 King Street, Carmarthen SA31 1BH Tel: 01267 233456
Peterfrancis@valuers.fsnet.co.uk
www.peterfrancis.co.uk

Warwickshire
Locke & England, 18 Guy Street, Leamington Spa CV32 4RT
Tel: 01926 889100
www.auctions-online.com/locke

West Midlands
Bonhams, The Old House, Station Road, Knowle, Solihull B93 0HT
Tel: 01564 776151

Fellows & Sons, Augusta House, 19 Augusta Street, Hockley, Birmingham B18 6JA
Tel: 0121 212 2131
info@fellows.co.uk
www.fellows.co.uk

Wiltshire
Woolley & Wallis, Salisbury Salerooms, 51–61 Castle Street, Salisbury SP1 3SU Tel: 01722 424500/411854
junebarrett@woolleyandwallis.co.uk
www.woolleyandwallis.co.uk

Yorkshire
BBR, Elsecar Heritage Centre, Elsecar, Barnsley S74 8HJ
Tel: 01226 745156
sales@onlinebbr.com
www.onlinebbr.com

Dee, Atkinson & Harrison, The Exchange Saleroom, Driffield YO25 6LD Tel: 01377 253151
info@dahauctions.com
www.dahauctions.com

Andrew Hartley, Victoria Hall Salerooms, Little Lane, Ilkley LS29 8EA Tel: 01943 816363
info@andrewhartleyfinearts.co.uk
www.andrewhartleyfinearts.co.uk

Tennants, The Auction Centre, Harmby Road, Leyburn DL8 5SG
Tel: 01969 623780
enquiry@tennants-ltd.co.uk
www.tennants.co.uk

AUSTRALIA
Leonard Joel Auctioneers, 333 Malvern Road, South Yarra, Victoria 3141 Tel: 03 9826 4333
decarts@ljoel.com.au or jewellery@ljoel.com.au
www.ljoel.com.au

Shapiro Auctioneers, 162 Queen Street, Woollahra, Sydney NSW 2025
Tel: 612 9326 1588

AUSTRIA
Dorotheum, Palais Dorotheum, A–1010 Wien, Dorotheergasse 17, 1010 Vienna Tel: 515 60 229
client.services@dorotheum.at

BELGIUM
Bernaerts, Verlatstraat 18–22, 2000 Antwerpen/Anvers
Tel: +32 (0)3 248 19 21
edmond.bernaerts@ping.be
www.auction-bernaerts.com

CANADA
Ritchies Inc, Auctioneers & Appraisers of Antiques & Fine Art, 288 King Street East, Toronto, Ontario M5A 1K4
Tel: (416) 364 1864
auction@ritchies.com
www.ritchies.com

MEXICO
Galeria Louis C. Morton, GLC A7073L IYS, Monte Athos 179, Col Lomas de Chapultepec CP11000 Tel: 52 5520 5005
glmorton@prodigy.net.mx
www.lmorton.com

MONACO
Bonhams, Le Beau Rivage, 9 Avenue d'Ostende, Monte Carlo MC 98000 Tel: +41 (0)22 300 3160

NETHERLANDS
Sotheby's Amsterdam, De Boelelaan 30, Amsterdam 1083 HJ Tel: 31 20 550 2200 www.sothebys.com

REPUBLIC OF IRELAND
James Adam & Sons, 26 St Stephen's Green, Dublin 2
Tel: 00 3531 676 0261
www.jamesadam.ie/

Hamilton Osborne King, 4 Main Street, Blackrock, Co Dublin Tel: 353 1 288 5011 blackrock@hok.ie
www.hok.ie

SWEDEN
Bukowskis, Arsenalsgatan 4, Stockholm Tel: +46 (8) 614 08 00
info@bukowskis.se
www.bukowskis.se

USA
Du Mouchelles, 409 East Jefferson, Detroit, Michigan 48226
Tel: 313 963 6255

Jackson's International Auctioneers & Appraisers of Fine Art & Antiques, 2229 Lincoln Street, Cedar Falls IA 50613
Tel: 319 277 2256/800 665 6743
www.jacksonsauction.com

James D. Julia, Inc, PO Box 830, Rte 201, Skowhegan Road, Fairfield ME 04937 Tel: 207 453 7125
www.juliaauctions.com

New Orleans Auction Galleries, Inc, 801 Magazine Street, AT 510 Julia, New Orleans, Louisiana 70130
Tel: 504 566 1849

R. O. Schmitt Fine Art, Box 1941, Salem, New Hampshire 03079
Tel: 603 893 5915
bob@roschmittfinearts.com
www.antiqueclockauction.com

Sotheby's, 1334 York Avenue at 72nd St, New York NY 10021 Tel: 212 606 7000 www.sothebys.com

Bloomington Auction Gallery, 300 East Grove St, Bloomington, Illinois 61701 Tel: 001 309 828 5533
joyluke@aol.com www.joyluke.com

Key to Illustrations

Each illustration and descriptive caption is accompanied by a letter code. By referring to the following list of auctioneers (denoted by ➤) and dealers (⊞), the source of any item may be immediately determined. Inclusion in this edition no way constitutes or implies a contract or binding offer on the part of any of our contributors to supply or sell the goods illustrated, or similar articles, at the prices stated. Advertisers in this year's directory are denoted by †.

If you require a valuation, it is advisable to check whether the dealer or specialist will carry out this service and if there is a charge. Please mention Miller's when making an enquiry. A valuation by telephone is not possible. Most dealers are willing to help you with your enquiry; however, they may be very busy and consideration of the above points would be welcomed.

A&O ⊞ Ancient & Oriental Ltd Tel: 01664 812044 alex@antiquities.co.uk
AAN No longer trading
AH ➤† Andrew Hartley, Victoria Hall Salerooms, Little Lane, Ilkley, Yorkshire LS29 8EA Tel: 01943 816363 info@andrewhartleyfinearts.co.uk www.andrewhartleyfinearts.co.uk
AL ⊞ Ann Lingard, Ropewalk Antiques, Rye, East Sussex TN31 7NA Tel: 01797 223486 ann-lingard@ropewalkantiques.freeserve.co.uk
AMB ➤ Ambrose, Ambrose House, Old Station Road, Loughton, Essex IG10 4PE Tel: 020 8502 3951
AMH ⊞† Amherst Antiques, Monomark House, 27 Old Gloucester Street, London WC1N 3XX Tel: 01892 725552 info@amherstantiques.co.uk www.amherstantiques.co.uk
ANG ⊞† Ancient & Gothic, PO Box 5390, Bournemouth, Dorset BH7 6XR Tel: 01202 431721
AnS No longer trading
AUC ⊞ Aurea Carter, PO Box 44134, London SW6 3YX Tel: 020 7731 3486 aureacarter@englishceramics.com www.englishceramics.com
AWI ⊞ American West Indies Trading Co Antiques & Art, USA awindies@worldnet.att.net www.goantiques.com/members/awindiestrading
B ➤ Bonhams, 101 New Bond Street, London W1S 1SR Tel: 020 7629 6602 www.bonhams.com
B(Kn) ➤ Bonhams, Montpelier Street, Knightsbridge, London SW7 1HH Tel: 020 7393 3900
B(L) ➤ Bonhams, 17a East Parade, Leeds, Yorkshire LS1 2BH Tel: 0113 244 8011
B(NW) ➤ Bonhams, New House, 150 Christleton Road, Chester, Cheshire CH3 5TD Tel: 01244 313936
B(W) ➤ Bonhams, Dowell Street, Honiton, Devon EX14 1LX Tel: 01404 41872
B(WM) ➤ Bonhams, The Old House, Station Road, Knowle, Solihull, West Midlands B93 0HT Tel: 01564 776151
B&L ➤ Bonhams and Langlois, Westaway Chambers, 39 Don Street, St Helier, Jersey, Channel Islands JE2 4TR Tel: 01534 722441
BAC ⊞ The Brackley Antique Cellar, Drayman's Walk, Brackley, Northamptonshire NN13 6BE Tel: 01280 841841 antiquecellar@tesco.net
BaN ⊞ Barbara Ann Newman Tel: 07850 016729
BBe ⊞ Bourton Bears Tel: 01993 824756 help@bourtonbears.co.uk www.bourtonbears.com
BBR ➤ BBR, Elsecar Heritage Centre, Elsecar, Barnsley, S. Yorks S74 8HJ Tel: 01226 745156 sales@onlinebbr.com www.onlinebbr.com

Bea ➤ Bearnes, St Edmund's Court, Okehampton Street, Exeter, Devon EX4 1DU Tel: 01392 207000 enquiries@bearnes.co.uk www.bearnes.co.uk
BELL ⊞ Bellhouse Antiques, Chelmsford, Essex Tel: 01268 710415 Bellhouse.Antiques@virgin.net
BERN ➤ Bernaerts, Verlatstraat 18–22, 2000 Antwerpen/Anvers, Belgium Tel: +32 (0)3 248 19 21 edmond.bernaerts@ping.be www.auction-bernaerts.com
BEX ⊞† Daniel Bexfield, 26 Burlington Arcade, London W1J 0PU Tel: 020 7491 1720 antiques@bexfield.co.uk www.bexfield.co.uk
BLm ⊞ Lyn Bloom & Jeffrey Neal, Vault 27, The London Silver Vaults, Chancery Lane, London WC2A 1QS Tel: 020 7242 6189 bloomvault@aol.com www.bloomvault.com
Bns ⊞ Brittons Jewellers, 4 King Street, Clitheroe, Lancashire BB7 2EP Tel: 01200 425555 info@brittons-watches.co.uk www.brittons-watches.co.uk www.antique-jewelry.co.uk
BrL ⊞ The Brighton Lanes Antique Centre, 12 Meeting House Lane, Brighton, East Sussex BN1 1HB Tel: 01273 823121 peter@brightonlanes-antiquecentre.co.uk www.brightonlanes-antiquecentre.co.uk
BrW ⊞ Brian Watson Antique Glass, Foxwarren Cottage, High Street, Marsham, Norwich, Norfolk NR10 5QA Tel: 01263 732519 brian.h.watson@talk21.com By appointment only
BUK ➤ Bukowskis, Arsenalsgatan 4, Stockholm, Sweden Tel: +46 (8) 614 08 00 info@bukowskis.se www.bukowskis.se
BWL ➤ Brightwells Fine Art, The Fine Art Saleroom, Easters Court, Leominster, Herefordshire HR6 0DE Tel: 01568 611122 fineart@brightwells.com www.brightwells.com
Byl ⊞ Bygones of Ireland Ltd, Lodge Road, Westport, Co Mayo, Republic of Ireland Tel: 00 353 98 26132/25701 bygones@anu.ie www.bygones-of-ireland.com
C&W ⊞ Carroll & Walker, Scotland Tel: 01877 385618
CAL ⊞ Cedar Antiques Ltd, High Street, Hartley Wintney, Hampshire RG27 8NY Tel: 01252 843222 or 01189 326628
CB ⊞ Christine Bridge Antiques, 78 Castelnau, London SW13 9EX Tel: 7000 445277 christine@bridge-antiques.com www.bridge-antiques.com www.antiqueglass.co.uk
CCO ⊞ Collectable Costume, Showroom South, Gloucester Antiques Centre, 1 Severn Road, Gloucester GL1 2LE Tel: 01989 562188

CCs ⊞ Coco's Corner, Unit 4, Cirencester Antique Centre, Cirencester, Gloucestershire Tel: 01452 556 308 cocos-corner@blueyonder.co.uk

CGC 🔨 Cheffins, Clifton House, 1 & 2 Clifton Road, Cambridge CB1 7EA Tel: 01223 271966 www.cheffins.co.uk

CHAC ⊞ Church Hill Antiques Centre, 6 Station Street, Lewes, East Sussex BN7 2DA Tel: 01273 474 842 churchhilllewes@aol.com www.church-hill-antiques.co.uk

CHTR 🔨 Charterhouse, The Long Street Salerooms, Sherborne, Dorset DT9 3BS Tel: 01935 812277 enquiry@charterhouse-auctions.co.uk www.charterhouse-auctions.co.uk

CoCo ⊞ Country Collector, 11–12 Birdgate, Pickering, Yorkshire YO18 7AL Tel: 01751 477481 www.country-collector.co.uk

COF ⊞ Cottage Farm Antiques, Stratford Road, Aston Subedge, Chipping Campden, Gloucestershire GL55 6PZ Tel: 01386 438263 info@cottagefarmantiques.co.uk www.cottagefarmantiques.co.uk

CoHA ⊞ Corner House Antiques and Ffoxe Antiques, Gardners Cottage, Broughton Poggs, Filkins, Lechlade-on-Thames, Gloucestershire GL7 3JH Tel: 01367 860078 jdhis007@btopenworld.com www.corner-house-antiques.co.uk

CoS ⊞ Corrine Soffe Tel: 01295 730317 soffe@btinternet.com

CuS ⊞ Curious Science, 319 Lillie Road, Fulham, London SW6 7LL Tel: 020 7610 1175 curiousscience@medical-antiques.com

DA 🔨 Dee, Atkinson & Harrison, The Exchange Saleroom, Driffield, East Yorkshire YO25 6LD Tel: 01377 253151 info@dahauctions.com www.dahauctions.com

DAN ⊞ Andrew Dando, 34 Market Street, Bradford on Avon, Wiltshire BA15 1LL Tel: 01225 865444 andrew@andrewdando.co.uk www.andrewdando.co.uk

DD 🔨 David Duggleby, The Vine St Salerooms, Scarborough, Yorkshire YO11 1XN Tel: 01723 507111 auctions@davidduggleby.com www.davidduggleby.com

Del ⊞ Delomosne & Son Ltd, Court Close, North Wraxall, Chippenham, Wiltshire SN14 7AD Tel: 01225 891505

DFA ⊞ Delvin Farm Antiques, Gormonston, Co Meath, Republic of Ireland Tel: 353 1 841 2285 info@delvinfarmpine.com john@delvinfarmpine.com www.delvinfarmpine.com

DMC 🔨 Diamond Mills & Co, 117 Hamilton Road, Felixstowe, Suffolk IP11 7BL Tel: 01394 282281

DN 🔨 Dreweatt Neate, Donnington Priory, Donnington, Newbury, Berkshire RG14 2JE Tel: 01635 553553 donnington@dnfa.com www.dnfa.com/donnington

DN(BR) 🔨 Dreweatt Neate, formerly Bracketts Fine Art Auctioneers, The Auction Hall, The Pantiles, Tunbridge Wells, Kent TN2 5QL Tel: 01892 544500 tunbridgewells@dnfa.com www.dnfa.com/tunbridgewells

DN(Bri) 🔨 Dreweatt Neate, formerly Bristol Auction Rooms, St John's Place, Apsley Road, Clifton, Bristol, Gloucestershire BS8 2ST Tel: 0117 973 7201 bristol@dnfa.com www.dnfa.com/bristol

DN(EH) 🔨 Dreweatt Neate, formerly Edgar Horns, 46–50 South Street, Eastbourne, East Sussex BN21 4XB Tel: 01323 410419 eastbourne@dnfa.com www.dnfa.com/eastbourne

DOL ⊞ Dollectable, 53 Lower Bridge Street, Chester, Cheshire CH1 1RS Tel: 01244 344888/679195

DORO 🔨 Dorotheum, Palais Dorotheum, A-1010 Wien, Dorotheergasse 17, 1010 Vienna, Austria Tel: 515 60 229 client.services@dorotheum.at

DPC ⊞ Devon Pottery Collectors Group, Mrs Joyce Stonelake, 19 St Margarets Avenue, Torquay, Devon TQ1 4LW Tel: 01803 327277 Virginia.Brisco@care4free.net

DRU ⊞ Drummonds Architectural Antiques Ltd, The Kirkpatrick Buildings, 25 London Road (A3), Hindhead, Surrey GU26 6AB Tel: 01428 609444 www.drummonds-arch.co.uk

DSG ⊞ Delf Stream Gallery, Bournemouth, Dorset Tel: 07974 926137 nic19422000@yahoo.co.uk www.delfstreamgallery.com

DuM 🔨 Du Mouchelles, 409 East Jefferson, Detroit, Michigan 48226, USA Tel: 313 963 6255

E 🔨 Ewbank, Burnt Common Auction Rooms, London Road, Send, Woking, Surrey GU23 7LN Tel: 01483 223101 antiques@ewbankauctions.co.uk www.ewbankauctions.co.uk

EAL ⊞ The Exeter Antique Lighting Co, Cellar 15, The Quay, Exeter, Devon EX2 4AP Tel: 01392 490848 www.antiquelightingcompany.com

ETO ⊞ Eric Tombs, 62a West Street, Dorking, Surrey RH4 1BS Tel: 01306 743661 ertombs@aol.com www.dorkingantiques.com

F&F ⊞ Fenwick & Fenwick, 88–90 High Street, Broadway, Worcestershire WR12 7AJ Tel: 01386 853227/841724

FAC ⊞ Faganarms, Box 425, Fraser, MI 48026, USA Tel: 586 465 4637 info@faganarms.com www.faganarms.com

FHF 🔨 Fellows & Sons, Augusta House, 19 Augusta Street, Hockley, Birmingham, West Midlands B18 6JA Tel: 0121 212 2131 info@fellows.co.uk www.fellows.co.uk

FOF ⊞ Fossack & Furkle, PO Box 733, Abington, Cambridgeshire CB1 6BF Tel: 01223 894296 fossack@btopenworld.com www.fossackandfurkle.freeservers.com

FOX ⊞ Fox Cottage Antiques, Digbeth Street, Stow-on-the-Wold, Gloucestershire GL54 1BN Tel: 01451 870307

G(B) 🔨 Gorringes Auction Galleries, Terminus Road, Bexhill-on-Sea, East Sussex TN39 3LR Tel: 01424 212994 bexhill@gorringes.co.uk www.gorringes.co.uk

G(L) 🔨 Gorringes inc Julian Dawson, 15 North Street, Lewes, East Sussex BN7 2PD Tel: 01273 478221 auctions@gorringes.co.uk www.gorringes.co.uk

G&G ⊞ Guest & Gray, 1–7 Davies Mews, London W1K 5AB Tel: 020 7408 1252 info@chinese-porcelain-art.com www.chinese-porcelain-art.com

GAK 🔨 Keys, Off Palmers Lane, Aylsham, Norfolk NR11 6JA Tel: 01263 733195 www.aylshamsalerooms.co.uk

GBr ⊞ Geoffrey Breeze Antiques, Top Banana Antiques Mall, 1 New Street, Tetbury, Gloucestershire GL8 8OS Tel: 01225 466499 antiques@geoffreybreeze.co.uk www.antiquecanes.co.uk

GGD ⊞ Great Grooms of Dorking, 50/52 West Street, Dorking, Surrey RH4 1BU Tel: 01306 887076 laurence@greatgrooms.co.uk www.great-grooms.co.uk

GRe ⊞ Greystoke Antiques, 4 Swan Yard,
(off Cheap Street), Sherborne, Dorset DT9 3AX
Tel: 01935 812833

GRI ⊞ Grimes House Antiques, High Street,
Moreton-in-Marsh, Gloucestershire GL56 0AT
Tel: 01608 651029 grimes_house@cix.co.uk
www.grimeshouse.co.uk
www.cranberryglass.co.uk

GS ⊞ Ged Selby Antique Glass, Yorkshire
Tel: 01756 799673
By appointment only

GWR ⊞ Gwen Riley, Stand 12, Bourbon Hanby Antique
Centre, 151 Sydney Street, Chelsea, London
SW3 6NT Tel: 020 7352 2106

H&G ⊞ Hope & Glory, 131A Kensington Church Street,
London W8 7LP Tel: 020 7727 8424

HAA ⊞ Hampton Antiques, The Crown Arcade,
119 Portobello Road, London W11 2DY
Tel: 01604 863979 info@hamptonantiques.co.uk
www.hamptonantiques.co.uk

HAL ⊞ John & Simon Haley, 89 Northgate, Halifax,
Yorkshire HX1 1XF Tel: 01422 822148/360434
toysandbanks@aol.com

HarC ⊞ Hardy's Collectables, Dorset Tel: 07970 613077
www.poolepotteryjohn.com

HEL ⊞ Helios Gallery, 292 Westbourne Grove, London
W11 2PS Tel: 077 11 955 997
info@heliosgallery.com www.heliosgallery.com

HiA ⊞ Rupert Hitchcox Antiques, Warpsgrove, Nr
Chalgrove, Oxford OX44 7RW Tel: 01865 890241
www.ruperthitchcoxantiques.co.uk

HL ⊞ Honiton Lace Shop, 44 High Street, Honiton,
Devon EX14 1PJ Tel: 01404 42416
shop@honitonlace.com www.honitonlace.com

HO ⊞ Houghton Antiques, Houghton, Cambridgeshire
Tel: 01480 461887

HOLL 🔨 Holloway's, 49 Parsons Street, Banbury,
Oxfordshire OX16 5PF Tel: 01295 817777
enquiries@hollowaysauctioneers.co.uk
www.hollowaysauctioneers.co.uk

HTE ⊞ Heritage, 6 Market Place, Woodstock, Oxfordshire
OX20 1TA Tel: 01993 811332/0870 4440678
dealers@atheritage.co.uk www.atheritage.co.uk

HUX ⊞ David Huxtable, Saturdays at: Portobello Road,
Basement Stall 11/12, 288 Westbourne Grove,
London W11 Tel: 07710 132200
david@huxtins.com www.huxtins.com

HYD 🔨 Hy Duke & Son, The Dorchester Fine Art
Salerooms, Weymouth Avenue, Dorchester,
Dorset DT1 1QS Tel: 01305 265080
www.dukes-auctions.com

JAA 🔨 Jackson's International Auctioneers & Appraisers of
Fine Art & Antiques, 2229 Lincoln Street, Cedar
Falls, IA 50613, USA Tel: 319 277 2256/800 665
6743 www.jacksonsauction.com

JACK ⊞ Michael Jackson Antiques, The Quiet Woman
Antiques Centre, Southcombe, Chipping Norton,
Oxfordshire OX7 5QH Tel: 01608 646262
mjcig@cards.fsnet.co.uk
www.our-web-site.com/cigarette-cards

JAd 🔨 James Adam & Sons, 26 St Stephen's Green,
Dublin 2, Republic of Ireland
Tel: 00 3531 676 0261 www.jamesadam.ie/

JAS ⊞ Jasmin Cameron, Antiquarius, 131–141 King's
Road, London SW3 4PW Tel: 020 7351 4154 or
077 74 871257 jasmin.cameron@mail.com

JBL ⊞ Judi Bland Antiques, Surrey Tel: 01276 857576
or 01536 724145

JDJ 🔨 James D Julia, Inc, PO Box 830, Rte 201
Skowhegan Road, Fairfield, ME 04937, USA
Tel: 207 453 7125 www.juliaauctions.com

JeH ⊞ Jennie Horrocks, Gloucestershire
Tel: 07836 264896 info@artnouveaulighting.co.uk
www.artnouveaulighting.co.uk

JHo ⊞ Jonathan Horne, 66 Kensington Church Street,
London W8 4BY Tel: 020 7221 5658
JH@jonathanhorne.co.uk
www.jonathanhorne.co.uk

JMC ⊞ J & M Collectables, Kent Tel: 01580 891657 or
077135 23573 jandmcollectables@tinyonline.co.uk

JPr ⊞ Joanna Proops Antique Textiles & Lighting,
34 Belvedere, Lansdown Hill, Bath, Somerset
BA1 5HR Tel: 01225 310795
antiquetextiles@aol.co.uk
www.antiquetextiles.co.uk

JTS ⊞ June & Tony Stone Fine Antique Boxes,
PO Box 106, Peacehaven, East Sussex BN10 8AU
Tel: 01273 579333 rachel@boxes.co.uk
www.boxes.co.uk

JUP ⊞ Jupiter Antiques, PO Box 609, Rottingdean,
East Sussex BN2 7FW Tel: 01273 302865

KEY ⊞ Key Antiques of Chipping Norton, 11 Horsefair,
Chipping Norton, Oxfordshire OX7 5AL
Tel: 01608 644992/643777 info@keyantiques.com
www.keyantiques.com

L 🔨 Lawrences Fine Art Auctioneers, South Street,
Crewkerne, Somerset TA18 8AB Tel: 01460 73041
www.lawrences.co.uk

L&E 🔨 Locke & England, 18 Guy Street, Leamington Spa,
Warwickshire CV32 4RT Tel: 01926 889100
www.auctions-online.com/locke

LaF ⊞ La Femme Tel: 07971 844279
jewels@joancorder.freeserve.co.uk

LAY 🔨 David Lay (ASVA), Auction House, Alverton,
Penzance, Cornwall TR18 4RE Tel: 01736 361414
david.lays@btopenworld.com

LBe ⊞ Linda Bee Art Deco, Stand L18–21, Grays Antique
Market, 1–7 Davies Mews, London W1Y 1AR
Tel: 020 7629 5921

LBr ⊞ Lynda Brine lyndabrine@yahoo.co.uk
www.scentbottlesandsmalls.co.uk
By appointment only

LGU ⊞ Linda Gumb, Stand 123, Grays Antique Market,
58 Davies Street, London W1K 5LP Tel: 020 7629
2544 linda@lindagumb.co.uk

LHA 🔨 Leslie Hindman, Inc, 122 North Aberdeen Street,
Chicago, Illinois 60607, USA Tel: 312 280 1212
www.lesliehindman.com

MAR 🔨 Frank R. Marshall & Co, Marshall House,
Church Hill, Knutsford, Cheshire WA16 6DH
Tel: 01565 653284

MB ⊞ Mostly Boxes, 93 High Street, Eton, Windsor,
Berkshire SL4 6AF Tel: 01753 858470

MCA 🔨 Mervyn Carey, Twysden Cottage, Scullsgate,
Benenden, Cranbrook, Kent TN17 4LD
Tel: 01580 240283

McP ⊞ R & G McPherson Antiques, 40 Kensington Church
Street, London W8 4BX Tel: 020 7937 0812
rmcpherson@orientalceramics.com
www.orientalceramics.com

MDL ⊞ Michael D. Long Ltd, 96–98 Derby Road,
Nottingham NG1 5FB Tel: 0115 941 3307
sales@michaeldlong.com www.michaeldlong.com

MFB ⊞ Manor Farm Barn Antiques Tel: 01296 658941
mfbn@btinternet.com
btwebworld.com/mfbantiques

MIL ⊞ Millennia Antiquities, Lancashire
Tel: 01204 690175 millenniaant@aol.com
www.AncientAntiquities.co.uk

MIN ⊞ Ministry of Pine, Timsbury Village Workshop,
Unit 2, Timsbury Industrial Estate, Hayeswood
Road, Timsbury, Bath, Somerset BA2 0HQ
Tel: 01761 472297 ministryofpine.uk@virgin.net
www.ministryofpine.com

Mit ⚒ Mitchells, Fairfield House, Station Road,
Cockermouth, Cumbria CA13 9PY
Tel: 01900 827800

ML ⊞ Memory Lane, Bartlett Street Antiques Centre,
5/10 Bartlett Street, Bath, Somerset BA1 2QZ
Tel: 01225 466689/310457

MLa ⊞ Marion Langham Limited, Claranagh, Tempo,
Co Fermanagh, Northern Ireland BT94 3FJ
Tel: 028 895 41247 marion@ladymarion.co.uk
www.ladymarion.co.uk

MLL ⊞ Millers Antiques Ltd, Netherbrook House,
86 Christchurch Road, Ringwood, Hampshire
BH24 1DR Tel: 01425 472062
mail@millers-antiques.co.uk
www.millers-antiques.co.uk

MSh ⊞ Manfred Schotten, 109 High Street, Burford,
Oxfordshire OX18 4RG Tel: 01993 822302
www.antiques@schotten.com

MTay ⊞ Martin Taylor Antiques, 323 Tettenhall Road,
Wolverhampton, West Midlands WV6 0JZ
Tel: 01902 751166/07836 636524
enquiries@mtaylor-antiques.co.uk
www.mtaylor-antiques.co.uk

MURR ⊞ Murrays' Antiques & Collectables, Dorset
Tel: 01202 823870

NOA ⚒ New Orleans Auction Galleries, Inc,
801 Magazine Street, AT 510 Julia, New Orleans,
Louisiana 70130, USA Tel: 504 566 1849

NSal ⚒ Netherhampton Salerooms, Salisbury Auction
Centre, Netherhampton, Salisbury, Wiltshire
SP2 8RH Tel: 01722 340 041

OIA ⊞ The Old Ironmongers Antiques Centre,
5 Burford Street, Lechlade, Gloucestershire
GL7 3AP Tel: 01367 252397

OLA ⊞ Olliff's Architectural Antiques, 19–21 Lower
Redland Road, Redland, Bristol, Gloucestershire
BS6 6TB Tel: 0117 923 9232
marcus@olliffs.com www.olliffs.com

P&T ⊞ Pine & Things, Portobello Farm, Campden Road,
Nr Shipston-on-Stour, Warwickshire CV36 4PY
Tel: 01608 663849 www.pinethings.co.uk

PaA ⊞ Pastorale Antiques, 15 Malling Street, Lewes,
East Sussex BN7 2RA Tel: 01273 473259 or
01435 863044
pastorale@btinternet.com

Penn ⊞ Penny Fair Antiques Tel: 07860 825456

PEZ ⊞ Alan Pezaro, 62a West Street, Dorking, Surrey
RH4 1BS Tel: 01306 743661

PF ⚒ Peter Francis, Curiosity Sale Room, 19 King Street,
Carmarthen SA31 1BH, Wales Tel: 01267 233456
Peterfrancis@valuers.fsnet.co.uk
www.peterfrancis.co.uk

PFK ⚒ Penrith Farmers' & Kidd's plc, Skirsgill Salerooms,
Penrith, Cumbria CA11 0DN Tel: 01768 890781
info@pfkauctions.co.uk
www.pfkauctions.co.uk

POL ⊞ Politico Book Shop, 8 Artillery Row, London
SW1 Tel: 020 7828 0010

POLL ⊞ Pollyanna, 34 High Street, Arundel, West Sussex
BN18 9AB Tel: 01903 885198

PSA ⊞ Pantiles Spa Antiques, 4, 5, 6 Union House,
The Pantiles, Tunbridge Wells, Kent TN4 8HE
Tel: 01892 541377 psa.wells@btinternet.com
www.antiques-tun-wells-kent.co.uk

PT ⊞ Pieces of Time, (1–7 Davies Mews), 26 South Molton
Lane, London W1Y 2LP Tel: 020 7629 2422
info@antique-watch.com www.antique-watch.com

RAY ⊞ Derek & Tina Rayment Antiques, Orchard House,
Barton Road, Barton, Nr Farndon, Cheshire SY14
7HT Tel: 01829 270429/07860 666629 and
07702 922410 raymentantiques@aol.com
www.antique-barometers.com

RBA ⊞ Roger Bradbury Antiques, Church Street, Coltishall,
Norfolk NR12 7DJ Tel: 01603 737444

RCo ⊞ Royal Commemorative China Tel: 020 8863 0625
royalcommemorative@hotmail.com

RdeR ⊞ Rogers de Rin, 76 Royal Hospital Road, London
SW3 4HN Tel: 020 7352 9007

RdV ⊞ Roger de Ville Antiques Tel: 01629 812496 or
07798 793857 www.rogerdeville.co.uk

RICC ⊞ Riccardo Sansoni

ROSc ⚒ R. O. Schmitt Fine Art, Box 1941, Salem, New
Hampshire 03079, USA Tel: 603 893 5915
bob@roschmittfinearts.com
www.antiqueclockauction.com

RTo ⚒ Rupert Toovey & Co Ltd, Spring Gardens,
Washington, West Sussex RH20 3BS
Tel: 01903 891955 auctions@rupert-toovey.com
www.rupert-toovey.com

RWA ⊞ Ray Walker Antiques, Burton Arcade,
296 Westbourne Grove, London W11 2PS
Tel: 020 8464 7981 rw.antiques@btinternet.com

S(Am) ⚒ Sotheby's Amsterdam, De Boelelaan 30,
Amsterdam 1083 HJ, Netherlands
Tel: 31 20 550 2200

S(O) ⚒ Sotheby's Olympia, Hammersmith Road, London
W14 8UX Tel: 020 7293 5555 www.sothebys.com

S(P) ⚒ Sotheby's France SA, 76 rue du Faubourg,
Saint Honore, Paris 75008, France
Tel: 33 1 53 05 53 05

S(S) ⚒ Sotheby's Sussex, Summers Place, Billingshurst,
West Sussex RH14 9AD Tel: 01403 833500

SaH ⊞ Sally Hawkins, Nottinghamshire Tel: 01636 636666
sallytiles@aol.com

SAS ⚒ Special Auction Services, Kennetholme, Midgham,
Reading, Berkshire RG7 5UX Tel: 0118 971 2949
www.invaluable.com/sas/

SAT ⊞ The Swan at Tetsworth, High Street, Tetsworth,
Nr Thame, Oxfordshire OX9 7AB
Tel: 01844 281777 antiques@theswan.co.uk
www.theswan.co.uk

SCO Peter Scott Tel: 0117 986 8468 or 07850 639770

SDA ⊞ Stephanie Davison Antiques, Bakewell Antiques
Centre, King Street, Bakewell, Derbyshire
DE45 1DZ Tel: 01629 812496
ask@chappellsantiquescentre.com
www.stephaniedavisonantiques.com/

SEA ⊞ Mark Seabrook Antiques, PO Box 396,
Huntingdon, Cambridgeshire PE28 0ZA
Tel: 01480 861935 enquiries@markseabrook.com
www.markseabrook.com

SMI ⊞ Skip & Janie Smithson Antiques, Lincolnshire
Tel: 01754 810265 smithsonantiques@hotmail.com

Som ⊞ Somervale Antiques, 6 Radstock Road, Midsomer
Norton, Bath, Somerset BA3 2AJ
Tel: 01761 412686
ronthomas@somervaleantiquesglass.co.uk
www.somervaleantiquesglass.co.uk

STA ⊞ George Stacpoole, Main Street, Adare, Co Limerick, Republic of Ireland Tel: 6139 6409 stacpoole@iol.ie www.georgestacpooleantiques.com

SV ⊞ Sutton Valence Antiques, North Street, Sutton Valence, Nr Maidstone, Kent ME17 3AP Tel: 01622 843333/01622 675332 svantiques@aol.com www.svantiques.co.uk

SWB ⊞† Sweetbriar Gallery Paperweights Ltd, 3 Collinson Court, off Church Street, Frodsham, Cheshire WA6 6PN Tel: 01928 730064 sales@sweetbriar.co.uk www.sweetbriar.co.uk

SWO ⚒ Sworders, 14 Cambridge Road, Stansted Mountfitchet, Essex CM24 8BZ Tel: 01279 817778 auctions@sworder.co.uk www.sworder.co.uk

TASV ⊞ Tenterden Antiques & Silver Vaults, 66 High Street, Tenterden, Kent TN30 6AU Tel: 01580 765885

TDG ⊞ The Design Gallery 1850–1950, 5 The Green, Westerham, Kent TN16 1AS Tel: 01959 561234 sales@thedesigngalleryuk.com www.thedesigngalleryuk.com

TEN ⚒ Tennants, The Auction Centre, Harmby Road, Leyburn, Yorkshire DL8 5SG Tel: 01969 623780 enquiry@tennants-ltd.co.uk www.tennants.co.uk

TH ⊞ Tony Horsley, PO Box 3127, Brighton, East Sussex BN1 5SS Tel: 01273 550770

TIC ⊞ Tickers, 37 Northam Road, Southampton, Hampshire SO14 0PD Tel: 02380 234431 kmonckton@btopenworld.com

TIM ⊞ S. & S. Timms, 2–4 High Street, Shefford, Bedfordshire SG17 5DG Tel: 01462 851051 info@timmsantiques.com www.timmsantiques.com

TLA ⊞ The Lanes Armoury, 26 Meeting House Lane, The Lanes, Brighton, East Sussex BN1 1HB Tel: 01273 321357 enquiries@thelanesarmoury.co.uk www.thelanesarmoury.co.uk

TMA ⚒† Tring Market Auctions, The Market Premises, Brook Street, Tring, Hertfordshire HP23 5EF Tel: 01442 826446 sales@tringmarketauctions.co.uk www.tringmarketauctions.co.uk

TOM ⊞† Charles Tomlinson, Chester Tel: 01244 318395 charlestomlinson@tiscali.co.uk

TOP ⊞† The Top Banana Antiques Mall, 1 New Church Street, Tetbury, Gloucestershire GL8 8DS Tel: 0871 288 1102 info@topbananaantiques.com www.topbananaantiques.com

TPC ⊞ Pine Cellars, 39 Jewry Street, Winchester, Hampshire SO23 8RY Tel: 01962 777546/867014

TRM ⚒ Thomson, Roddick & Medcalf Ltd, 60 Whitesands, Dumfries, Scotland DG1 2RS Tel: 01387 255366 trmdumfries@btconnect.com www.thomsonroddick.com

VB ⊞ Variety Box Tel: 01892 531868

VK ⊞ Vivienne King of Panache, Somerset Tel: 01934 814759 or 07974 798871 Kingpanache@aol.com

WAA ⊞ Woburn Abbey Antiques Centre, Woburn, Bedfordshire MK17 9WA Tel: 01525 290350 antiques@woburnabbey.co.uk

WAC ⊞ Worcester Antiques Centre, Reindeer Court, Mealcheapen Street, Worcester WR1 4DF Tel: 01905 610680 WorcsAntiques@aol.com

WADS ⊞† Wadsworth's, Marehill, Pulborough, West Sussex RH20 2DY Tel: 01798 873555 info@wadsworthsrugs.com www.wadsworthsrugs.com

WAL ⚒† Wallis & Wallis, West Street Auction Galleries, Lewes, East Sussex BN7 2NJ Tel: 01273 480208 auctions@wallisandwallis.co.uk grb@wallisandwallis.co.uk www.wallisandwallis.co.uk

WD ⚒ Weller & Dufty Ltd, 141 Bromsgrove Street, Birmingham, West Midlands B5 6RQ Tel: 0121 692 1414 sales@welleranddufty.co.uk www.welleranddufty.co.uk

WeA ⊞ Wenderton Antiques, Kent Tel: 01227 720295 By appointment only

WiB ⊞ Wish Barn Antiques, Wish Street, Rye, East Sussex TN31 7DA Tel: 01797 226797

WilP ⚒ W&H Peacock, 26 Newnham Street, Bedford MK40 3JR Tel: 01234 266366

WL ⚒ Wintertons Ltd, Lichfield Auction Centre, Fradley Park, Lichfield, Staffordshire WS13 8NF Tel: 01543 263256 enquiries@wintertons.co.uk www.wintertons.co.uk Photos: Courtesy of Crown Photos Tel: 01283 762813

WRe ⊞ Walcot Reclamations, 108 Walcot Street, Bath, Somerset BA1 5BG Tel: 01225 444404 rick@walcot.com www.walcot.com

WSA ⊞† West Street Antiques, 63 West Street, Dorking, Surrey RH4 1BS Tel: 01306 883487 weststant@aol.com www.antiquearmsandarmour.com

WW ⚒ Woolley & Wallis, Salisbury Salerooms, 51–61 Castle Street, Salisbury, Wiltshire SP1 3SU Tel: 01722 424500/411854 junebarrett@woolleyandwallis.co.uk www.woolleyandwallis.co.uk

YC ⊞ Yesterday Child Tel: 020 7354 1601 or 01908 583403

YT ⊞ Yew Tree Antiques, Woburn Abbey Antiques Centre, Woburn, Bedfordshire MK17 9WA Tel: 01525 872514

Index to Advertisers

Ancient & Gothic ....*back jacket*
Daniel Bexfield 159
Amherst Antiques 281
Andrew Hartley..113
Lambert & Foster..31
Miller's Publications...........................217, 233
Sweetbriar Gallery...185
Tombland Antique Centre............................81
Charles Tomlinson...269
Top Banana Antiques Mall 97
Tring Market Auctions...................................161
Wadsworth's...265
Wallis & Wallis 2
West Street Antiques 237

Index

Bold numbers refer to information boxes.

A

Adam-style furniture 19, 50
Adams, George 151
Adie & Lovekin 163, 165
Admiral Fitzroy barometers 215, 216
Aesthetic Movement 50
Afghani *ensis* 262
Afshar rugs 265
alabaster
  antiquities 220
  architectural antiques 230
  clocks 200
  sculpture 270–2
alarm watches 208, 212
Alcock, Samuel & Sons 110
Allen, Thomas 121
alms dishes 261
Amberina glass 167
American
  arms and armour 236
  clocks 197, 203
  furniture 15, 29, 49
  glass 167, 168, 184, 190
  mirrors 46
  money boxes 246
  silver 142, 150
  watches 209
amulets 220, 221, 223
anatomical models 267
Anderson & Sons 267
Andreyev, Vasili Ivanovich 161
aneroid barometers 215
Angell, George 147
Angell, Joseph 157
animals
  bears 89
  cats 91, 271
  dogs 92–4, 272
  elephants 155
  fish 272
  horses 93
  lions 92
  sculpture 271, 272
  sheep 93
  see also birds
Ansonia 197
antiquities 219–23
apothecary boxes 267
apprentice chests of drawers 37
architectural antiques **224**, 224–33
armchairs 27
  child's 24
  open 19, 22, 23
  tub 20, 28
  Windsor 22, 26
  wing 26
  see also chairs
armoires 41, 42
arms and armour 234–7
Arnold, Max Oscar 245
Arnold & Sons 266, 267

B

Art Deco 256
Art Nouveau 163, 164
Arts and Crafts 50, 228
ashtrays 129
Aspreys 160
assay bowls 134
Austrian
  ceramics 108
  clocks 204
  sculpture 271–3
  silver 134, 137, 139, 159
Avallon, S. 259

Baccarat **184**, 185
bagfaces 262
bags 275
Baillon, Jean Baptiste 210
Baker 236
Bakhtiari carpets 264
Bannister, J. 209
banquettes 16
Barbedienne, F. 272
barber's bowls 87
bargeware 108, 118
Barnard, W. & J. 152
Barnaschina, C. 215
barometers 192, 214–16
Barringer Wallis & Manners 258
basins 50
baskets
  ceramic 65–6
  silver 133–4, **134**
Bass & Co 117
Bateman 151
Bateman, Anne 150
Bateman, Peter 150
bayonets 236
beadwork 274–7
beakers
  ceramic 70, 71, 75
  glass 174
  silver 146–8
bears 247
bedroom chairs 19
beds 15, 49
bedside cabinets 41
Bell, John 91
bell pulls 229
bell pushes 227
Belleek 66, 70, 85, 118, 122
bells, brass 227, 229
benches 16
Benetfink & Co 194
bentwood furniture 15
bergère cradles 15
bergère settees 49
bergères 25
Bergman 273
Berlin ceramics 71, 74, 116
Bernasconi, F. & Son 215
Betham, James 148
Betjemann, George & Sons 172, 279

Bevington 207
bidets 58
birds
  bronze 273
  ceramic 88, 90
  silver 165
biscuit barrels 108
bisque
  dolls 244–6
  figures 88, 89, 92
blanket boxes 29–31
blotters 161
blue and white ware 78
boardroom tables 60
Bohemian glass 167, 171, 174, 176, 183, **188**, 189, 191
boilers 230
bonbon baskets 133
bonbonnières 191
bone china 69, 99, 101, 116
bonnets 274
book presses 280
book slides **279**, 279
bookcases 17–18
boot jacks 226, 281
boot stands 51
Boote, T. & R. 120
Boston & Sandwich Glassworks **188**
botanical decoration, ceramics **83**
bottles 169–72, **170**
  see also scent bottles
Bouhon Frères 233
boulle clocks 202
Bourne, Charles 85
Bow
  animals 93
  candlesticks 67
  cups 77
  dishes 84
Bowie knives **237**, 237
bowls
  antiquities 219, 221
  ceramic 78–87
  demon **221**, 221
  glass 167–8
  silver 133–4
  wooden 278
boxes 238–43
  apothecary 267
  ceramic 65–6
  microscope slide 269
  puzzle 278
  silver 135–9
  tortoiseshell **238**, 238, 240, 242, 243
  Tunbridge ware 279, 280
  work 239, 280
bracket clocks 193
Bramah, John **145**
branding irons 261
brandy dispensers 172
brandy saucepans 164

Branhamware 123
Brannam, C.H. 112
brass 258–61
  architectural antiques **224**, 224–9
  candlesticks 261
  clocks 194–6, 198, 201, 205
  kitchenware 252
  lighting 256
  mirrors 48
  scientific instruments 266, 268, 269
Brasted, F. 136
braziers 261
bread forks 150
bread plates 96, 100
breakfast cups 68
breakfast tables 59, 61
Brewer 73
bronze 260, 261
  antiquities 219, 222–3
  lighting 255, 256
  sculpture 270–3
Brooke Bath 169
Brown-Westhead, Moore & Co 91
Brownfields 129
brushes, silver 162
buckles, silver 162
buffets 59, 62
bureau de dame 44
bureaux 44, 45
Burgess & Leigh 68
Burmantofts 107, 113
Burmese glass **168**, 168
busts 91, 270–1, 273
butcher's blocks 253
Butler, Frank 77
butler's trays 63
butter boats 85, 87
butter dishes 248
butter knives 149, 153
butter pots 108
butter stamps 248–9, 251
Byzantine antiquities 222

C

cabaret services 115
cabinets 38–42
  bedside 41
  display 38, 39, 42
  music 39–40
  sewing 39
  side 40
  table 38, 39
  work 38
caddy spoons 152
cake baskets 134
cake plates 96
Caldas-style wine carriers 110
cameo glass 168, 187
cancellation lines **97**
candelabra 140, 141, 256

candle boxes 240
candle extinguishers **90**, 90, 131
candle lanterns 254
candlestands 51
candlesticks
  brass 261
  ceramic 67
  Sheffield plate 140
  silver 141
Canton ceramics 66, 85, 126
card boxes 242, 243
card cases 135, 138
card tables 57
cards, playing 245
Carpenter, Richard 207
Carpenter, Thomas 207, 209
carpets see rugs and carpets
Carr, Alwyn 138
carriage clocks **194**, 194–6
Carter, Salisbury 199
cartonnage masks 222
carver chairs 25
caskets 66, 239, 241, 242
cast-iron see iron
Caughley 80, 83, 119
Cauldon 95
ceiling lights 256
celadon 117
celery dishes 167
centre tables 56, 62
centrepieces, silver 157
ceramics 64–131
  antiquities 219–23
  baskets and boxes 65–6
  botanical decoration **83**
  cancellation lines **97**
  candlesticks 67
  clobbering **105**, 105
  clocks 199
  cups, mugs and tea bowls 68–77
  dishes and bowls 78–87
  faïence and Delft **72**
  figures 88–94
  flatware 95–106
  jardinières 107
  jars and canisters 108
  jugs and ewers 109–12
  kitchenware 250–2
  lighting 257
  Linthorpe **97**, 97
  pâte-sur-pâte **105**, 105
  plaques 113–14
  services 115–16
  stands 117
  tea, coffee and chocolate pots 118–19
  tiles 120–1
  vases 65, 122–7
  Willow pattern **108**
Cervine 211
Chad Valley 244
chairs 19–28
  carver 25
  child's 19–26
  correction/deportment 25
  desk 26, 27
  dining 26–8
  elbow 19, 21–3
  hall 20, 22, 23, 26
  high 21, 25

library 21
  nursing 22
  Oxford 23
  rocking 23–5
  side 20, 24
  Windsor 20, 22, 25, 26
  see also armchairs
Chamberlain's Worcester 67, 75, 76, 81
chambersticks 67, 140, 141, 259
champagne glasses 180
champlevé enamel 200, 202
chandeliers 257
chargers 101, 104, 106
Chawner, William 152
cheese dishes 79
cheese domes 129
cheese strainers 130
Chelsea 97, 103
chessboards 247
chests 29–31
chests of drawers 32–7, 44
chests-on-stands 34
cheval mirrors 48
chiffoniers 56
children's furniture 19–26, **21**
Chiltern 247
chimney ornaments 258
Chinese
  cabinets 42
  embroidery 277
  silver 164
Chinese ceramics
  animals 93
  bowls 79, 80, 83, 85
  chargers 105
  cheese strainers 130
  cups 72
  dishes 79, 81, 83, 84
  ecuelles 82
  jardinières 107
  kendi 130
  meat plates 97
  mugs 74
  plates 102, 103
  salts 131
  saucer dishes 85
  stands 117
  tea bowls 70, 76
  teapots 118
  trios 73
  vases 126, 127
Chippendale-style furniture 23, 53
christening mugs 147
christening sets 153, 163
chronographs 206, 209
chrystoleum paintings 190
cider caskets 250
cider pitchers 110
cigar dispensers 281
cigarette cases 138
clamps, Tunbridge ware 281
claret jugs 154, 155, 182
clerk's desks 43
Clichy **184**, 184–6
clobbering **105**, 105
clocks 192–205
  bracket 193
  carriage **194**, 194–6

mantel 197–202
  mignonettes **194**, 195
  wall 203–4
Clodion 271
cloisonné enamel 165, 261
clothes 277
  doll's 245
clothes presses 41
coaching tables 58
coal purdoniums 38
coal scuttles 227
Coalbrookdale 233
Coalport 66, 73, 116
codd bottles 169
coffee cans and cups 68, 69, 72, 73, 77
coffee grinders 252, 253
coffee pots 118–19, 159, 251
coffee services 116
coffers 29–31
Coker, Ebenezer 157
Cole, Thomas 205
Colombar, J. 214
coloured glass **182**
commemorative ware
  cups 69, 71
  egg cups 128
  mugs 68–70, **70**, 76
  plates 95, 96, 99
commodes 32, 37
commodes, night 35
compasses 258
comports 129, 191
Comyns, William 136, 187
condiments, silver 142–5
console tables 59
Continental
  arms and armour 235
  ceramics 66, 92, 108, 114, 128, 131
  chairs 24
  chests 31
  chests of drawers 33
  clocks 198
  silver 135, 151, 153, 155
  tables 58
  watches 213
  wood 281
Copeland 95, 116
copper
  architectural antiques 224, 228
  kitchenware 249, 250, 253
  measures 260
cordial glasses **175**
Corn Laws **110**
corner cupboards 39
correction/deportment chairs 25
cots 15
crackleware 126
cradles 15
cranberry glass
  bowls 167
  jugs 182
  lighting 254
  models 191
  preserve dishes 168
cream jugs 154–5
cream skimmers 81, 252

creamware
  barber's bowls 87
  dishes 83
  mugs 74, 77
  sauce boats 112
  strainers 128
  tureens 78
cribbage boards 278
Crouch, Henry 268
Crown Derby 115
Crown Devon 108
crucifixes 270
cruets
  ceramic 129
  glass 190
  silver 143–5
cupboards 38–42
cups and saucers
  ceramic 68–77, 220
  silver 146–8
curtain ties 276
cushions **274**, 274
cutlery, silver 149–53
cutlery boxes 242
cylinder bureaux 45
Cypriot antiquities 219, 221

D
dairy bowls 278
Daniel, H. & R. 96
Darly 213
Davenport 126
davenports 45
Davie, William 157
Davies, J. & Son 141
decanters 170–2
decoration, furniture **31**
Delft **72**
  animals 89
  dishes 79, 105
  meat plates 105
  plates 97, 99, 100, 102, 103, 105, 106
  tiles 120, 121
demon bowls **221**, 221
Dent 205
Derby
  animals 93
  candlesticks 67
  dishes 82
  figures 88, 92
  loving cups 77
  mugs 68, 73, 74
  saucer dishes 97
  tea bowls 75
Derringer 235
desk chairs 26, 27
desk stands 278
desks 43–5
dessert plates 97
dessert services 106, 115
Diana cargo 76
dining chairs 26–8
dining tables 58
dinner services 115, 116
dish covers 134
dishes
  antiquities 222
  ceramic 78–87, 106
  glass 167–8
  silver 133–4
display cabinets 38, 39, 42

Ditisheim, Paul 210
Dixon, Thos. 201
Dr Soules hop bitters 169
dolls 244–7
doll's clothes 245
doll's furniture 246
door furniture 224–8, 230
doors 230, 231
Doucai 85
Doulton 70, 124, 127
  see also Royal Doulton
Doulton Lambeth 77, 127
draughts sets 281
Dresden 89, 94
Dresser, Christopher **97**
dressers 40, 41
dresses 277
dressing mirrors 46–7
dressing table boxes 136
drinking glasses 173–81
drop-leaf tables 58
Dubinin, D.N. 174
dumps, glass 184
Dutch
  chairs 22
  mirrors 46
  silver 135
Dutch Delft 72, 79, 100, 120

E

earthenware see ceramics
East, John 165
East European chests 30
East India Company 234
écuelles 82
Edwards, J.C. 121
Edwards, Thomas 139
egg crocks 250
egg cups 128
egg frames 163
Egyptian antiquities 219–21,
  223
Egyptian revival armchairs 27
elbow chairs 19, 21–3
Elder & Co 159
electroplate candelabra 140
Eley, William II 159
Elkington & Co 154, 158
embroidery 277
Emes & Barnard 134
Empire style clocks 201, 202
enamel
  clocks 200, 202
  kitchenware 251
  kovshes 165
  vases 261
  watches 208, 211
Enfield 236
engine turning, silver **139**
English delft 99, 102, 105,
  106
ensis 262
entrée dishes 134
épergnes 189
Ersari ensis 262
étuis 260
ewers
  ceramic 109, 111–12
  glass 182
  silver 154
Excise Duty, glass **181**
excise wine glasses **181**, 181

F

face screens 276
faïence **72**
  antiquities 219, 220
  cruets 129
  dishes 79
  jardinières 107
  mugs 72
  plaques 113
  tazzas 117
famille rose
  bowls 79, 85
  dishes 79, 84
  meat plates 97
  plaques 114
  plates 103
  tea bowls 70
  teapots 118
  vases 126, 127
famille verte
  bowls 83
  dishes 79
  plates 102
  teapots 118
  vases 126
Favell, Rupert 144
Federzeichnung glass 189
felt dolls 244
fenders 225, 229, 230, 233
Feraghan rugs 262, 263
ferners 190
Fesana, J. 215
figured woods **28**
figures
  antiquities 220, 222, 223
  ceramic 88–94
  sculpture 270–3
finger bowls 167
finger plates 224, 226–8,
  230
Finnish silver 146
Firderen, Samuel 203
fire accessories 225, 229,
  230, 232, 233
fire surrounds 231
firing glasses 177
fish knives and forks 153
fish servers 149, 152
flagons, antiquities 223
flasks 90, 219
flatware, ceramic 95–106
Flavelle, Henry 137
Flaxman, John 87
Fleming, William 164
Flemish
  lace 275
  tapestry 277
Flight & Barr 75
flintlock pistols 234–5, 237
flour shakers 251
flower pots 107
fob watches 207
footstools 53
forks
  kitchenware 253
  silver 149–51, 153
  silver plate 153
four-poster beds 15
Fox, Charles II 144
frames
  mirrors 46–8
  silver 163, 164

French
  architectural antiques 226,
    230, 233
  armoires 41
  boxes 241
  ceramics 92, 99, 107, 110,
    127
  chests of drawers 35
  clocks 193–6, 198–202,
    204
  cradles 15
  glass 170, 182
  kitchenware 249, 252,
    253
  lighting 256
  medical instruments 268
  metalware 259
  paperweights **184**, 184–6
  scientific instruments 266
  silver 137, 139, 146, 163
  tables 55, 62
  watches 210, 211
Frodsham 204
Frodsham, Charles 209
frog mugs **77**, 77
Fugakawa 123
Fuller, Alfred 145
furniture 15–63
  children's **21**
  decoration **31**
  doll's 246
  figured woods **28**
  hardwoods **34**

G

Gardener 93
Garella, Professor 272
garnitures, clock 198
gas lamps 256
gateleg tables 62
Gaudy Welsh 68, 96
German
  arms and armour 236, 237
  ceramics 72, 73, 94, 105,
    122, 130
  chests 30
  chests of drawers 33
  dolls 244–7
  figures 88, 89
  glass 181
  sculpture 270, 271
  silver 137, 146
  teddy bears 247
  watches 211
  wood 281
Gerrard, T. 267
Gill 237
Gillows 281
ginger jars 108
girandoles 47
glass 166–91
  baskets, bowls and dishes
    167–8
  bottles and decanters
    169–72, **170**
  Burmese **168**, 168
  coloured **182**
  drinking glasses 173–81
  Glass Excise Duty **181**
  inkwells 160
  jugs 182
  lemon-squeezer feet **175**

  lighting 254–7
  lustres 183
  paperweights and dumps
    184, 184–6
  rinsers **167**, 167
  scent bottles 162, 187
  stained-glass windows 231
  vases 188–9
glove stretchers 163
goblets, glass 174, 176, 178
Godwin, W. 121
gold watches 206–13
Goldsmiths & Silversmiths Co
  194
Gorham & Co 142
Gothic-style
  chairs 26
  doors 230
  mirrors 48
Gouda 129
grain measures 248
Grainger's Worcester **80**, 80,
  116
grandfather chairs 27
Grant, J.D. 204
Grecian-revival lighting 256
Greek antiquities 223
Green, T.G. 252
Greenaway, Kate 121
griddles 251
Griffiths, Alfred 154
Grimwade 251
Guerin, W. & Co 110

H

Haas Puivat & Co 207
Hadley, James 94
Hadley's Worcester 126
Haentges Frères 16
Hahnstedt, Lars Anders 146
Halden, J. & Co 214
half-hunter watches 206–8
Hall, E. 133
hall chairs 20, 22, 23, 26
hall stands 50
Hamadan rugs 262, 263,
  265
hanging cupboards 39
hardwoods **34**
Harrach Glass Co **188**, 188
Harris, Charles Stuart 143,
  154, 158
Harrison, John **97**
hat pin stands 163
Haviland & Co 115
Hayes, R. 147
Hayes, Thomas 142
'haystack' measures 260
Hebe jugs 112
Hellenistic antiquities 221,
  222
helmets 237
Hepplewhite-style chairs 22
Herati carpets 263
herb choppers 248
Heriz carpets 265
Heubach, Ernst 246, 247
Hibbut, Harriet E. 127
high chairs 21, 25
Hirado 88
hock glasses 177
Hoi An Hoard **128**, 128

Hollis & Sheath 235
horn footstools 53
Hornby 245
Horner, Jack 230
horse harnesses 219
hot water pots 158
housekeeper's cupboards 42
humidors 238
Hutton, Edward 159
Hutton, Messrs 146

I
Imari
  beakers 71
  bowls 79, 87
  chargers 104
  dishes 82, 83
  plates 102
  tea bowls 72
  vases 123
incense burners 222
Ingraham, E. & Co 197
inkstands 160, 161
inkwells
  bronze 261
  glass 160, 184
  silver 160, 161
Irish
  ceramics 66, 70, 122
  cupboards 38, 40
  dressers 40, 41
  kitchenware 251
  mirrors 47
  settle beds 49
  silver 133, 136
  stools 16
iron
  architectural antiques 225,
    226, 228, 231–3
  branding irons 261
  kitchenware 250, 252, 253
  money boxes 246
irons 250
ironstone
  ewers 111
  mugs 68
  plates 99
  tureens 78
Italian
  boxes 242
  ceramics 106, 113
  furniture 16–18
  sculpture 271–3
ivory
  boxes 242, 243
  chessboards 247
  pencils 161
  scientific instruments 266
  sculpture 270

J
Jackson, J. 133
Jacob, Samuel 141
Jaeger-LeCoultre 212
Japanese
  metalware 261
  silver 152
Japanese ceramics
  animals 88
  bowls 78, 80, 87
  cups and tea bowls 68,
    69, 71, 72

dishes 78, 80, 81, 87
  plates 95, 96
  vases 123
Japy Frères & Co 199
jardinières 107
jars, ceramic 108
Jaschinov, A. 145
jasper ware **67**, 67, 79, 87
jelly moulds 250, 251
jewellery
  antiquities 219
  necklaces 219
jewellery boxes 239, 241,
  242
Johnson, Edmund George
  145
Johnson & Collins 234
jotters 258
jugs
  antiquities 221
  ceramic 109–12
  glass 182
  kitchenware 252
  silver 154–5

K
Karadja rugs 263
kendi 130
Kenrick 252
kerosene lamps 254
kettles 253
keys 219
Khamseh rugs 265
Khlebnikov, Ivan 165
kitchenware 248–53
Klett, H. 271
kneehole desks 45
knives
  Bowie **237**, 237
  silver and plate 149, 152,
    153
knockers 225
kovshes 165
Kraak porcelain 130
Kurdish rugs 262, 263
Kurzer and Wolf 137
Kutani 78, 91, 96, 103, 118

L
lace 275
lace irons 250
ladles 151
Lambeth 99
Lamport, John 151
lamps *see* lighting
Langlands, J. 152
lantern clocks 205
lanterns 254
Larroux, Antonin 272
latches 225, 226
lazy Susans 279
Le Gallais, John 143
Le Roy, Julien 211
Lee & Wigfull 163
Leeds Pottery 78, 87, 112
lemon-squeezer feet, glass
  175
letter openers 161
letter plates 224, 227
Levo, H. 269
Lewis & Towers 169
Lias Brothers 153

Libbey 168
library chairs 21
lighters 260
lighting 254–7
Limbach 92
Limoges 110, 115, 130, 245
linen presses 41, 42
Linthorpe **97**, 97
Liverpool 111
Liverpool delft 103, 121
Lock, Joseph 147
locks 231
Loetz 189
London delft 97, 106
Longines 213
Longquan 117
Lori rugs 264
loving cups 77
Low Ford Pottery 74
Lowestoft 101
Lupton, Eliza 124
lustre ware
  cups 71
  jugs 111–12
  mugs 77
  tea services 115
lustres, glass 183
Luvate, D. 215
Lyon velvet 274

M
Macintyre 69, 78
Mackay Cunningham & Co
  205
magazine racks 162
maiolica 113
majolica
  animals 90, 92
  bread plates 100
  chargers 106
  cheese domes 129
  comports 129
  dishes 85
  jugs 109
Maling 251
Mandarin 73
mantel clocks 197–202
mantels 46
Manzoni, A.C. 124
Mappin & Webb 140
marble
  antiquities 221
  clocks 199–201
  sculpture 271, 273
  tables 56
Margaine 195
Märklin 246
Markwick, Markham &
  Perigal 207
marquetry
  boxes 242
  cabinets 39
  coffers 31
  davenports 45
  tables 60
Marseille, Armand 244, 246,
  247
Marsh, Charles 155
Marshall & Rutter 164
Martin, R. 133
Martin Hall & Co 157
Mary Gregory glass **188**, 188

Masonic
  cribbage boards 278
  glass 168
  watches 211
Mason's Ironstone 111, 115
matchboxes 279
Matthews, H. 133, 155
Maw, Soloman 269
Measham 118
measures 248, 260
meat plates 97, 101, 104,
  105
medical instruments 266–9
Megnin, G. 202
Meissen
  animals 92, 94
  beakers 75
  boxes 66
  coffee pots 119
  dishes 82
  figures 91
  paperweights 94
  salts 130
  saucers 97
memorial boxes 241
Mêne, Pierre Jules 272
Mesopotamian antiquities
  221
metalware 258–61
Mettlach 112
microscope slide boxes 269
microscopes 266–9
microscopic lamps 266
mignonettes **194**, 195
Miles, A. 203
militaria
  secretaire chests 44–5
  watches 212, 213
milk jugs 111
milking stools 16, 52
Mills, Nathaniel 138
miner's tobacco tins 258
miniature chests of drawers 37
miniature glasses 173
Minton
  bowls 81
  figures 91
  jugs 111
  plates 105
  services 106
  teapots 119
  tiles 120, 121
  vases 125
mirrors 46–8
models
  anatomical 267
  glass 191
Moitte, Alexandre 107
money boxes 65, 246
Monroe, C.F. 190
Monte Christo 106
Moore & Co 120
Moore Bros 257
Mordan, Sampson & Co
  145, 145, 161, 268
Mordaunt & Co 165
Morland, George 111
Morton, Richard 161
mother-of-pearl
  boxes 238–42
  opera glasses 259, 260
Mottoware 70

moulds **250**, 251
Mount Washington Glass Co **168**
Mourey, P.H. 199
Moyr Smith, J. 121
mugs
ceramic 68–74, 76–7
commemorative 68–70, 70, 76
frog **77**, 77
silver 147, 148
Mühlhaus 188
mule chests 29
Müller, Berthold 155
music boxes 241
music cabinets 39–40
mustard pots 143–5
mustard spoons 152

N

Nanking cargo 79
napkin rings 165
Nathan, G. 136, 147
nécessaires 240
necklaces 219
needlework boxes 239, 240
needlework tables 59
Neolithic antiquities 219
nests of tables 61
New England Glass Co 184
New Hall 82
niello **138**, 138, 148, 152, 153
night commodes 35
Nippon 78, 95
Noritake 69
North Country furniture 23, 36
Norwegian wood 281
novelties, glass 191
nursery ware 71, 96, 99
nursing chairs 22
Nye, Edmund 279

O

occasional tables 55
oil lamps 254–7
Omega 206, 213
opaline glass 183, 189
open armchairs 19, 22, 23
opera glasses 259, 260
opium pipes 164
ormolu 200, 201, 255
Owen, Edward 162
Oxford chairs 23
oyster dishes 85

P

padlocks 258
paintings
chrystoleum 190
glass paste 190
panels, wall 232, 233, 281
paper clips 160, 258, 260
paperweights 94, **184**, 184–6
papier-mâché chairs 19
Parian ware 89, 91, 113
Paris porcelain 107, 127
patch boxes 139
pâte-sur-pâte **105**, 105
Patek Philippe 206, 211
Pearce & Sons 202
pearlware

flower pots 107
jugs 112
meat platters 104
mugs 71
teapots 118
vases 123
pedestal desks 43–5
pedestals 230
peg dolls 247
Pemberton, Samuel 136
Pembroke tables 54, 57, 61
pen wipes 260
pencils, silver 161
penknives 161
pepper pots 142–3, 145
perfume bottles *see* scent bottles
Perlington & Batty 133
Persian rugs 262–5, **263**
pestles and mortars 259
Peugeot François 252
Philpot, George 207
Phipps, Thomas 138
Phoenician antiquities 219
photograph frames 163, 164
piano stools 52
pickle dishes 86
pickle forks 149
pillboxes 238
Pillischer, M. 268
pin cushions **165**, 165
pin trays 156
Pinxton 111
pipes, opium 164
pistols 234–7
pitchers 110, 182
Pitkin and Brooks 167
plafonniers 256
plant stands 50
plaques, ceramic 113–14
plates 95–106, 167
playing cards 245
pocket watches 206–11
poison bottles 169
police rattles 280
porcelain *see* ceramics
porter mugs 73, 74
portraits, glass 190
Portuguese ceramics 110
postal scales 268, 269
potpourri vases 126
pottery *see* ceramics
powder boxes 135
preserve dishes 168
preserve spoons 150
Preston, William 209
pricket stands 117
prie dieus 20
primitive chairs 26
Pringle, Robert 162
prune forks 151
Prussian glass 172
pumps, water 226
punch bowls 85
purdoniums, coal 38
purses 275, 276
puzzle boxes 278

R

Ramsden, Omar 138
rattles, police 280
reading tables 55

Red Cliff Ironstone 78
redware, antiquities 220
regulators 204
Reilly, C. 143
Renaissance-style tables 56
Reni, Guido 114
Reuthes 235
revolvers 235, 236
revolving bookcases 18
ribbonwork 274
Richards, George John 144
Richardsons of Stourbridge 187
Ridgway 102
rifles 235
Riley, John & Richard 95
Rindskopf, Josef 188
rinsers, glass **167**, 167
Roberts, Florence C. 127
Roberts, W. 208
Robertson, J. I 152
Robinson, Edward 138
rock-crystal tazzas 146
rocking chairs 23–5
Rococo revival sofas 49
Rolex 210, **213**, 213
rolling pins, glass 190
Roman antiquities 219, 220, 222, 223
Rose, John 83
Round, John 156
Royal Doulton 70, 109, 113
see also Doulton
Royal Worcester
candlesticks 67
coffee services 116
dishes 81
figures 94
jugs 110
plates 97, 101
snuffers 90, 131
vases 65, 124–6
see also Worcester
Rugendas 75
rugs and carpets 262–5, **263**
rules 266
rummers 173–7
runners 262, 263, 265, 274
Russian
ceramics 106
glass 174
silver 138, 145, 147, **148**, 148, 152, 153, 161, 165

S

safe plaques 258
St Louis **184**, 186
salad bowls 168
salon suites 49
salt-glazed stoneware 90, 106, 122, 131
salts 130, 131, 142–5
salvers 156–7
samplers **275**, 275–7
Samson 74, 92, 163, 210
Sarab rugs 264
Satsuma 71, 80, 86, 87, 123
sauce boats 111, 112, 154
saucepans 164, 249
saucer dishes 79, 85, 86, 97, 101
see also cups and saucers
Saunders, C. 144

scales, postal 268, 269
scent bottles
ceramic 89, 128–30
glass 162, 187
silver 162, 165
Schuco 247
scientific instruments 266–9
Scott 193
Scottish silver 150
screens, face 276
sculpture 220, 221, 270–3
seats, iron 232–3
secretaire chests 44–5
services 106, 115–16, 191
Seth Thomas Clock Co 203
settees 49
settles 49
Sèvres 102, 103, 113
Sewell, J. 203
sewing cabinets 39
sewing étuis 260
shaving mirrors 46
Shaw, Thomas 139
Sheffield plate 140, 163
shelves 17–11
Shepherd, F. 144
Sheraton-style tables 58
Sherwin & Cotton 120, 121
Shirley, Frederick **168**
Shoolbred, Jas & Co 19
shovels, grain 249
Sibley, Arthur 144
side cabinets 40
side chairs 20, 24
side tables 54–9, 61, 62
sideboards 60, 61
silk 274
silver and plate 132–65
barometers 215
baskets, bowls and dishes 133–4
boxes and cases 135–9
candlesticks and chambersticks 140–1
clocks 194, 195
condiments 142–5
cups, mugs and tankards 146–8
cutlery and serving implements 149–53
engine turning **139**
jugs and sauce boats 154–5
lighting 256, 257
medical instruments 268, 269
niello **138**, 138, 148, 152, 153
pin cushions **165**, 165
Russian **148**
salvers and trays 156–7
scientific instruments 267
silver-mounted glass 170, 174
tea, coffee and chocolate pots 158–9
watches 206–11
wear **156**
writing equipment **160**, 160–1
Sitzendorf 255
skeleton clocks 205
skeleton mirrors 46
slag glass lamps 255
slipware 103

smelling salts bottles 169
Smith & Wesson 236
snuff boxes 135, 137–9
snuffer trays 157
snuffers **90**, 90
sofa tables 60
sofas 49
Solon, Marc-Louis **105**
soup plates 99
soup tureens 78, 86
Spanish
  architectural antiques 232
  arms and armour 234
  metalware 261
  sculpture 270, 273
spelter 198, 273
Sperry, Henry & Co 197
spice towers 253
spill vases 90, 123–5
Spode 99, 122, 123, 129
spoons, silver 149–53
Springfield 235
Staffordshire
  candlesticks 67
  dinner services 116
  figures 90–1, 93
  plates 104, 106
  sugar sifters 131
  teapots 119
stained-glass windows 231
stands 50–1, 117
Steiff 245
stethoscopes 268
Stevenson, Andrew 86
Stilton dishes 79
stone antiquities 219
stoneware
  jugs and ewers 109
  kitchenware 250
  loving cups 77
  mugs 76
  perfume bottles 128
  vases 127
  see also salt-glazed
  stoneware
stools 16, 52–3
Storer, G. 143
Stourbridge 184
strainers, ceramic 128, 130
string dispensers 136
Strutt, William 190
sucriers 86
Suffolk latches 225, 226
sugar bowls
  ceramic 81, 83, 84
  glass 168
  silver 133
sugar casters 144
sugar sifter spoons 149
sugar sifters 131
sugar tongs 150, **151**, 151
suites
  glass 191
  salon 49
Sunderland 74, 77, 112
Sutherland tables 61
Swift, John 147
swing-handle baskets, silver **134**
Swiss
  music boxes 241
  watches 206, 207, 210–13
swords 234, 236, 237

table boxes 243
table cabinets 38, 39
table lamps 254, 255
table runners 274
tables 54–62
  boardroom 60
  breakfast 59, 61
  card 57
  centre 56, 62
  coaching 58
  console 59
  dining 58
  drop-leaf 58
  gateleg 62
  needlework 59
  nests of tables 61
  occasional 55
  Pembroke 54, 57, 61
  reading 55
  side 54–9, 61, 62
  sofa 60
  Sutherland 61
  tea 55
  tripod 54, 56, 60
  wine 60
  work 55–7
Tabor, George Hugo 127
tankards 148, 281
tantaluses 172
tape measures 279
tapestry 274, 277
Tassie, James 190
Taylor, Joseph 165
tazzas 117, **146**, 146
tea caddies and canisters
  108, 137, 165, 240, 242–3
tea chests 241
tea services 115, 116, 158
tea tables 55
tea bowls, ceramic 70, 72,
  73, 75–6
teacups see cups and saucers
teapot stands 117, 157
teapots 118–19, 158–9
teddy bears 247
telescopes 191
Templetown, Lady 87
terracotta 220, 231
textiles 274–7
thatching tools 278
thermometers, medical 269
thimbles 163
Thomas, David 204
Thompson & Vine 203
Thwaites & Reed 204
tie-backs 259
Tiffany & Co 150, 255
tiles 120–1
tin-glazed ceramics 65, **72**,
  72, 78
tobacco boxes 138
tobacco jars 108
tobacco tins 258, 260
Toby jugs 109
toddy ladles 151
toilet mirrors 46, 48
Tokey, James 150
toleware 227
tongs, silver 150, **151**, 151
torchères 51
tortoiseshell

boxes **238**, 238, 240, 242,
  243
crucifixes 270
  medical instruments 267
  watches 207, 211
Touliet, John 164
toys 244–7
training chairs 20
trains, toy 245, 246
trays
  beadwork 277
  butler's 63
  silver and plate 156, 157
  wooden 280
trinket boxes 65, 241
trios 73, 74
tripod tables 54, 56, 60
trivets 228
truncheons 235
tub chairs 20, 28
Tunbridge ware **278**, 278–81
tureens 78, 86
Turkoman bagfaces 262
tygs 77

U

umbrellas, silver-mounted 162
Unite & Hilliard 153
uranium glass 254
urn stands 51
urns 124, 228, 231
ushabti figures 220

V

vaseline glass 183
vases
  antiquities 223
  ceramic 65, 122–7, 163
  cloisonné enamel 261
  glass 188–9
  silver-mounted 163
Vauxhall 86
Venetian mirrors 47
vents, cast-iron 225
verge watches **208**, 208,
  209, 211
Vienna
  bronzes 271–3
  ceramics 72, 104
Vietnamese ceramics **128**, 128
Viking antiquities 219
Villeroy and Boch 101
vinaigrettes 135, 136, 139
Vincenti et Cie 200
vodka cups 147
Vung Tau cargo 79

W

Wakely, James 158
Walker & Hall 156
walking sticks 162
wall brackets, porcelain 131
wall clocks 203–4
wall cupboards 42
wall lights 255
wall mirrors 46–8
wall plates 103
Walley, Joseph 148
Waltham 209
wash boards 252
wash boilers 230
washstands 50, 51

watches
  pocket 206–11
  Rolex 213
  verge **208**, 208, 209, 211
  wristwatches 212–13
Watcombe Pottery 107, 108
water jugs 110, 182
water pumps 226
Watson, J. & Son 140
Watson & Sons 267
wax dolls 244, 246
wax jacks 140
weapons 234–7
Webb, Thomas & Sons **168**,
  168, **187**, 187
Wedgwood 190
  cream skimmers 81
  jasper ware **67**, 67, 79, 87
  tiles 120
Wellington chests 45
West, Matthew 133
West Country chairs 25
whatnots **63**, 63
wheel barometers 214–16
Wheeler, Frank 158
Whieldon 104
whip stands 51
whistles 164
Whytock & Sons 137
Willow pattern **108**
Wilmore, Joseph 139, 152
windows, stained-glass 231
Windsor chairs 20, 22, 25, 26
wine bottles 169–72
wine carriers 110
wine glasses 173, **175**,
  175–81
wine tables 60
wing chairs 26
Winkle, George 150
wood 278–81
  figured **28**
  hardwoods **34**
  kitchenware 248–53
  sculpture 270, 273
Woodall, George **187**
Worcester
  bowls 80, 84, 86
  butter boats 85, 87
  chambersticks 67
  coffee pots 119
  cups 73, 75
  Grainger's Worcester **80**, 80
  mugs 76
  pickle dishes 86
  plates 100
  sugar bowls 81
  teapots 119
  trios 74
  vases 126
  see also Royal Worcester
work boxes 239, 280
work cabinets 38
work tables 55–7
wristwatches 212–13
writing boxes 242
writing equipment **160**, 160–1
wrought-iron see iron
wucai 107

Z

Zimmermann, A. & J. 160, 161